THE POLITICS OF CULTURAL CAPITAL

THE
POLITICS
OF
CULTURAL
CAPITAL

China's Quest for a Nobel Prize in Literature

JULIA LOVELL

UNIVERSITY OF HAWAI'I PRESS

HONOLULU

Library of Congress Cataloging-in-Publication Data
Lovell, Julia.
The politics of cultural capital : China's quest for a Nobel Prize
in literature / Julia Lovell.
p. cm.
Includes bibliographical references and index.
ISBN-13: 978-0-8248-2962-9 (hbk : alk. paper)
ISBN-10: 0-8248-2962-X (hbk : alk. paper)
ISBN-13: 978-0-8248-3018-2 (pbk. : alk. paper)
ISBN-10: 0-8248-3018-0 (pbk. : alk. paper)
1. Chinese literature — Social aspects.   2. Intellectuals —
China.   3. Nobel Prizes.   I. Title.   II. Title: China's
quest for a Nobel Prize in literature.
PL2273.L68 2006
895.1'09 — dc22
2005036470

University of Hawai'i Press books are printed on acid-free
paper and meet the guidelines for permanence and
durability of the Council on Library Resources.

Designed by April Leidig-Higgins

Printed by The Maple-Vail Book Manufacturing Group

CONTENTS

ACKNOWLEDGMENTS

WORK ON THIS BOOK began in 1999 when I started researching a dissertation at the University of Cambridge. I owe enormous thanks, first and foremost, to my supervisor Susan Daruvala for her constant generosity with her time and insights and for guiding me always judiciously with her inspiringly vast knowledge of Asian and Western literature and history. Many thanks are due as well to Michel Hockx, who has supported and encouraged the project from its beginnings as well as making extremely timely interventions and suggestions at important moments of thinking and writing. Bonnie McDougall most generously provided both crucial source material and a remarkably close and helpful reading of the manuscript at a moment that was extremely inconvenient to her. I have also profited from the comradeship of my fellow Ph.D. students at Cambridge, particularly Lim Song Hwee and Sy Ren Quah, both of whom provided me with invaluable source material and counsel at key points; and I am most grateful to Red Chan, for kindly sending me a copy of her thesis on Chinese literature in translation.

I would like to thank especially Bai Ye, for offering me huge amounts of useful advice about navigating the literary scenes of Beijing and Shanghai and for generously opening up to me his address book and enabling me to make contact with a great many of the Chinese writers and critics I interviewed for the book. Thanks are owed also to these writers and critics, who patiently listened to my interminable lists of questions. I am particularly grateful to Han Shaogong, who not only agreed to be interviewed, but in addition hospitably threw in a bonus tour around Hunan.

The writing of the thesis was generously funded by research grants from the University of Cambridge and from Emmanuel College, Cambridge. The completion of the book was made possible by a research fellowship at Queens' College, Cambridge. Over the past two years I have benefited greatly from the relaxed, supportive research atmosphere of this college community.

Many thanks also to Pamela Kelley, my editor at University of Hawai'i Press, for her thoughtful and stimulating responses to the manuscript and to Terre Fisher for the care with which she copyedited the manuscript. I am extremely grateful to the two anonymous readers who provided exceptionally thorough and helpful reports, both of which have much improved the book. The errors and shortcomings that remain are entirely my own.

One of my largest debts is undoubtedly to my family: to my husband, Robert Macfarlane, for his patient ruthlessness in hunting down faulty syntax and mixed metaphors (those that are left are exclusively my own doing) and for his invaluable guidance on European poetry and ideas of authorship; to my mother, Thelma Lovell, for her painstaking editing, for working out what I was meaning to say long before I had much of an idea, and for her insights, among many things, into Plato and Romanticism; to my brother, Stephen Lovell for help with Russian sources and advice about the painful business of thesis writing. And in a broader sense, this book would never have been finished without the endless support and encouragement of my husband, parents, brother, and sister.

AN EARLIER VERSION of Chapter Five appeared in *Modern Chinese Literature and Culture* 14, no. 2 (Fall 2002) as "Gao Xingjian, the Nobel Prize, and Chinese Intellectuals: Notes on the Aftermath of the Nobel Prize 2000."

An extract of a verse by Carl David af Wirsén from *The Nobel Prize in Literature* by Kjell Espmark (G. K. Hall, 1991) is reprinted by permission of the Gale Group.

PROLOGUE

O n 12 October 2000, when Gao Xingjian (1940–), a Chinese-born novelist and playwright then living in France, was awarded the Nobel Prize for Literature, China's century-long quest for Nobel glory finally came to an end.[1] Chinese intellectuals and politicians had worried for decades over when a Nobel Literature Prize would come to China, but the lack of a Chinese laureate was now, it seemed, resolved and the mystique of the prize dispelled. A Chinese writer had been acclaimed "for an oeuvre of universal validity, bitter insights and linguistic ingenuity, which has opened new paths for the Chinese novel and drama."[2] Gao's work, the Swedish Academy explained, was in touch both with Western modernism and the flow of sources from popular Chinese drama. Chinese literature could live happily ever after, basking in its global significance.

Reactions to Gao's prize soon dashed such hopes, however, as rumors and accusations of politicization began to circulate on both sides of the East-West ideological divide and throughout the global Chinese community. The government in Beijing responded by denouncing the "political purposes" of the Nobel Prize, declaring the prize had lost legitimacy and calling Gao a "French writer." Outside China, Gao was an unknown quantity. In the wave of panic that swept the Western media on the afternoon of October 12 — Who is he? What's he written? How's his name pronounced? — many reached for one of the first security blankets of nonspecialist reporting on contemporary Chinese culture and literature: Gao Xingjian is an exiled dissident. Writers in China displayed mixed feelings. Although pleased by this symbolic recognition for literature in Chinese and critical of the government's knee-jerk condemnation of the prize, many were ambivalent about the political significance of honoring an exile who was relatively unknown in China at the time of the award.[3] Chinese people in other parts of the world, meanwhile, were delighted that Gao as a Chinese had won a Nobel, even though Gao had for some time disassociated himself from China the nation-state and had shown little interest in being published or reaching readers there since his 1987 departure for France. Finally, a closer look at the Swedish Academy's commendation of

1

Gao reveals that despite praise for his "universal validity" — thereby implying that his prize was awarded for the universal artistic value of his oeuvre — the Academy's press release and presentation speech commended by name only those of his works that make reference to, and largely adopt a dissident stance towards, Chinese politics: his two novels *Lingshan* (Soul mountain) and *Yige ren de shengjing* (One man's bible), and his play *Taowang* (Fleeing).[4] All these imputations, refutations, and confusions of identity show that writing in Chinese on a global stage — especially if it wins a Nobel Prize — is still a highly contested undertaking.

CHAPTER ONE

Introduction

Diagnosing the Complex

T he question of why China — a country, so it is often claimed, with five thousand years of culture and a language spoken by one fifth of the world's population — had failed for almost a century to win a Nobel Prize began to be raised with increasing urgency during the 1980s, following the Mainland's reentry into the international political, economic, and cultural realm. The quest for a Nobel Prize was promoted to the level of official policy and Nobel anxiety evolved into a "complex" (*Nuobeier qingjie*) that drew in writers, critics, and academics. The task of securing a Nobel Literature Prize — viewed as a passport to world recognition as a modern civilization — generated conferences, a national literature prize, delegations to Sweden and countless articles. In the 1990s, following changes in the national politico-literary climate after the crackdown of 4 June 1989, the Nobel question was dislodged from its prominent public position but continued to rumble underground, reemerging on periodic waves of media hype. Through both decades the issue also mobilized worldwide interest among diasporic Chinese communities. There was a resurgence of Nobel anxiety in 2000: as the prize approached its centenary, Chinese journalists once again prepared articles on why a writer from China had still not won what was seen as the literary Olympics, on how the great modern Chinese writers Lu Xun (1881–1936), Lao She (1899–1966), Shen Congwen (1902–1988), and Ba Jin (1904–) missed out by a hair's breadth, and so on and so forth.[1]

The question invites the rebuttal: why *should* China win a Nobel Prize? With due respect, how can any committee of individuals effectively judge the "most outstanding work of an idealistic tendency" that has conferred the "greatest benefit to mankind," as stipulated vaguely in Alfred Nobel's prize testament? Why should China care about, or even find anything illogical or unfair in the fact that a group of Swedish judges — almost all lacking the ability to read

Chinese—had failed to appreciate its modern literature? In the West, public debate about Nobel rights and wrongs is seldom heard outside the media coverage that erupts around the annual announcement made in October (the private hopes of writers are, of course, another matter). The fact that some European countries have failed to win a prize hardly makes a story, let alone a book. Dutch commentators, for example, are not embarrassed to admit that a prize would be desirable, but the issue does not annually generate dozens of articles in academic and literary circles. But the question takes on a larger significance when we note similarities between the "Nobel Complex" and the preoccupations that have engaged the dominant Chinese intellectual experience of modernity: anxiety about China's international status, ambivalence towards Western influences and values, and the relationship between Chinese intellectuals (especially writers) and national politics. The plausible barriers between China and the Nobel Prize, namely, ignorance on the part of the outside world, the workings of different literary value systems, and linguistic differences, have often been forgotten in face of the broader anxieties of significant numbers of Chinese intellectuals in the global arena: what is so *wrong* with Chinese literature that it cannot join the modern world literary order symbolized by the Nobel Prize?

The term "complex" started to be used in the 1980s to discuss Chinese Nobel anxiety and is in itself revealing of the broader context of modern Chinese history. It first of all suggests a psychoanalytical path of enquiry. The Nobel Literature Prize had become a cause of a psychological disorder, a token whose value and authority as imagined in China was inflated out of all proportion to its real importance or exchange value in international letters. In Freudian terms it was an object of desire, the lack of which became a larger symbol for the impotence of Chinese intellectuals in the modern world. Secondly, in addition to its general significance in psychoanalysis, the word "complex" carries very particular connotations in the modern Chinese context. It taps into powerful discourses of sickness and the inferiority of the Chinese character first formulated by modern intellectuals such as Sun Yat-sen (1866–1925) and Lu Xun that have survived into intellectual discussions of the post-Mao period. Chinese intellectuals at the turn of the twentieth century imbibed imperialist views of Chinese racial inferiority, and the project of curing the diseased national character underlay much intellectual reformism. Lu Xun, still the paradigm of modern Chinese intellectual integrity today, saw the question of national character as central to the crisis of modern China, and his prestige and influence sealed the link between literature and national sickness. It is hard to overestimate the degree to which his conviction has permeated the modern Chinese intellectual consciousness. Lydia Liu points out that, as transforming the national character (*gaizao guominxing*) became the dominant theme in the narrative of Chinese modernity,

> many began to accept modern literature as the best means to remedy China's problems . . . the theory of national character led [Lu Xun and his peers] to justify Chinese literary modernity as a national project whose importance to China's nation-building efforts fundamentally outstripped that of state wealth, military power, science and technology, and the like.[2]

Medical and anatomical tropes, Liu notes, have dominated Chinese debates on literary modernity, implying both a fundamental disorder or weakness within China and its literature, and the healing power of literary intellectuals. Lu Xun began training as a doctor before undergoing a famous conversion to literary writing when confronted with evidence of the craven, ignoble Chinese character: "I felt that medical science was not so important after all; when the people of a nation were ignorant and weak citizens, it mattered little whether or not they were physically strong . . . the important thing to do was to transform people's spirit, and literature and art were the best means to that end."[3] A term such as the "Nobel Complex" is thus compromised from its very inception in the discourses of nationalism and national inferiority that have dogged the Chinese intellectual experience of modernity, in the condition it aims to expose and (by implication) remedy. While directed at rectifying China's perceived failure to win a Nobel, the Nobel Complex is itself produced by and reinforces this same sense of national inferiority.

It is important to specify what is meant here by the term "Chinese intellectual," which, at its widest application, can refer to anyone in possession of a high-school education; the bibliography on the subject in both Chinese and Western languages is similarly broad. In the present study the term "literary intellectual" is used to refer to those professionally engaged in literary work: writers, critics, editors, scholars, and so on. The more general term "Chinese intellectual," however, carries with it a complex package of political, social, and ideological commitments. Indeed, as Vera Schwarcz points out in her account of the May Fourth movement, *zhishi fenzi*, the modern Chinese phrase for intellectual, directly emerged out of the sociopolitical challenges of the 1920s.[4] Schwarcz herself views Chinese intellectuals as an educated elite occupying the forefront of social and political reform efforts.[5] Perry Link, similarly, in his survey of Chinese intellectual attitudes in the 1980s, *Evening Chats in Beijing*, identifies an important vein of political and social engagement running through the mindset of educated Chinese.[6] The engaged stance of Chinese intellectuals has also been characterized famously by C. T. Hsia as an "obsession with China": an anxious cultural nationalism.[7]

Despite the general validity of these observations about the intellectual "obsession with China" and nationalism, a consistent, uniform stance throughout China's intellectual community must not be assumed. In analyzing Chinese intellectual attitudes to nationalism, internationalism, and the Nobel Complex, it is crucial to differentiate as precisely as possible between groups and individuals that fall into the general category of "intellectuals" and "literary intellectuals." At various points during China's troubled twentieth century, intellectuals (both literary and nonliterary) have combined resentment of China the nation-state with patriotism for the motherland: modernizing iconoclasm has coexisted with affection for and pride in aspects of traditional, premodern Chinese culture. Attitudes to national and international values have, moreover, become increasingly unstable in the contemporary era of transnational media, migration, and globalization.[8] In exploring the significance of the Nobel Complex and cultural nationalism within such an amorphous and diverse category as "Chinese intellectuals," this study will focus primarily on literary intellectuals, whose attitudes in turn vary both between groups (poets, novelists, critics, and editors; men and women; different age cohorts) and between individuals within those groups. I do not expect the conclusions I draw about certain literary intellectuals to apply uniformly to Chinese intellectuals as a whole, and this book will attempt to avoid the dangers of over-generalization by closely specifying the subjects of its discussion. I have, however, made judgments throughout this study, and particularly in this introductory chapter, about what I consider to be fairly dominant and widespread modes of modern intellectual consciousness, such as anxiety about the vigor and viability of a national Chinese culture in comparison with Western nations. It should be noted that these dominant modes of consciousness are frequently those held and propagated by male intellectuals.

The Nobel Complex is itself a metonym for C. T. Hsia's diagnosis of "obsession with China" in many modern Chinese intellectuals and writers: their "obsessive concern with China as a nation afflicted with a spiritual disease."[9] Having reinvented China as a nation-state and invested so much hope in its salvational narratives of modernity and progress, certain intellectuals have sought all possible affirmation of their efforts in this direction, namely recognition from the (imperialist) inventor of modernity and progress, the West. In the post-Mao era this desire for recognition has manifested itself in the near-pathological yearning for international prizes and "face" — for the Nobel Prize, for the prestige of hosting the Olympic Games and qualifying for the football World Cup, for entry to the WTO. This yearning has intensified since the 1990s, when rapid economic development and the growth of (particularly urban) incomes have fueled a confident sense of nationalistic entitlement to markers of international prestige.[10] Even during the Maoist era, although Western prizes were regarded as capitalist and bourgeois, China initially remained eager for recognition from new, politically respectable international sources of authority (such as the Stalin Prize).

But the Chinese yearning to recover the luster of lost glory through winning international recognition is also doomed to ambivalence and frustration, since the global authority from which China has sought recognition is dominated by the West, the very source of China's international humiliations. China's sense of entitlement to Western-based international plaudits reveals both a confident belief in China's superiority *and* an anxious need for that belief to be affirmed by the West. Modern Chinese have combined an admiration for Western modernity with a resentful inferiority complex towards Western strength and a fear that the Chinese national essence will be lost in the process of modernization. Insecurity about Chinese national identity and the obsession with a diseased Chinese culture have often produced their inverse: a cultural machismo, angrily sensitive to slights and humiliations, that asserts China's cultural uniqueness. Debate concerning China's desire for a Nobel Prize has frequently swung from self-criticism to aggression. Geremie Barmé has summarized this as the tendency towards "self-hate and self-approbation" in modern Chinese culture: China is perceived both as a glorious five-thousand-year-old civilization deserving of recognition and a humiliated modern culture inferior to the global standard.[11]

Intense Chinese interest in the idea of a Chinese writer winning the Nobel Literature Prize crystallizes the tensions inherent in China's move towards a "global" culture in the modern era; it also neatly illustrates the degree to which the responsibility for achieving this task has been laid on the shoulders of literature at various points in the twentieth century.[12] All spheres of cultural and social activity—economics, politics, sports—have been drawn into modern China's quest for international prestige, but literature, the traditional medium for intellectual expression, has been given special weight in this effort. The Nobel Prize is awarded for the natural sciences, medicine, economics, and peace, yet for decades it has been the literature prize that has been the principal focus of Chinese hopes and worries. Despite the controversy generated by the award of the 1989 Nobel Peace Prize to the Dalai Lama, hopes for a peace prize have not matched the fervor of China's desire for a Nobel Prize in literature. Interest in the science prize has, admittedly, grown throughout the post-Mao period. A Central China Television (Zhongyang dianshi tai) program of 29 April 2000, for example, asked "How far are we from a Nobel [Science] Prize?" and featured interviews with Chinese-born Nobel science laureates who won their prizes for research done in the United

States and either already were or later became U.S. citizens. Again, however, the quest for science prizes has not matched the enthusiasm, urgency, and national and political sensitivity that have surrounded the literature prize. While the Chinese state has proved willing to establish friendly public relations with Chinese-born winners of the science prizes long resident in the West, the case of Gao Xingjian, who spent the first forty-seven years of his life on the Mainland but whom Beijing immediately dismissed as a "French writer" after the Nobel announcement, demonstrates this sensitivity. It is the dissident, oppositional tendencies of Chinese writers in exile (including Gao, whose play *Taowang* denounced the Tian'anmen massacre of 1989) that have made the Chinese state so suspicious of international recognition for these authors. This suspicion is emblematic of the troubled relationship between individual literary intellectuals and a centralized, political national identity, that has endured throughout China's twentieth-century quest for modernity. International achievements in the spheres of sports and science are judged by criteria far less contentious than those used for literature. Unlike literature —an elite intellectual form—sport provides a far more straightforwardly populist symbolic framework for representing the nation: athletes train their bodies to win Olympic gold medals as members of the larger national body. The development and the denouement of China's literary Nobel Complex demonstrate the particularly sensitive and problematic status attached to the Chinese literary language and tradition as mediators between national identity and international standing in twentieth-century modernizing schemas.

Changing attitudes to the prize from as far back as the 1920s shed light on the contradictory mix of admiration, resentment, and anxiety that intellectuals and writers have felt towards "international" (i.e., Western) values as they attempted to forge a modern Chinese literary and cultural identity. That so much attention has been paid to an external source of valuation indicates the continued uncertainty of Chinese writers as to their aims and audience, caught as they have been between admiration for the West and anxiety about their role in forging and positioning China's own cultural identity: should Chinese literature serve a global audience or the nation? Should it address the masses or intellectuals? In short, the Chinese Nobel Complex reveals pressure points in a modern intellectual identity not entirely sure of itself.

The complex also provides a case study for the politics of world literature, highlighting, through the local example of China, the position occupied by non-Western literatures in the world literary economy. Firstly, although intellectual anxieties about modernity and nationhood may appear to be especially acute in the Chinese context, they are in fact part of the broader, global phenomenon of nation-building discourses, in particular as experienced in the non-West.[13] Secondly, the sense of inferiority and weakness raised in China by exclusion from the Nobel Prize must beg the question: what, precisely, is the nature of this global culture in relation to which China feels marginal and excluded? Moreover, with all this talk of "global culture," why raise the question of national identity at all? Is the contemporary global system not ruled by free-flowing postmodern forces that disregard national boundaries and any assertion of dominant positions?

It is true that the international profile of East Asia has risen dramatically since the 1960s, largely due to economic progress in the region, and that cultural products from the non-West have in recent years been making deeper inroads into mainstream global culture. The international success in 2001 of Ang Lee's martial arts film *Crouching Tiger, Hidden Dragon* is a case in point. Since Mao's death, moreover, Mainland China has thoroughly distinguished itself in international sports.[14] Yet literature has proved an altogether more intractable medium for globalization, and the state of world literature is very different from that of global popular culture. Here, the significant fact is that the sector of the world literary market (particularly, of the economically and culturally powerful Anglophone market) occupied by Chinese literature in translation is tiny, far smaller than the sector occupied by books on China written directly into Western languages.[15] The sense of failure and disappointment resulting from writers' inability to reach a global audience has in turn been heightened by post-Mao China's rapid international success in cinema, sports, and economics. Winning a Nobel Prize represents a highly significant gain in cultural and economic capital for a nation aspiring to become an equal participant in "world literature." Yet while it is pledged to ignore national boundaries, the Nobel Prize has long been dominated by Western writers and languages. When we come to examine the prize's more multicultural, geographically inclusive policy of recent years, we will see that the inclusion of more non-Western writers does not necessarily signal the victory of pluralism. Closer examination of and attempts to define the fashionable concept of global culture reveal that boundaries and norms are still being set in tune with Eurocentric values, and nation-states remain key players in matters political, economic, *and* cultural.

This introductory chapter sets Chinese intellectual and literary concerns within a global framework of modernity, awareness of which marks one of the crucial points of departure for modern Chinese intellectual consciousness. The quandary of Chinese intellectuals is shared by countless others who find themselves outside the mainstream of modern Western economic and political development. How can they win, or even participate equally, in a game (viz., the right to represent China on a modern global stage) whose rules and values belong to a Western-based power structure built on social, economic, and political factors that are centuries old? What, ultimately, lies behind the modern idea of "global culture" and the Chinese experience of the term? Finally, we will consider here the specific issue of world literature and Chinese literature's position within the modern world literary market.

Nationalism, Modernity, Globalization

Scholarship of the last twenty years has rendered increasingly explicit the ties between intellectuals, nation building, modernity, and globalization, starting from the early modern period in the West. Benedict Anderson views the "imagined community" created by fiction and mass print culture as a prerequisite to the formation of a national community, thereby underlining the imaginative, ideas-based origins of nationalism.[16] The works of Liah Greenfeld on Europe and the United States and John Fitzgerald on China have emphasized the role of intellectual elites in forging the idea of the nation.[17] The causal links between nationalism and modernity are more contested. While Greenfeld portrays nationalism as the powerful symbolic resource through which elites since the sixteenth century have transformed their own identities and the social structures in which they lived, Anderson and Ernest Gellner take the view that nationalism was only made possible by the advent of modernity and its concomitant systems of communication and organization, such as mass education and new media.[18] In her analysis of nationalism and modernity in China, Susan Daruvala traces the complex links between these two phenomena; her arguments are helpful in understanding one of the products of their interaction, globalization, or its more abstract companion concept, universality. Daruvala uses the term "second-order modernity" to describe the form of global modernity influenced by the spread of nationalism and imperialism from the West. The fact of this influence in turn has brought ambivalence and inequality both to the expression of the modern global ideal and to China's bids to attain it.[19]

The leap from the specificity of modern nationalism to the universalism of globalization is somewhat paradoxical and has long bemused scholars.[20] Benedict Anderson articulates the problem as "the formal universality of nationality as a socio-cultural concept — in the modern world everyone can, should, will 'have' a nationality, as he or she 'has' a gender — vs. the irremediable particularity of its concrete manifestations, such that, by definition, 'Greek' nationality is sui generis."[21] The rise of nationalism in both political theory and practice coincided with the heyday of the Enlightenment ideal, universal human reason. In Enlightenment conceptualizations such as Hegel's

(1770–1831) influential *The Philosophy of History*, only the individualistic self-awareness of reason leads to a proper understanding of History. If History is the mode of being (namely, a consciousness of past, present, and progress) and the condition which allows the possibility of modernity, "the nation-state is the agency, the subject of History which will realize modernity."[22] Just as everyone has a gender and possesses reason, they must have a nationality or risk being left behind by History.[23]

If Hegel provided philosophical arguments for tying nationalism to a global universal model, the legal and political underpinnings of this development had been put in place much earlier. The interstate basis of membership to the international, eventually global community had a legislative precedent in the 1648 Treaty of Westphalia that ended the Thirty Years War. The Westphalian model holds that the world consists of sovereign territorial states, recognizing no superior authority; the processes of law making are in the hands of these individual states. This treaty continued to serve as a model for international law and regulation from 1648 to 1945; some contend that it still holds now.[24] Today, even the most ardent advocates of globalization theory find it almost impossible to break free of the international relations structures imposed by the network of sovereign states. For better or for worse, the nation-state and its complex of Enlightenment ideas provide one of the foundation stones for twentieth-century globalization.

These ideas lay behind the traumatic sense of awakening Chinese intellectuals experienced from the late nineteenth century onward regarding the global order and China's place therein. Before the incursions by the West, Chinese understanding of the world order had been shaped by sinocentric ideas that went back to the Han dynasty (206 BC–220 AD). According to the Han five-zone (*wu fu*) theory, the known world had been divided into five concentric zones since the time of the mythical Xia dynasty (c. second millennium BC): the Chinese king directly ruled the inner three, while the outer two were occupied by barbarians. The world, in other words, revolved around China. The barbarian zones were tied to the Chinese center by a system of tributary relations; inhabitants of all five zones owed tribute to the center, thus affirming their status as dependent vassals.[25] The reality of imperial China's foreign relations was very different from this ideal: between the Han and Qing dynasties, part and sometimes all of China was repeatedly conquered by tribes from the northern steppe; the last of these conquering tribes founded Qing rule in 1644. Nevertheless, the idea that China occupied the center of the world retained a hold on the Chinese imagination until its gradual erosion following the introduction of the treaty port system in the mid-nineteenth century.[26] For a substantial part of the period from Han to Qing, China was not wholly unjustified in its politico-cultural self-confidence. Long the dominant culture in the East Asia region, China was arguably one of the most powerful nations in the world during the Ming and early Qing dynasties (c. fifteenth to eighteenth centuries).[27]

In the *longue durée* of Chinese history, however, the impact of Western aggression in the mid-nineteenth century represents a highly significant, albeit relatively recent and still short-term, rupture of self-confidence that finally forced the Chinese government by the start of the following century to abandon its sinocentric approach to foreign relations and deal with the "barbarians" as powerful and vigorous diplomatic equals, rather than as tributary vassals. "It was the contraction of China from a world to a nation in the world," wrote Joseph Levenson, "that changed the Chinese historical consciousness."[28] The intellectual and journalist Liang Qichao (1873–1929) can thus be defined as the mind of modern China, the paradigmatic thinker who visualized China's place in a new world order of modern nation-states. Liang was one of the first to tackle discursively the perceived need for a completely different kind of subjectivity — modern nationalism — after becoming aware of the existence of five continents and many flourishing nations beyond the Middle Kingdom. For Liang, nationalism signified modernity "not only because it explains the arrival of the modern world in terms of national revolution and collective progress but also because nationalist discourse mandates a new spatiotemporal regime."[29] In Liang's understanding, the modern world was made up of individual nations; global modernity, defined as a world historical moment, could thus only be induced by nationalism as an ideology for change. It was this sense of the modern world, of the "great stage" of national and world history on which China suddenly found itself, that threw old-style Confucian universalism into a provincial and complacent light.

Such an analysis of Chinese modernity privileges a very particular form of modern consciousness, namely nation building stimulated by contact with the imperialist West. It is important, however, not to revert to the kind of viewpoint that for decades trapped understanding of Chinese modernity within the nationalistic, revolutionary boundaries of May Fourth and Communist historiography, that considered the story of Chinese modernity to be one of national liberation from semi-feudalism and semi-colonialism. From its beginnings, the Chinese modernizing project has encompassed multiple aims: to make China rich and powerful (*fuqiang*), to achieve female emancipation, establish a modern autonomous aesthetic, and so on. Scholarship of the last decade has determinedly challenged the May Fourth account of Chinese modernity. Rey Chow and David Der-wei Wang have turned the old revolutionary May Fourth and Communist paradigms of modernity on their heads, showing the Westernized and reformist May Fourth thought to have been traditional and reactionary. At the same time, they have identified a state of immanent modernity in the decadence of more traditional Chinese literary forms under pressure from external stimuli, such as the new popular public sphere that took shape in the treaty ports in the late Qing and early decades of the twentieth century.[30] Leo Lee's consideration of the early twentieth-century "Shanghai Modern" through consumer and print culture, cinema, and literature points to the virtual absence of terms generally associated with Marxist nation-building models of modernity in his subject material.[31] Yet a significant common point emerges from these various models: nineteenth- and twentieth-century Chinese modernity was a product of the intersection of international, including imperialist, cultures with Chinese society. A combination of historical, cultural, and political factors within China then ensured that the political goal of nation building would become the dominate mode of modern intellectual consciousness and underlie many of the concomitant goals of modernization.

Perry Link has written of three traditional assumptions underlying the stance of modern Chinese writers: that written Chinese embodies moral and political power, that a literary intellectual has a responsibility to help set the world in order, and that he can reasonably expect the state to make use of his talents.[32] The nation-building schemas pioneered by intellectuals such as Yan Fu (1854–1921) and Liang Qichao rendered more explicit these links between state and (literary) intellectuals, and brought them closer in the era of modern nationalism. Influenced by examples from the West and Japan, Liang concluded that the "development of science, material well-being, liberal democratic polities, and modern national power was the universal process of the contemporary world."[33] The principle that through literature the Chinese people, as citizens of the Chinese nation, could be co-opted and cultivated lay at the base of the modern Chinese intellectual and literary manifesto. Both Liang and Yan seized upon vernacular literature, and fiction in particular, as the key to national salvation, on the grounds of its broad popularity and their perception of the role it had played in strengthening national consciousness in the West and Japan.[34]

The development of these ideas through the May Fourth period and beyond is described in Fitzgerald's account of China's national awakening during the first four decades of the twentieth century. Examining diverse cultural forms, including fiction, fashion, architecture, autobiography, ethics, ethnography, literature, journalism, and history, Fitzgerald conveys the range and power of nationalist discourse across all spheres of intellectual activity. He traces the process by which individual awakening turned into a new collective national consciousness and describes the impulse of "awakened" twentieth-century intellectuals to awaken others — the "marriage of ethics and action."[35] Fitzgerald notes no significant qualitative difference in the calls to collective action of Sun Yat-sen and the Nationalists (Guomindang, GMD), and Mao Zedong (1893–1976) and the Chinese Communist Party (CCP). In the 1930s and 1940s, intellectual preoccupations with the nation on both the Left and Right crystallized into the high political demands made of writers by both Mao and the GMD.

Yet even as the discourse of national, and hence international, modernity and transformation took hold in China, its intellectual proponents were quick to note the contradictions it contained. Chinese nation building was stimulated by consciousness of a larger global whole and by the desire to gain membership in this community through the passport of nationhood. If one of the primary tasks faced by Chinese intellectuals in the twentieth century was that of establishing, in the face of imperialism, a national literature, the desire to pursue that end was at the same time "a desire for a kind of universal justice — a justice in the eyes of which Chinese literature and culture would become legitimate internationally rather than simply 'Chinese.'"[36] Nationalism and universality are almost always two sides of the same coin in twentieth-century China, from Liang Qichao to Mao Zedong and beyond. Liu Kang, for example, characterizes Mao, the inventor of sinicized Marxism, as "a universalist or internationalist in his revolutionary utopian aspirations . . . nationalism, as a strategy in his revolutionary schema, is always subjugated to Mao's overall vision of the 'emancipation of all mankind.'"[37] Yet Liang Qichao's original vision of Chinese identity as one national culture among many in the global network immediately created a logical dilemma: "The same moment the modern world space makes possible a universal human history, the geopolitical reality exploited by the system of nation-states also keeps that prospect at bay."[38] Moreover, what kind of "universal justice" has after all been delivered by the value systems of modernity and progress in which Chinese intellectuals have invested so much hope?

Despite the heavy emphasis on awakening *Chinese* national consciousness in modern China, and despite the local and universal claims of nationalism, a deep ideologically ambivalent vein of Western-based imperialism runs within discourses of modern nation building in China and other countries outside the developed West: nationalism, the instrumental logic behind Western imperialist domination and racism, is reproduced under leaders of national liberation movements such as Mao. This propagates a global model of nationalism intertwined with imperialism, a second-hand modernity that never quite delivers the liberating universalism it promises.[39] Bin Zhao expresses the derivative nature of the struggle thus:

Ever since the idea of progress, invented some 250 years ago in a cold corner of Western Europe, conquered the imagination of the rest of the world through violence and enticement, the frenzied pursuit of modernization has become a central concern for the so-called "Third World." Modernity, the most formidable achievement of the West, questioned and criticized at home since its inception, remains a potent dreamland for the rest of the world. The vision of many cultural and political elites in poor countries has been so dazzled by its powerful display that their imagination of other possibilities for development has been seriously blunted.... The history of desperately seeking modernity has been littered with sufferings, failures, frustrations, and disasters.[40]

Although Bin Zhao here is discussing "modernization," the term "nation building" — a key ingredient in the Western European recipe for progress over the past 250 years — could be substituted equally well. China, represented by its intellectual elite, has turned out to be one of the twentieth century's most determined aspirants to this understanding of progress. Yet if the general idea of progress is split into two concepts, modernization (such as institutional reforms, and economic and technological development) and modernity (a form of consciousness), we can identify one feature that has repeatedly frustrated Chinese efforts. While modernization is linked to material developments such as science, capitalism, and the like, modernity (an abstract outlook) is rooted in the ideas of progress, movement, unrepeatable time, innovation and originality. Modernity demands a new kind of subjectivity, one that can cope with the influx of new influences brought by the modern era and a new envisioning of the global spatiotemporal realm. This emphasis on novelty implies that, having embarked on modernity, there is no turning back, but only a ceaseless pursuit of renewal and change.[41] Until very recently, the dominant cultural and historical geography of modernity has insisted that the initiative in this process lies with the West, leaving those outside doomed to a perpetual game of catch-up. Such assumptions have long formed the problematic basis of China's attempts to join the global structures that symbolize success in the modern world.[42]

Its pretensions to universal emancipation notwithstanding, nationalism, as it has spread throughout the modern world, has been deeply implicated in this game of catch-up. Indeed, scholars have often adopted a domino-effect analytical model to describe nationalism's advance. Greenfeld, for example, traces the process by which nationalism spread from England, to France, Russia, the United States, and Germany, driven by the *ressentiment*, or the competitive desire of national elites for the sense of uniqueness and prestige generated by consciousness of national identity. When the creeds of modernization and nationalism spread beyond the West, there was an altogether more powerful propagating force at work — namely, imperialism — equipped with its full arsenal of modern Western reason, science, and capital. The mode of historical thinking tied to Enlightenment reason, in turn, has had a bearing on all kinds of social, political, and cultural production, particularly in East Asian societies, which, in Prasenjit Duara's view, have adopted the Enlightenment model of history perhaps more wholly than other non-Western societies.

> The last two centuries have established [Enlightenment] History as we know it — a linear, progressive history — not only as the dominant mode of experiencing time, but as the dominant mode of being. That is to say, time overcomes space — a condition in which the Other in geographical space will, *in time*, come to look like earlier versions of us . . . History enables not simply the justification of world mastery by the West, but . . . the appropriation of the Other as a form of knowledge.[43]

This sets down the hierarchy that governs the rhetoric of much political and cultural interaction between the developed and developing world in the modern era and provides the philosophical background to the phenomenon that Edward Said calls Orientalism. In Orientalist discourse, Orientals by themselves lack the requisite objective reasoning abilities to survive in the Western vision of the world order.[44] This phenomenon is neatly captured by Partha Chatterjee's term for nationalist thought in the colonial world — "a derivative discourse."[45] Chatterjee raises an acute objection even to Benedict Anderson's approach, which theorizes the spread of imagined national communities made possible by the growth of vernacular literatures. "If nationalisms in the rest of the world have to choose their imagined community from certain 'modular' forms already made available to them by Europe and the Americas, what do they have left to imagine? History, it would seem, has decreed that we in the postcolonial world shall only be perpetual consumers of modernity . . . even our imaginations must remain forever colonized."[46]

The cultural implications of this point, directly relevant to Chinese intellectuals' desire for the Nobel Prize as part of their desire for modernity, have been probed by Gregory Jusdanis in *Belated Modernity and Aesthetic Culture*, in which he describes the efforts of Greek elites to catch up with more advanced European nations in their quest for modernity.[47] Jusdanis makes the observation, highly pertinent to the close links between modernity, nation, and literature in China, that the tensions created by the opposition of Greek tradition with Western modernity were resolved by the modern construct of the autonomous aesthetic. His discussion of the institutions of this autonomous "aesthetic" — literary criticism, canon making, and so on — highlights the process by which it has been established as a powerful, independent system of symbolic values (arbitrated by organizations such as the Nobel Committee) that represents nationhood and hence functions as a passport to membership of the modern global whole. These Enlightenment–Romantic discourses of nation building — the belief that the world is made up of nations, each comprised of creative individuals who belong to and reflect a unique national culture — have had enormous influence on modern understandings of how a universalistic autonomous aesthetic is constituted.[48] However, as Pierre Bourdieu's work suggests, although modern ideas of art define it as an independent value system, this claim conceals and implicitly denies the concepts of nationality, class, and gender that inevitably shape this process.[49]

The persuasive superiority of Western enlightenment, progress, and science was widely embraced by Chinese reformers, to whom it promised national empowerment even as it took away discursive control. Addressing the question of the national character and national emancipation, modern Chinese writers such as Ba Jin and Shen Congwen could not but engage with, and thus reinforce with varying degrees of reflective self-consciousness, the very Orientalist critiques they sought to refute.[50] Anxiety about the Nobel Prize, as an external and specifically Western source of valuation, expresses the ambivalence of Chinese intellectuals concerning their relation to the global order and to the basis of membership to the global whole, nationhood, as mediated by the autonomous aesthetic and the institutionalization of a national literature. The establishment of a national literary criticism in twentieth-century China provided a discursive tool by which literary intellectuals could theoretically work out relations with international and national communities, but more often than not these efforts foundered on deeply politicized contention over who constituted and represented these communities.[51]

A useful theoretical perspective on the troubled psychology behind intellectual nation-building discourses in China is provided by Xueping Zhong's work on the modern Chinese intellectual "marginality complex." In her analysis of masculinity in the modern Chinese literary identity, Zhong asserts that Chinese cultural and literary politics of the twentieth century and in particular of the post-Mao era, can be read in terms of a beleaguered (male) subjectivity. The modern Chinese encounter with the West produced an intellectual identity that struggled to detach itself from tradition while desiring to catch up with and win recognition from the West, the source of "universal modernity." Feelings of inferiority deriving from the historical encounter between Chinese tradition and the West engendered both a sense of rootless marginality (a "male marginality complex") and — the kickback from patriarchalism and sinocentrism — a desire to recover a central (read modern, national, global, universal) position. "Instead of embracing the marginality . . . the Chinese male marginality complex is filled with the desire to overcome the marginalized position by moving toward the center" and ultimately supporting the center.[52]

This, however, is the search for a center that is not fixed or even attainable, given the two-way pull between marginal and central aspirations, between nationalistic pride and global ambitions. Intellectuals both yearn for what they see as rightful recognition *and* suspect that things Chinese will never quite reach the imagined global standard.

Finally, it should not be forgotten that the Nobel Literature Prize is given to individuals and not nations, a fact often obscured in China's Nobel discussions. The Chinese identification of literature with national prestige in the international arena (signified by the Nobel Complex) has proved continually troublesome. It in effect holds literature — an elite form in which the role of the creative individual is nowadays paramount — ransom to a collective, centralized national identity. Yet although Chinese intellectuals have brought the particularities of their own local experience to bear on the problem of modern national identity and literature, the self-contradictory notion of a universal literary (and civilizational) system constituted by individual geniuses representative of their national cultures is not unique to China; similar convictions have been held, and indeed originated, in the modern West.

Chinese preoccupation with a powerful cultural institution such as the Nobel Prize is part of the uncomfortable play-off in the modern era between China, the West, and the quest for universality. If desire for the prize is equivalent to the Chinese yearning to represent China on a global, Western-dominated stage, it is deeply enmeshed in these century-old discourses of inferiority and insecurity. The struggles to reclaim and represent the nation in the twentieth century, struggles in which literature has often been at the center, testify to the hold these discourses have taken on the Chinese intellectual imagination. The hope that literature can carry Chinese aspirations forward demonstrates the faith in modern China, as in Greece, that the autonomous aesthetic can effectively resolve tensions between West and East, modernity and tradition, the nation and the world. However, the often tumultuous and heavily politicized workings of this aesthetic and of the search for a Nobel Prize in twentieth-century China also point to real-world imbalances and inequalities that belie the universalistic promise of national and world literatures.

Post-Second World War Globalization and the Nation-State

Although nationhood over the last fifty-odd years has largely continued to be the key to membership in the modern international order, the relationship between the nation and the process of globalization has not remained static and currently forms the crux of debates on global transactions at the start of the new millennium. The second half of the twentieth century appears to have been the golden age of the nation-state, and hence, theoretically, of the Western-dominated model of modernity that has long been viewed as lying behind the nation-state: the number of internationally recognized states more than doubled between 1945 and the early 1990s, and the importance of interstate relations to the contemporary global order was formally institutionalized with the establishment of the United Nations in 1945.

At the same time, however, the growth of multinational organizations and transnational flows of capital, information, people, and culture has meant that politics, economics, and culture in the majority of nation-states (barring anomalies such as North Korea) have become increasingly subject to forces and influences from the outside that exhibit little respect for national sovereignty. Since the fall of the Soviet bloc in 1989 and the accelerated advancement of market forces within the People's Republic of China in the 1990s, socialism no longer presents an alternative to global capitalism; indeed, it has been almost totally discredited. Martin Jacques characterizes the 1990s ethos as that of "neutral, interest-free globalization," consigning "the past to the dustbin of history — ideology, left, right, socialism, capitalism, imperialism (hopelessly old hat) and the rest." Although this decade saw the emergence of the United States as a global hyperpower, remarks Jacques, the U.S. strove "to construct a global alliance, its multilateralist instincts still predominant," rather than unilaterally asserting its national interests.[53] Even after the radical change in global politics brought about by September 11, 2001, when the Americans became increasingly willful in their interventions on the international stage, scholarly analysts of the globalization debate have continued to position themselves somewhere in or between two extreme camps: skeptics, who believe that the sovereign nation-state remains the crucial unit in the organization of the world; and believers in globalization, who see instead one world, shaped by extensive, intensive, and rapid flows across regions and between continents.[54]

Few hard-and-fast conclusions can be drawn from this debate, beyond the fact that since the 1960s globalization has emerged as a respectable analytic term. This is not to say that scholars of globalization such as David Held and Anthony McGrew are agnostic about its contemporary practice, or view it as heralding the emergence of a truly inclusive, egalitarian global system. Joining their voices with those of the swelling worldwide ranks of antiglobalization protestors, they point out that, given the accelerating gap between rich and poor nations, globalization poses significant questions about the kind of world order being constructed and whose interests it serves.[55] The principal beneficiary, indeed the architect of an open global realm, is still capital; those who enjoy and gain most benefit from capital and the political and cultural influence it generates are, of course, those who hold most of it, namely the developed nations of the West. Yet scholars such as Arjun Appadurai counter claims that globalization is synonymous with Western economic, political, and cultural imperialism by asserting that global flows occur in and through growing disjunctures between different spheres of global activity. The question of agency (contested between consumers and producers), argues Appadurai, is now thoroughly confused, and globalization exists in tension between homogenization and heterogenization.[56]

Appadurai's emphasis on the blurring of agency and on processes of decentering and pluralism in the global arena indicates that there is some overlap between theories of globalization on the one hand, and postcolonial and postmodernist theory (the former term current by the 1980s, the latter a decade earlier) on the other. If so, the age of globalization should herald the death of Enlightenment thought. Starting with *Orientalism* in 1978, the Eurocentrism of Enlightenment-derived schemas of knowledge has endured an uncomfortable two decades in academia. Said laid bare the Occidental construction of the Orient, likening Western knowledge of the East to subordination by a strong, knowing West of the weak, knowable, and therefore controllable East. Nationalism, another Enlightenment model, has also slipped out of fashion, replaced by the postmodern free-for-all of global capitalism. Indeed, even though the nation-state remains the chief unit of political organization in the world today, new globalizing orthodoxies assert the world is ruled instead by neutral flows of transnational capital, arbitrated by transnational corporations. The idea of the nation has thus become a little passé, even distasteful to those in the West who have moved on (postcolonial intellectuals included). As non-Western peoples and regimes gained access to the special formula of nationalist liberation (membership in the United Nations grew from 51 at its founding in 1945, to 156 in 1981, the new members largely third-world states released from crumbling empires), the West was tiring of it. By the 1970s, writes Chatterjee, the West started to view the nation as a slightly embarrassing export, as "the reason why people in the Third World killed each other. . . . Nothing, it would seem, was left in the legacy of nationalism to make people in the Western world feel good about it."[57]

Admittedly, nationalism has made quite a comeback in the West in the twenty-first century, particularly in the United States, which has abandoned the multilateralism of the Cold War and the 1990s in favor of a unilateral, or at best bilateral (with Britain) course of action in international relations. But in the world of cultural studies, the advent of globalization in the 1960s has made the search for a more evenly weighted, less Western-focused understanding of global transactions a continuing and major concern. Tainted by cultural imperialism, nationalism and the other companion concepts of Enlightenment modernity have in Western academic circles been superseded by the epistemic developments associated with postmodern and postcolonial theory, two flagships of global multiculturalism. While both these terms encompass a broad range of theories and theorists, academic postcolonial criticism shares with postmodernist theory and culture the aim of contesting master narratives: Eurocentrism, Orientalism, and nationalism, "those modes of thinking which configure the Third World in such irreducible essences as religiosity, underdevelopment, poverty, nationhood, non-Westernness."[58] Manifestations of culture and criticism labeled "postmodern," similarly aim to accept and represent with relativistic inclusiveness all classes and races in rebellion against the suffocating embrace of European modernity.[59]

Both postmodernism and postcolonialism thus seek a cultivated indeterminacy that has spread into all spheres of thought: philosophy, science, history, literature, and cultural criticism. The very porosity of national boundaries (former markers of the modern) seems to be the hallmark of our globalized contemporary era. Already the victory of decentered, genuinely universalistic plurality over earlier, Western-dominated models of global modernity has been celebrated: for instance, in Frederick Buell's *National Culture and the New Global System*. This work, endorsed by the prominent theorist of postmodernism Fredric Jameson, takes an overall optimistic view of the interaction between national and global culture, questioning both the ability of the West to impose unmediated cultural imperialism over distant corners of the globe and the authenticity of local "traditions."[60] Buell traces the historical process behind the contemporary ideal of indeterminate globalization, from the formation of the global network of nations, via the Three Worlds system, to the decentered single system that developed over the two decades before the early 1990s. In short, he finds at work a "fruitful paradox" in which, "as the world draws more tightly together into a single system, it multiplies its circulation of differences."[61] He denies the existence of any one center: the shifting and overlapping of agency permits none. As the ultimate gesture of postmodern magnanimity, he even offers an oblique thanks to Johann Gottfried von Herder (1744–1803), Enlightenment theorizer *par excellence* of the nation, for the latter's attachment to referential cultural boundaries that could later be so easily attacked as a sociocultural construction rather than supported by objective social science.[62] This echoes the conviction of the postcolonial critic Homi Bhabha that the nation is no more than a notion.[63]

So much, it seems, for Enlightenment thinking and nationalism in the postcolonial era of globalization. What is the significance of this newly inclusive, multicultural universalism for those non-Western countries, such as China, that found themselves forever lagging behind in the race for global modernity as defined by this same Enlightenment thinking and nationalism? Thoughtful critics are not convinced by claims of victory for a decentered, universalistic multiculturalism. Although the binary views of the West and its Other seem "already to have been erased by the global condition of modernity," Daruvala writes, "this does not solve the issue at all . . . since the idea of a global (post)modernity — which is often seen as leading to the supercession of the nation-state — is still deeply indebted to the Enlightenment mode of history. Postmodernity and modernity are conjoined, in that both are posited on a rupture with the past. More suspiciously, capitalism is still the beneficiary of whatever changes may have taken place."[64] These are points that Buell acknowledges but does not allow to seriously qualify his celebratory account of globalization. To back up his conclusions, he approvingly quotes a satire on anti-immigrant American chauvinism that meticulously chronicles the non-American origin of practically every component of the daily American routine: clothing, mirrors, coffee, sugar, china, and so on.[65] Yet he overlooks one crucial element of the power play involved: the "Hundred Percent American" is the consumer and primary beneficiary of all these exotically derived everyday commodities.

Arif Dirlik and Ziauddin Sardar have taken issue with the multiculturalist triumphalism of postcolonialism and postmodernism. In provocative and stimulating critiques, both view, to varying degrees, these "post-isms" as creating an indeterminate mishmash that undermines rigorous, constructive academic debate while duplicitously strengthening Western-derived value systems and continuing to marginalize the non-West. Dirlik's reservations concerning postcolonialism are on four general counts. Firstly, postcolonialism, with its emphasis on local subjectivities, denies and erases real global historical phenomena such as the spread of capital, which are related to complex networks of Eurocentrism that survive up to the present day (in the form, for example, of Western economic dominance).[66] Secondly, the subversive potential of postcolonialism has been, and always will be, limited by the fact that it issues from intellectuals of third-world origin located in the centers of power, producing, arguably, an equation between multiculturalism and postcolonial Eurocentrism.[67] Thirdly, the ritualized attacks on the Enlightenment in the name of postcolonialism suppress the complexities of the historical Enlightenment, in its time a source of new critiques of oppression and exploitation within and without Europe. Finally, postcolonialism takes aim at universalist Enlightenment modes of thinking while itself being a product of globalization and a new universal vision for global cultural relations; even a multiculturalist critic such as Buell acknowledges resonance between his project and Enlightenment aspirations clearly enough: "Vastly more than eighteenth-century concepts of universal citizenship," Buell writes of multiculturalism, "these developments represent an attempt to form a global civil culture."[68] Multiculturalism has thus become the new universalistic dogma: "Be hybrid, or die!"[69]

Taking the ethics of marginality (recentering of non-Western "Other worlds") as a crucial underpinning of postmodernism, Sardar concludes that "far from being a new theory of liberation,

> postmodernism, particularly from the perspective of the Other, the non-western cultures, is simply a new wave of domination riding on the crest of colonialism and modernity . . . postmodernism avoids, by glossing over, the politics of non-western marginalization in history by suddenly discovering Otherness everywhere. . . . We are all Others now, can appropriate the Other, consume artefacts of the Other, so what does it matter if Others want something different in their future.[70]

Rather than merely repudiating colonialism and modernity, postmodernism instead soars far above them both: "Postmodernism is about appropriating the history and identity of non-western cultures as an integral facet of itself, colonizing their future and occupying their being."[71] The world of postmodernism is still being made by the nations of the West, with the mendacious assurance that it is tolerantly, inclusively internationalist. Sardar's array of examples ranges from Disney's historicist "edutainment" to The Body Shop's one-way, parasitic sampling of indigenous exotica for the benefit of Western consumers.

Of relevance to the present study's focus on literature is Sardar's reservation of some of his most passionate criticisms for the phenomenon of postmodern fiction such as magical realism, the genre by which non-Western authors have managed, it seems, most successfully to gain entrance on their own terms to the contemporary world canon. Magical realism, he asserts, was already present in Kafka (1883–1924), Beckett (1906–1989), and Kipling (1865–1936); its boom in the non-West "gives the appearance of speaking from the perspective that incorporates the Other but in so doing it merely utilizes that conception of the Other that fits within the established conventions of the west."[72] The idealized culture of liberal democracy, acclaimed by postmodernists as the only culture in which a desirable plurality can function, while declaring the indefensibility of all values, is in fact declaring the defensibility of two ideologies, capitalism and democracy. Everything else, however, can and should be ironized and mocked. Sardar's locus classicus here is Salman Rushdie's (1947–) celebration of postmodern secularism and demonization of faith, *The Satanic Verses*. Rushdie's book, Sardar asserts, represents the capitulation of a non-Western author to the logic of the West. Rushdie, like authors of Latin American magical realism, writes in European languages, and therefore chooses to operate within a recognizably Western linguistic and literary tradition. Rather than even-handedly representing values of pluralistic tolerance, Rushdie uses the economic might of a powerful Western publishing house to promote the Western orthodoxy of secular art. More than simply privileging the voice of secularism over others, Rushdie's fiction claims the position of god and becomes an arch ideology of Western art.

It is significant that, once more, suspiciously in common with Enlightenment modernity and nationalism, the idea of the autonomous aesthetic (in the form of Western secular art) aspires to play a powerful emancipatory role within the universalistic schema of postmodernism. Yet, as before, its claims to autonomy require scrutiny. In face of the triumph of Western secular art, other cultures find their own distinct voices severely muffled, and subject to an agenda determined by the secular imagination. Pluralism is being simulated, while the underlying structures of dominance (America, the West) continue to rule.

Both Dirlik's reservations about postcolonial theory and Sardar's attack on postmodernism are far from the last word on either subject. Dirlik is ungenerous in assessing the contribution made by postcolonial theory to creating a less Western-centric scholarly framework of analysis (a framework to which the present study is itself heavily indebted). In his anxiety to denounce what he sees as the manifestations of postmodernism in contemporary global culture, Sardar neglects to engage in a careful way with the critical and oppositional possibilities inherent within analyses by postmodern critics such as Fredric Jameson.[73] Sardar refuses also to consider the subversive tendencies of the postmodern aesthetic, for example its parodic potential and its ability to combine ironic distance from, and complicity with, mainstream culture and society.[74] But both Dirlik's and Sardar's criticisms provide bracing insights into the workings of a contemporary global culture that, while lauding the values of multicultural universalism, continues to be dominated by the economic might of the West, a dominance that has so far been only slowly and partially challenged by the rise of alternative power centers in Asia (Japan's now faltering economic miracle, and the considerable but far from even growth achieved in Mainland China since the 1980s). Less polemical arguments about the failings of "post" theories have, moreover, been advanced by scholars such as Leela Gandhi, Rey Chow, and Ien Ang. Gandhi and Chow rightly applaud the pluralistic, oppositional achievements within the Western humanities associated with developments in postmodernist and postcolonial theory, including poststructuralism, cultural studies, and *Orientalism*-inspired critiques.[75] Yet at the same time, they express strong caution about premature multiculturalist triumphalism. While the broad schools of postmodernist and postcolonial theory certainly open the door to multiculturalism, they have not yet erased certain key power relations within global culture and within Western academe: for example, the problem of postcolonial, multicultural theory being rooted in the West and the danger that exists for postcolonial or subaltern studies of collapsing into "identity politics" that reaffirm the old-style essentializations of imperialist nationalism. In *On Not Speaking Chinese*, meanwhile, Ien Ang argues convincingly about the failure of "identity" and "diaspora" politics to erode nationalism and racism.[76]

These reservations about the ability of postcolonialism and postmodernism to globalize and eradicate enduring forms of Western-centrism and nationalistic bias in cultural transactions are borne out by noting the selective application of these theories in China between the late 1980s and early 1990s. Postmodernism first seized Chinese intellectual imaginations in 1985, following a series of lectures given by Fredric Jameson in Beijing. After 1989 the ever-more-visible manifestations of globalization, combined with disillusionment over the failure of Westernized ideals of enlightenment and progress of the 1980s, resulted in an even more enthusiastic embrace of postmodernism and postcolonialism as models for understanding China's situation. Critics in the West such as Dirlik and Xudong Zhang have also seized upon postmodernism as a new, fruitful way of envisioning contemporary Chinese cultural identities, moving beyond "the increasingly problematic status of the nation as a unit of analysis, as it is undermined by forces from both within and without."[77] Dirlik and Zhang hold that China's incorporation into the global economy, and the growing influence and prosperity of the Chinese global diaspora, dictate a rethinking of modernist notions of a unified and unquestioned Chinese identity put forward by the socialist state. Within Mainland China alone, uneven development and the dislocation between a socialist system in apparent meltdown and capitalism with global characteristics suggest the need to question the possibility of any coherent teleological narrative.

The 1994 manifesto of "post-studies" (*houxue*), "From Modernity to Chineseness," coauthored by Zhang Fa, Zhang Yiwu, and Wang Yichuan, sought a postmodern, postcolonial model for understanding China's experiences of the modern. Its authors defined modernity as an exclusively Western, hegemonic model of knowledge to be abandoned in the 1990s in favor of a new Chinese vision. The manifesto, in short, aspired to fulfill an emancipatory function — unlocking China from the relations of domination inherent to the Western notion of modern progress by unleashing the powerful theoretical forces of postmodernism and postcolonialism. Rather than distancing themselves from the idea of nation as an inseparable component of Western Enlightenment modernity, however, these theorists seemed to reassert essentialized national characteristics.

Ever since postmodernist theory arrived in China, cultural critics have pointed out the nationalist uses to which it has been put. Jing Wang scornfully characterizes the earliest manifestations of the postmodernism debate as permeated by the "Great Leap Forward" mentality, namely, an Enlightenment-like desire for cultural progress, for China to stride to the forefront of civilizational developments.[78] After the Maoist model of nationalism and universalism had been discredited, Chinese intellectuals in the 1980s first introduced a Western-oriented notion of modernity. The rapid succession of literary and cultural imports was driven by the familiar intellectual desire for Chinese culture to modernize, catch up, and "march towards the (center of the literary) world" (*zou xiang shijie*); the desire to capture a Nobel Prize slotted naturally into this schema. But the enthusiastic reception of these imports was always mediated by anxious cultural nationalism and by ambivalence concerning their non-Chinese origins. Postmodernism, however, the most up-to-date intellectual trend to enter China in the 1980s, offered the bonus feature of combining a new and inclusive global vision with privileging the local over some dominant center. Thus the attraction of postmodernism in the 1980s, Jing Wang maintains, lay in its pliability to the ends of cultural nationalism, in its promise to help shape and legitimize a sinified vision of global (post)modernity. Even critics such as Dirlik and Zhang, who have endorsed the use of "postmodernism" in the Chinese context, note the irony: "While the ultimate justification for the use of the term may lie in spatial fracturing and temporal dissonance, which call into question any claims to cultural authenticity, Chinese postmodernists insist nevertheless on marking Chinese postmodernity as something authentically Chinese."[79]

Critics such as Ben Xu and Henry Yiheng Zhao, both now resident in the West, have reached even more profoundly critical conclusions concerning the functioning of postmodernist and postcolonial theory in 1990s China.[80] While following the postcolonial and postmodernist privileging of local "marginal" subjectivities, they assert, Chinese cultural nativist theory has developed along with a growing intellectual nationalism that focuses resentment at past humiliations and failures onto attacks on the West. This is, moreover, a stance welcomed by the post-1989 government interested in encouraging an antiforeign nationalism to secure its claims to legitimacy. Xu notes inconsistencies in the postmodernist, postcolonial standpoints that indicate nothing less than a recapitulation of Chinese cultural nationalism and all the problems and sources of ambivalence that have dogged China's quest for the modern. China's "post-ist" scholars repudiate Western-derived ideas of progress, while presenting modern Chinese culture in teleological terms, progressing inexorably towards the postmodern emancipation of a Post-New Era, "a self-congratulatory process of national maturing that purposefully leaves out any possible historical reverse."[81] While thumbing a postmodernist nose at their Western-based targets, these critics themselves pose as absolute arbiters of truth, upholding the virtue of a mystically unique notion of "Chineseness" (comprising Chinese-style market economy, Chinese popular culture, and Chinese diversified values). Rather than decentered concepts open to redefinition, modernity and Chineseness become fixed entities, with the idea of "China" firmly reinstalled at the center of Chinese culture. Cultural nativists, Xu has little doubt, "rally under the banner of *nation*."[82] And, of course, the fact remains that these theories being used to criticize the West still originated in the West.[83]

Plus ça change, plus c'est la même chose: under the mantle of postmodernist and postcolonial theory, Enlightenment ideas of the modern have, at least in part, continued to color new, inclusive schemas of global culture and the "local" (marginal) milieus they are meant to privilege. China's *ressentiment* for modernity has lived on.[84]

Chinese Literature and the World Literary Economy

The evolution of global modernity in the twentieth century has set in place epistemological and aesthetic frameworks that base agency and power in the West, despite the leveling aspirations of contemporary theoretical and cultural developments. This state of affairs is played out in the world of literary production as it is in the worlds of economics and politics. Once more, agency for inventing universal cultural models has lain within the West, in the hands of theorizers and architects such as Goethe (1749–1832), Marx (1818–1883), and Alfred Nobel (1833–1896), who have tended to overlook or perpetuate various forms of Eurocentrism.

Goethe's 1827 schema for a world literary marketplace, based on principles of free trade (an antecedent of global capitalism) that would advance human civilization through mutual understanding and tolerance, is very much a philosophical product of its time, revealing both Enlightenment universalism and Romantic faith in an artistic realm that is both made up of and floats above national difference. The realization of his ideal, however, was compromised both by the global system of transnational exchange governed by economic inequalities, and by a barely concealed Euro- and Germanic-centrism.[85] Marx, who linked the spread of literature across national boundaries with the invasive, exploitative spread of capital, nevertheless also took a positive view of the universalistic potential of this development. "National one-sidedness and narrow-mindedness become more and more impossible, and from the numerous national and local literatures, there arises a world literature."[86] The power of Swedish capital accounts at least in part for the global authority of the Nobel Prize. A hierarchy of Western power and economics governs world literature and the Nobel Prize, the latter representing "a systemic designation of literary authority that rightly or wrongly has been established and accepted by the economically advanced Western nations; the rest of the world ignores it only at the peril of exclusion from this source of wealth and power."[87] The very idea of a prize surely contradicts Goethe's ideal: a truly universalistic world literature would not require arbitration by the possessors of wealth and power, but concentrate purely on global free-flows of literary translation and exchange.

The Nobel Prize occupies a very particular position in the global imagination as a unique institution of world literature (it is virtually the only international literary prize, certainly the most famous and lucrative). Yet the Nobel Prize is also very much a product of modern European philosophy, combining contradictory ideas about literature from the Enlightenment, the Romantic era, and the nineteenth century. In practice, the prize has not been a clearly centered or static institution, having veered confusingly between different criteria (shaped by the personal preferences of the committee members and unacknowledged Western systems of literary evaluation) in different epochs, including a Goethean "coolness of plasticity," universal accessibility, engaged writing, pioneering experimentalism, anticommercialism and ethnic marginalia.[88] It is neither a bastion of "pure" literary values nor a consistent arbitrator among literary styles and nations: its criteria have moved from artistic universalism to national characteristics depending on whether the laureate is Western or non-Western, from the "description of the human condition" to the nationally specific "spokesman for Arabic prose" (citations for 1985 and 1987, Claude Simon, France, and Naguib Mahfouz, Egypt, respectively).

The multiculturalist record of the Nobel Prize speaks for itself. In its first one hundred years, the prize went to only six (black) African or Asian laureates (Rabindranath Tagore, Yasunari Kawabata, Wole Soyinka, Naguib Mahfouz, Kenzaburo Oe, Gao Xingjian), two of whom (Tagore and Soyinka) won the prize principally for works written in English. Four of these prizes, however, have been concentrated in the last twenty years, from which it could be inferred that the Nobel Committee has shifted its attention towards universality. In the period following the Second World War, Nobel committees have increasingly singled out "difficult" oeuvres that claim artistic universality and autonomy through their obscurity, floating above the realm of national sociopolitical specificity. Since the 1970s committees have also sought to honor writers from "marginal" literatures. More women have received the prize and the committee has sought to break away from Nobel's worthy stipulation of "idealism," honoring instead avant-garde jokers and skeptics like Dario Fo (1997) and Gao Xingjian. What are the implications of this trend for the reception of a "marginal" national literature such as China's within a world literary economy — the contemporary heir to Goethe's ideal of World Literature — in transition from the modern to the postmodern?

Even as China aims at the start of a new millennium to take an ever-more-active part in "global culture," and even as a Chinese-born writer whose most important work was written in Chinese has finally taken Nobel laurels, reception of Chinese literature is still caught up in tortuous aesthetic and ideological wrangles that illuminate the true dynamics of the world literary economy. Despite strenuous efforts on the part of Chinese politicians, critics, and writers, along with Western translators, Chinese literature has not achieved mainstream recognition in the global canon as defined by the publishing markets and literary institutions (such as organs of literary review, prizes, academic curricula) of the politically and culturally dominant West.[89] Although translations from Chinese into Western languages have been on the increase since the death of Mao, relatively little Chinese literature is translated and published in English (only 181 book-length translations were produced between 1976 and 2002).[90] The translations that do come out are rarely produced by prestigious commercial publishers able to afford generous publicity budgets.[91] Translations are more often picked up by academic presses, ensuring that Chinese literature tends to remain in an academic ghetto.[92] Where translations are produced by commercial literary publishers, these presses rarely devote the editorial resources necessary to achieve the stylistic standards expected in works written directly in English or translated from other languages.[93] Works of Chinese literature in translation are seldom reviewed in mainstream arenas of literary criticism, such as the book pages of national broadsheet newspapers or review journals such as *The New York Review of Books* or *The London Review of Books*. Even the relative boom in translations since the death of Mao has "failed to generate either best-sellers or accepted points of reference in

Western literary criticism."[94] Why is Chinese literature rarely, if ever, appreciated as literature in the West?

It is not the intention here to consider at length the question of whether modern China has produced literary works of sufficient quality to merit further Nobel Prizes or a more central position in the world canon. Such an approach would imply a faith in a universal standard of evaluation in world literature, and it is one of the aims of this book to demonstrate the fallacy of such a notion. True enough, the weaknesses in modern Chinese literature are sufficiently obvious even for specialists in the field to admit.[95] A few of the principal criticisms can be summarized thus: the ruptures brought about by the literary revolutions ongoing since the start of the twentieth century have interrupted the maturation process of a modern literature; the intrusion of politics into the literary realm, particularly after 1949, has stifled literary creativity as Chinese writers, critics, and editors have not been able to withstand these incursions; in the 1990s, as overt politicization of literature has decreased, "serious" writers have been unable to resist new commercial temptations and have consequently neglected literary quality. Other commentators have pointed to the poor quality of translations as a factor contributing to the low popularity of Chinese literature in the West.[96] "It is perfectly comprehensible that [Westerners] may choose not to read widely in modern Chinese literature, since the greater part of it lacks grace, wit and sensibility," Bonnie McDougall asserts. "Even its natural audience in its native country would, in strict confidence, agree that it is a sad comedown from the glories of the Chinese literary tradition."[97]

Works of indifferent or even poor artistic quality have not, however, prevented a good many writers from winning a Nobel Prize. The list of awards is peppered with names that literary history has long forgotten: Sully Prudhomme, the first laureate, is a case in point. At present, moreover, several national literatures in the West probably possess as few writers of obviously Nobel stature as China does. In Britain, for example, it is hard to think of more than one or two potential Nobel laureates. Chinese literary history is, admittedly, strikingly barren between 1949 and the 1970s, but the pre- and post-Mao periods have undoubtedly produced works that could compare in terms of quality certainly with the worst and probably with a few of the best of Nobel-winning oeuvres; some of these have been skillfully translated into Western languages.[98] Rather than arguing endlessly about the strengths and weaknesses of various literary works, this section instead seeks to root the relative marginality of such a large national literature as China's within the world literary economy in the international politics of publishing, translation, and reception.

First of all, the term "world literary economy" as used here requires further definition. It is both divided between the various discrete national reading markets, and unified by ever-growing multinational publishing consortiums based in the West such as HarperCollins and Bertelsmann. The advertising and distributing power of these principally Anglophone publishing giants has resulted in the phenomenon of multinational best-sellers. The linguistic dominance of English has made translating and exporting global best-sellers a largely one-way process, from Anglophone nations into other languages. Compared to other national reading markets (including those in Europe), Anglophone reading markets have remained relatively impervious to translations.[99] By the mid-1980s the translation of English texts into other languages was five times more frequent than works in French, the second most popular language. There is little indication this trade deficit in translations has subsequently shrunk. In 2002 German publishers, for example, bought translation rights to 3,782 American books, while American publishers bought rights for only 150 German books.[100] This unequal exchange is replicated and intensified in the case of China, whose readers have long been voracious translators and consumers of Western books, while books translated from Chinese into European languages are rarely read outside specialist circles.[101] The market share of Chinese literature in English translation has long been dwarfed by that of books about China by Chinese-born authors writing directly in English.[102] In this skewed system of literary exchange, the kudos attached to winning a Nobel Literature Prize represents an important route to renown in the world literary economy for non-Anglophone and, in particular, non-European writers. Nobel and global success for works written in languages other than English, and particularly non-European languages, depends, of course, largely on translation into English or other European languages (most members of the Swedish Academy, arbiters of the Nobel Literature Prize, are proficient readers in English, French, and German as well as the Nordic languages, but at any one time, only one or two are able to read non-European languages in the original). The close links between translation and winning a Nobel Prize bring non-Anglophone literature back up against the first barrier to achieving success in the world literary economy — Anglophone disinclination towards reading translations.

Anglophone insularity and the disinterested publishing circle it generates explain in part the paucity of translations from Chinese into English and their failure to generate large sales, particularly given the additional difficulty of successfully translating a language as remote from English as Chinese. Aversion to reading translations, however, does not fully explain the low status of Chinese literature. Translated fiction from Japan (whose language and culture are historically as remote from the West as those of China) has carved out a place for itself in literary publishing in the West. A handful of modern Japanese authors — Yukio Mishima, Haruki Murakami, and Banana Yoshimoto — have become better known to a general Anglophone readership than even the two Japanese Nobel laureates, Yasunari Kawabata (1968) and Kenzaburo Oe (1994).[103] Perhaps thanks to Japan's postwar reinvention of itself as a pillar of global capitalism, a tiny portion of its literature has found some degree of comfortable acceptance in the West, acclaimed for its artistic worth rather than its sociopolitical interest.[104]

Chinese literature, however, remains marginal in Western, and particularly Anglophone, consciousness. Where it is read, it tends to be read — and often dismissed — for its political rather than its literary content, thus implying it is of insufficient quality to be read for artistic value beyond its immediate sociopolitical context. Reception of modern Chinese literature *as* literature in the West has long been stymied by its association with (national) politics — again, C. T. Hsia's "obsession with China." The historical roots for this lie in the long-standing relationship in China between politics, literature, and the human sciences, a connection that is seen as alien to modern liberal Western thought. This association tightened to an unprecedented degree after 1949, with the implementation of an ideology and administrative system in China that prioritized politics above all other spheres of life. The stain of ideology affects the perception of Chinese literature in the West, where it has tended to be seen as concerned with politics, history, and didacticism. As Sture Allén, then secretary to the Nobel Committee, remarked with some truth in 1998, "[T]here was something called the Cultural Revolution that happened there. It has been a problem for China. And it has been a problem for us."[105]

In Britain the earliest study of modern literary texts — as opposed to those written in the classical language — in university courses coincided with the foundation of the Communist regime. Teachers of the new discipline of modern Chinese studies accepted the modern works promoted by the Chinese state "without further critical attention. The result was that students of Chinese were burdened by inferior literary texts masquerading as modern masterpieces." Thanks to the influence of the Cold War, Chinese studies in the postwar United States, meanwhile, assumed a similarly political bent, drawing on contemporary literary texts approved by officialdom to illuminate policy formulation and implementation.[106] Where critics did exercise judgment over texts, appraisals were often aimed at detecting the presence or absence of political virtue, namely "literary dissent." "A simple syllogism emerged: such-and-such a work is propaganda for the Chinese government (or Communist Party); the Chinese government (or Communist Party) is bad/good; therefore this work is bad/good."[107] Small wonder, perhaps, that Anglophone readers associated modern Chinese literature with politics.

China has opened up politically, economically, and culturally since the death of Mao, permitting researchers and translators direct access to contemporary writers and the opportunity to break with official orthodoxy and select their own subjects of study. Yet sociopolitical considerations have continued to drive selection of texts and authors for translation. Many works published in English in the 1980s and 1990s continued to divide fairly tidily between political orthodoxy and dissidence, according to which of two routes to translation they had taken: through the state or through Western sinologists.

After 1979 the Chinese government set up ten new publishers with full-time in-house translators, in addition to the two that had existed since 1949, the Foreign Languages Press and the New World Press. The official press has produced 69 of the 181 translations of contemporary Chinese fiction published in the post-Mao period up until 2002; most of this translation work bears the heavy imprint of official literary orthodoxy. This corpus has left a general Western readership largely cold on grounds of both content (works are selected for their orthodoxy and are thus highly unrepresentative of the creative diversity of the contemporary literary scene) and style (works are usually translated by Chinese and only polished by native English speakers; production values are low, as is the Foreign Languages Press's expertise in overseas promotion and distribution). In 1990 W. J. F. Jenner, an in-house translator and polisher for the Foreign Languages Press in the 1960s and 1980s, summarized its deficiencies as follows: "Design, editing, translation, the choice of titles — all these need a lot of attention if the tremendous effort and expense invested in producing the books is not to be wasted."[108]

The translation efforts of non-Mainland sinologists have provided Chinese authors with an alternative route to Western audiences. For much of the period since 1979, however, the choice of works to be translated has remained politically driven to a significant degree, although the politics favored by Western publishers are dissident rather than conformist. A string of translations published in the 1980s and 1990s — especially anthologies — focused on works that illustrated sociopolitical issues in the Mainland. *The New Realism*, one of the earliest post-Mao collections, was edited by the Hong Kong journalist Lee Yee, who identified critical realism as the flagship style of contemporary Chinese literature and selected works accordingly. Lee's anthologizing efforts, notes Jeffrey Kinkley, "only confirmed Western impressions that the new Chinese literature cared far more about social critique than literary values."[109]

While finding much modern Chinese literature unappealingly politicized,

Western publishers and readers are nonetheless happy to encourage politicized Chinese literature, as long as the politics are correct. Since 1989 the rising public profile of a new Chinese dissidence has pressed Chinese writing published in the West still further into a corner occupied chiefly by memoirs of political persecution in Communist China.[110] The slur of "ideology" is erased by politics progressive enough to be congenial to Western audiences. Even though exiled poets, for example, do not produce such memoirs, it has become increasingly difficult for them to achieve any kind of artistic voice independent of their political significance. As Dian Li commented in 1996, despite attempts by the exiled poet Bei Dao (1949–) to seek "forms of distance" (the title of a 1994 collection of his poetry in translation) from his political persona, and despite the increasingly inward turn of his poetry by the mid-1990s, he is now inevitably read as a poet in exile, defined by his political associations.[111] Mentioning the words "Cultural Revolution" somewhere on the jacket of a work of Chinese literature has become, it seems, the most effective way to attract Western readers' attention, even if the book itself has nothing to do with those events. The best marketing strategy for Chinese literature is to emblazon "banned in China" on the cover.[112]

The politicized reception of Chinese writing in the West has not diminished since the 1990s, even as literature has became more artistically independent of politics and more pluralistic than at any other period since the founding of the People's Republic. Those anthologies that have emphasized stylistic experimentation — *The Lost Boat: Avant-garde Fiction from China, China's Avant-garde Fiction, Running Wild: New Chinese Writers* — have mostly been produced by small or by academic presses and have had little impact outside academic circles.[113] Even the efforts of Howard Goldblatt, translator of about a dozen Mainland and Taiwanese authors who has made available to Anglophone audiences a wide range of contemporary Chinese stylists, have failed to generate much of an audience for Chinese fiction as works of literature.[114] In a review of short stories written in English by Ha Jin, Justin Hill's sweeping and inaccurate comments in *The Times Literary Supplement* are perhaps representative of the Anglophone literary world's view of Chinese literature, which it sees as occupying one of two ends of the political spectrum and artistically null in either case: "The limited range of these stories is reminiscent of the moralizing tales of Mainland China with their neat Socialist Realist endings." The world's most populous country, he asserts, suffers from a "dearth of literary fiction. . . . The popularity in the West of *Wild Swans* . . . has spawned a slush pile of autobiographical 'misery' books, but few novels of any worth."[115]

Where Chinese literature is considered in terms of its formal literary characteristics, the once-sided cultural exchange that lies behind the rhetoric of world literature often deems much modern Chinese literature to be "derivative of outmoded Western models, and thus condemned to a perpetual, and futile game of catch-up."[116] Although, concurrent with the advent of postcolonial writing in the West, apparently non-Western multicultural influences have entered the mainstream of contemporary literature (examples include the success of Latin American magical realist fiction and novels such as Rushdie's *Midnight's Children*, Zadie Smith's *White Teeth* and Monica Ali's *Brick Lane*), these works are invariably written in European languages. Thus, despite their portrayal of societies and cultures other than those of white Europe and America, they retain reassuring bonds with Western linguistic and literary traditions, which tacitly remain the touchstone for literary creativity. Gregory Lee angrily argues that common interpretations of the channels of influence between Chinese poetry and Ezra Pound at the start and close of the twentieth century provide a case in point:

> That Pound should have had an impact on the modern practice of a poetic culture whose tradition he had earlier appropriated surely fits precisely the Orientalist presumptions of European modernity: the East, and the Third World in general, provides the tradition to be exploited and reinvented as the modern, and then offered back to the East as the "new," the Western, the superior. That the East should mimic the West is taken as an indication of a lack of originality and authenticity; that the West should recuperate the East is glossed as the inventive creativity of high modernist genius.[117]

These assertions are echoed by the comments of Stephen Owen, one of the West's greatest authorities on classical Chinese poetry. He identifies world poetry as "a version of Anglo-American or French modernism"; after an initial encounter with Romantic poetry, twentieth-century Chinese poetry "has continued to grow by means of the engagement with modernist Western poetry; and as in any cross-cultural exchange that goes in only one direction, the culture that receives influence will always . . . appear slightly 'behind the times.'"[118] Owen is under no illusions as to the historical causes of this one-way exchange between East and West: "Western cultural self-confidence arrived [in Asia] together with the reality of Western military and technical power."[119]

It is true that modern Chinese literature, particularly since the May Fourth period (1910s–1920s), has been deeply influenced by foreign, especially Western literatures. Seminal works of twentieth-century Chinese literature have drawn extensively on Western styles and models (romanticism, realism, modernism, free verse, the Chekhovian short story). Lu Xun's highly acclaimed "Kuangren riji" (Diary of a madman) was inspired by Gogol's story of the same name.

No post-Mao author will deny the impact that the resurgence of translated texts after the antiforeign literary drought of the Cultural Revolution has had on his or her writing.[120] Yet it is arrogant of the West to assume either that this exchange is exclusively one-way (consider, again, the influence of classical Chinese poetry on Ezra Pound's fashioning of a modern Anglo-American poetry) or that it produces no more than inferior literary derivatives, leaving creative initiative firmly rooted in the West. Although recent work by sinologists such as Lydia H. Liu and David Der-wei Wang has argued that modern Chinese writers creatively refashioned Western forms, many Western critics and readers still appear to have little interest in the possibility of a creative canon existing so far beyond their shores.[121] W. J. F. Jenner bluntly states the Western reader's prejudice against the idea of Chinese originality thus: "Anglophone readers have generally been offered not what is better than and different from their own and cognate literature, but inferior imitations and adaptations of nineteenth- and twentieth-century Western models. . . . Why should [Western readers] bother with Qian Zhongshu's *Weicheng* when they can read Evelyn Waugh's satirical writing in the original?"[122]

The only hope for Chinese writers then seems to be to imbue their works with exoticism (of a political nature or otherwise), thus providing curious Western readers with insights into China's society and psyche. This, of course, returns writers to the first problem, namely that of limiting themselves to reflecting "Chineseness" and neglecting "pure" literary qualities. It also means being read, willingly or no, as Orientalist artifacts, as exotica through which China can be "known" to the West. At the start of the 1990s, Stephen Owen accused Bei Dao of courting all constituencies with his "political virtue" and "local color," to the detriment of Chinese aesthetic complexity.[123] Low critical esteem for Chinese literature as art, its lack of popularity among a general readership, and its failure to generate best-sellers all contribute to low production values for translations of Chinese works. And in the increasingly commercial world of international publishing, low popularity and low production values form a vicious cycle that prevents Chinese literature from reaching a broader, more appreciative audience. These conundrums of Western reception indicate that it is not just the Chinese nation-state that has chained Chinese literature to national identity; the world literary economy, too, is "obsessed with China." Chinese literature is both censured for being too political and then praised only for being political.

On the surface, the awarding of the Nobel Prize to Gao Xingjian for the "universal validity" of his works seems to buck this pattern of literary reception.[124] Gao is a writer who has asserted his detachment from the nation-state and from all "obsession with China." Within literary circles both in Mainland China and in exile, he was until October 2000 a marginal figure who appeared to revel in his marginality, committed only to artistic experimentation in his body of drama concerned with modernist, universally existential themes. But the Swedish Academy's enthusiasm for the "universal" value of Gao's work becomes less convincing when we note that the Nobel judges focused primarily on his novels *Lingshan* and *Yige ren de shengjing*, both of which take an explicitly dissident stance on Chinese politics. For all the manifest appeal of the universalistic ideals touted by global institutions, careful scrutiny brings their inconsistencies to the surface.

Critics have been attempting for some time to come to terms with the relationship between nationhood and establishing a centralized value system for world literature. Probably the best-known discussion of recent years is Aijaz Ahmad's exchange with Fredric Jameson over the latter's essay "Third-World Literature in the Era of Multinational Capitalism."[125] Despite his overgeneralizations, Jameson's essay manifested a laudable desire to fashion a more genuinely *world* literature at the end of the twentieth century and to effect an adjustment of aesthetic valuation for the differing significance of the nation in the literatures of the third world and the postmodern West. His honesty in stating plainly the disappointment often elicited in Western audiences on reading works of noncanonical third-world literatures precedes an attempt to refigure Western-dominated aesthetic hierarchies in which the radical difference of the noncanonical texts he selects will always be judged wanting for failing to offer the satisfactions of Proust or Joyce. The sociopolitical emphasis of these works, Jameson asserts, tends "to remind us of outmoded stages of our own first-world cultural development and to cause us to conclude that 'they are still writing novels like Dreiser or Sherwood Anderson.'"[126] Jameson's intention here was to revalorize the sociopolitical within an aesthetics of world literature. The political and social reading of the personal and the psychological (what Jameson calls the "national allegory") in third-world texts, he believed, could offer a much-needed awakening of radicalism to those Western intellectuals slumbering under the anesthetic of late capitalism.

Ahmad, meanwhile, writing as a "third-world intellectual," expressed his deep affront at Jameson's essentializing of the third world, of the "other," and at his construction of a binary opposition between Western and non-Western cultural production. Is the third world — whatever that means — doomed to produce nothing but "national allegory"? Is there no middle ground between American postmodernism and third-world nationalism? Ahmad feels that non-Western literatures are simply being made to dance to the two-part tune of essentializing Orientalism and bored, apathetic fin-de-siècle Western theory: "Politically, we are Calibans all. Formally, we are fated to be in the poststructuralist world of Repetition with Difference; the same allegory, the nationalist one, rewritten, over and over again, until the end of time."[127] The whole exchange usefully highlights unresolved tensions underlying the ideal of world literature and one can sympathize with Jameson's belief, even in the face of Ahmad's searing criticism, that "these things were worth saying."[128] Even if this dispute failed to resolve the issue (only a remapping of modern world history or, equally impracticable, the anarchic dissolution of all concept of canon and of the institutions of literary criticism would accomplish that task), it drew attention to the splits within the universalistic ideal of world literature between "them" and "us," to the aesthetic hierarchy in which the universalist West speaks down from high to low at the nationally obsessed non-West.

The present book probes the links between literature, nationalism, and globalization via the local example of China. I examine from various angles the different levels of discomfort expressed by Chinese obsession and ambivalence over the Nobel Prize: the tension between intellectual and political identities in modern China, the sociopolitical demands placed on the shoulders of literature, and the position occupied by China within global culture. It is not my intention to dismiss universalism as an ideology practiced by the modern West to its own hegemonic advantage; the constituency of the term is much broader and vaguer than this. Whether we like it or not, global universalism is a part of the modern cultural identity and embraces laudable philosophical and theoretical aims. This book intends rather to conduct an enquiry into one institution of global culture — the Nobel Literature Prize — rarely subjected to close critical and historical examination, and into what it represents as a modern global arbiter of aesthetic evaluation. By the same token, multiculturalism should not be repudiated as an empty, self-deluding ideal. Contemporary multiculturalism in academia has already produced many useful insights and no scholar of modern Chinese culture can afford to ignore the inherent hybridity of his or her subject of study; discourses on modern China are already inextricable from discourses on the West. If aiming for a truly plural, multicultural global realm is a worthwhile concern, then the "global" ideal, in its various manifestations, requires constant scrutiny to prevent its lapsing into a glib buzzword.

The traditional relationship between Chinese politics and the arts adds a crucial extra dimension to the whole issue of China's position within world literature. The Platonic view of the direct connections between literature and the political regime found in *The Republic* has, it seems, more affinities with the Chinese experience than with that of modern Western societies. Yet the longevity of this debate in both the West and China suggests that the relationship between politics and literature is one of broad and persisting significance. The Nobel Prize proclaims itself arbiter of a neutral universal global aesthetic, a position that is the product of European ideas about literature and authorship that have evolved only since the Enlightenment. In Western Europe the idea of the creative artist as an autonomous spirit above the mundane laws of morality and culture that bind the ordinary citizen is indeed of relatively recent vintage; it is no more than two centuries old. The two-tier system of criteria used by the Nobel Committee identified here and in the next chapter — writers in the Western tradition are judged on their intrinsic artistic qualities, while non-Western writers are commended as representatives of their respective nation-states — indicates that national and sociopolitical realities still play an important role in defining the terms by which literature is evaluated. Despite the commercialization and inward turn of much Western literary production, and the increasingly esoteric and nonreferential nature of much contemporary art, the link between politics and literature thus remains a question of ongoing importance and interest.[129] The historical inconsistencies of how this relationship has developed in both the West and non-West will figure in later chapters, presenting a broader perspective on the problem. The questions posed here are of relevance both to the local issue of modern Chinese intellectual experience and to the more general issue of aesthetic values in the imperial and postimperial world.

Chapter Two will provide a detailed examination of the philosophy and practice of the Nobel Prize for Literature, analyzing the unique and controversial role it has played in arbitrating world literature and shaping ideas of a universal aesthetic over the past century. Chapter Three will give an overview of conflicting ideas about authorship in modern China from the late Qing to 1976, highlighting the tensions between national, global, and individual identities that have dogged many intellectual experiences of the modern. This narrative will include episodes relating to the Nobel Literature Prize: Lu Xun's alleged refusal to be nominated in 1927, the reception given to Tagore (1913 laureate) and Pearl Buck (1938 laureate) in 1920s and 1930s literary China, and Qian Zhongshu's (1910–1998) prescient satire on what would in fact become China's Nobel Complex in his story "Linggan" (Inspiration). Chapter Four will analyze the Nobel Complex of the post-Mao decades, during which China has striven most resolutely to participate in global culture. This chapter will explain the dramatic intensification of the complex after 1979, a development linked to the painful collapse of the Maoist anti-Western worldview and the subsequent spurning of Maoist values, the deep influence of pro-Western internationalism on Chinese political, economic, social, and cultural life, and the resurgence of intellectual culture during the 1980s. The fifth and concluding chapter will draw out the significance of Gao Xingjian's Nobel Prize, examining Gao's prize-winning works and reactions to his prize all over the world, particularly in Mainland China.

CHAPTER TWO

The Nobel Prize for Literature

Philosophy and Practice

The whole of my remaining realizable estate shall be dealt with in the following way: the capital shall constitute a fund, the interest on which shall be annually distributed in the form of prizes to those who, during the preceding year, shall have conferred the greatest benefit to mankind. The said interest shall be divided into five equal parts, which shall be apportioned as follows: . . . one part to the person who shall have produced in the field of literature the most outstanding work of an idealistic tendency; and one part to the person who shall have done the most or the best work for fraternity between nations. . . . It is my express wish that in awarding the prizes no consideration whatever shall be given to the nationality of the candidates, but that the most worthy shall receive the prize, whether he be a Scandinavian or not.

ALFRED NOBEL[*]

First awarded in 1901 in accordance with Alfred Nobel's testament, the Nobel Prizes have since come to embody the complex of contradictions that inhere in the modern idea of global culture. Founded to honor benevolent contributions to mankind, the prizes were established and financed by profits from the dynamite industry. Alfred Nobel was proclaimed in his own lifetime a "merchant of death" whose research into explosives had fueled the escalating arms race between nations towards the end of the nineteenth century, while his peace prize aimed to promote "fraternity between nations."[1] A 1947 biographer notes the irony that Nobel, a workaholic inventor throughout his life, died leaving his will hidden under plans for explosives. "In his desk, buried under designs for new tools of war, lay the peace testament."[2] The stipulated "idealism" of the literary prize jars with both its historical background and its practice. On the one hand, Alfred Nobel's will champions a realm of literary idealism far above the worldly temptations of the international artistic field; on the other, the prize drags literature and

41

writers down into an arena promising material rewards, in which unspoken personal prejudices, financial temptations, thoughts of worldly gain, and international rivalries jostle.

The concept of "global culture," embraced with enthusiasm throughout the twentieth century, has been consistently undercut by boundaries between nation-states and Western powers' dominance in global institutions. The United Nations, for example, is founded on modern ideals of a world community, raised above nationalisms to assert universal interests. Its history, however, has been punctured with failures to acknowledge Western sources of self-interest deriving from colonialism and Cold War power conflicts.[3] Much of the early interest in the Nobel Prize can be attributed to the growing spirit of national competition: the prize was viewed as a thinking man's Olympic Games (which were restarted in 1896, just five years earlier). Today, announcement of the prize winner's nationality is still a matter of general interest. None of this seems to shake widespread belief that the Nobel Prize and like institutions are a fundamentally sound idea; however unrealized, universalism remains a key underpinning of the modern identity. In *Sources of the Self*, Charles Taylor sets the parameters of modern (Western) moral behavior around the belief that "it would be utterly wrong and unfounded to draw the boundaries any narrower than around the whole human race."[4] And among the Nobel Prizes, literature, far more than science, has played a crucial role in promoting, if not necessarily realizing, the prizes' modern universalistic ideal.

I am not suggesting that the laudable aims of the Nobel Literature Prize should be dismissed due to the impracticability of fully carrying them out. It would be unreasonable to hope that selections are devoid of individual subjectivity. The Nobel Prize, particularly in the last three decades, at very least does service reviving interest in literature for at least one day a year and brings neglected authors and those ignored outside their homeland to an international audience. My purpose here is to analyze the constituent elements of the Nobel Prize philosophy, what it represents as a modern, global institution of aesthetic evaluation, and the bad fit between its self-presentation and the reality of its practice. Having examined the psychological, philosophical and historical principles behind such an institution, especially with respect to national literatures outside the global mainstream, we can more easily comprehend the temptations and frustrations it has presented to modern Chinese writers and readers.

It is important not to overestimate the stability of ideas about literature in the West, since the uses of literature in practically every culture remain a point of constant contention. In China, the Nobel Prize and modern Western ideas about literature have frequently been misread as espousing a pure artistic professionalism, in contrast with the sociopolitical uses to which literature has been put in twentieth-century China. The course of Nobel literary history is far more complex than this: Romantic, humanist and Enlightenment conceptions of art have interacted to create a literary realm that espouses autonomy and literary professionalism while reserving the right to intervene in society where it chooses. The Nobel Prize represents an uneasy mix of ideas about literature, and its history is studded with controversies that reveal the different directions Western literature has taken in the twentieth century: classicism, humanism, experimentalism, and so on. In comparison with China (and, indeed, most colonial and semicolonial nations), however, the West in the modern era has possessed a far greater degree of social, political, and cultural self-confidence, and in that respect has experienced a smoother general continuity in literary and cultural concepts. This environment ensures that an institution such as the Nobel Prize can survive for a century, absorbing a variety of changes and criticisms while remaining in place. The task below is to understand what these ideas about literature involve and how they have manifested themselves in Nobel practice.

Philosophy and Origins of the Nobel Prize

The Nobel Prize has become "an anointed ritual whose claims are accepted as part of the order of things."[5] During its existence, the expansion of the mass media in conjunction with the growing gulf between modern science and literature and the general public have helped it attain global repute. The Nobel Prize has served as a bridge between the mystique of modern letters and the mass marketplace; prize winners are a sober part of our modern celebrity culture.[6] The six prizes — physics, chemistry, medicine, literature, peace, and economics — cover a broad sweep of modern intellectual life, in combination augmenting the prestige of each other. The literature prize has been adjudicated since 1900 by the Swedish Academy (a committee of five is appointed to administer the selection procedure), whose eighteen members over the century have changed only slowly. Once elected, Academy members — who are generally a mix of scholars and writers, all Swedish — remain in place for life, although resignations have been known. As the only literary prize of global humanistic scope, the Nobel Literature Prize occupies a unique position in modern world letters.

Nobel Prizes are accompanied by a prudent amount of fuss and ritual. Members of the Nobel Committee keep their deliberations secret for fifty years and maintain quaintly genteel habits such as addressing each other as Mr., Miss, and Mrs., in meetings. The prize ceremony is relatively brief, but the presence of the Swedish king and queen furnishes the Nobel awards with an important touch of class. The Nobel ceremony avoids the media scrum of speculation that surrounds the British Man Booker or Whitbread prizes, since the winners are announced two months before. The occasion thus is a more sedate affair, marked by the dignity of a victory parade rather than the cheap thrills of a suspense-filled finish spun out by delaying speeches. The whole ceremony and banquet are the image of ordered restraint: precisely 1,288 guests are invited, all eating with and off special Nobel cutlery and porcelain. The banquet is the climax of the annual Nobel week, centered around the anniversary of Nobel's death on 10 December. Nobel prestige feeds off its resulting press coverage: winning a Nobel guarantees increased book sales, as new editions roll off the press, onto which "winner of the XXXX Nobel Prize" stickers are promptly slapped.

Naturally, Nobel authority stems also from the amount of money involved: the prizes are among the most lucrative in the world, offering in 2000 £615,000 to each winner. The Nobel Foundation is an industry in itself, generating an administrative expenditure of six million dollars in 1994.[7] It has produced various appropriate legitimizing devices, including a museum, journals, and patronage of hundreds of top intellects (the Nobel laureates), to whom and to whose ideas it lays a somewhat proprietorial claim. The Nobel Museum asserts a mission of unique scope; it is: "special . . . its 'acquisitions' are just those ideas that have served human beings and given them understanding and spiritual, yes, spiritual satisfaction. . . . A Nobel Museum recognises and praises the best in human beings."[8] The Nobel newsletter gives the distinct impression that winners of the Nobel Prize are absorbed into the Nobel fold at the expense of their individual, independent intellectual identities: mention of the latest post-Nobel work of laureates is subsumed under the telling heading, "Recent Literature on the Nobel Prize."

The nomination procedure for the literature prize is designed to avoid commercial pressures. While nominations for literary prizes such as the Man Booker in Britain come from the publishers themselves (and therefore appear more commercial), Nobel nominations give the prize the stamp of the expert's choice. Four kinds of people are qualified to nominate: members of the Swedish Academy and of other national academies, institutions and societies similar in membership and aims; university professors of literary history or languages; previous winners of the Nobel Prize for Literature; and presidents of authors' organizations representative of the literary activities of their countries (such as PEN).[9] Apart from membership of the Swedish Academy, none of these categories is nationally specific. Certain individuals, of course, are inevitably in a better position to nominate than others, and writers, their lobbyists, and their opponents have often waged campaigns — sometimes behind the scenes, sometimes very publicly — over the awards. Pablo Neruda "was fully obsessed with the Nobel Prize. . . . He once said he would outlive Ekelöf (the committee member opposed to his laureateship) and win the prize. And he did."[10] The Nobel's cautious selection procedure has also imbued the prize with a sense of gravitas: a writer may hover several years on the short list before being considered a safe choice by the Academy. Such prudence has sometimes resulted in awards made so late they either seem out-of-date (the 1999 award to Günther Grass, for example) or become unrealizable due to the untimely death of the would-be beneficiary (Paul Valéry in 1945, Shen Congwen in 1988).[11]

It is perhaps this particular aura of authority that accounts for the paucity of thorough historical analyses of the prize.[12] For years, studies of the Nobel phenomenon have either focused on the character of Alfred Nobel or simply described what has happened over the last century, with little analysis of the institution or the prize winners. (Nobel was certainly a curious personality — a brilliant, cosmopolitan inventor and poetry-writing millionaire whose misanthropy and unhappy private life coexisted with hope for the betterment of humanity.) However, both these approaches have added to the Nobel's time-honored mystique, dehistoricizing the actual practice of awarding the prizes and failing to subject their fundamental raison d'être to rigorous analysis. Kjell Espmark, a member of the Swedish Academy, has produced a study of the changing criteria behind the prizes; his work goes to the opposite extreme, emphasizing the precise historical circumstances that governed the selections of each era.[13] Useful as it is, to some extent it still impedes our understanding of the broader, unifying rationale behind the prizes, in addition to airbrushing literary and cultural prejudices: everything becomes eminently comprehensible, even reasonable, once it is explained away in its historical context. Such an approach is problematic because it glosses over failures and shortcomings in the history of the prize as historical contingency rather than as part of the prize's fundamental conceptualization, a contradictory mix of Enlightenment and Romantic convictions. In the adjudication of the prizes, these convictions have been put through the additional wringers of personal bias and historical circumstance. The only commonality in the mixture of philosophies behind the Nobel Prizes is their distinctly modern character.

The Nobel Prizes represent first of all an Enlightenment belief in the existence of a universal, rational, secular realm capable of judging and ordering contemporary human achievements, "a self-admiring mirror of our democratized, scientized, secularized modern culture."[14] Alfred Nobel was himself one of the most renowned scientists of his day, a compulsive innovator who researched and experimented tirelessly in the pursuit of scientific progress. The Nobel ethos attests to belief in an autonomous, rational self, a figure that gains control through disengagement—the correlative of objectification and mechanization—and in the commensurable achievements of such individuals.

Cutting into the Nobel Prize's Enlightenment philosophy is another set of modern ideas about literature and society that come under the umbrella of Romanticism. Nobel's vision of a universal, idealistic literature of benefit to mankind manifests a Romantic confidence in literature's capacity to exert a powerful transformative influence on humanity. Meanwhile, his call for a prize in which "no consideration whatever shall be given to the nationality of the candidates" denotes faith in a literature that transcends the everyday realm of human society and a Romantic belief in the supremacy and genius of the autonomous creator. Nobel was himself a great admirer and imitator of the English poet Percy Bysshe Shelley, "whose philosophy of life he absorbed both as regards its Utopian idealism and its religiously colored spirit of revolt."[15] From the age of eighteen, Nobel composed poems and plays full of overwrought Romantic emotions; his 1895 play *Nemesis* was written on the same theme as Shelley's Renaissance tragedy, *Beatrice Cenci*. The Enlightenment and Shelley exercised a deep intellectual influence on Nobel, leaving him with a hatred of religious dogmatism and the priesthood, and an enduring Romantic idealism.

Nobel's schema and its subsequent realization manifest all the contradictions inherent in its Enlightenment and Romantic tendencies. Nobel invoked a literary realm that was both secular and in possession of miraculously transformative powers. His vision reflects the parallel processes of secularization and divinization that shaped attitudes towards literature throughout the nineteenth century. In the 1860s, Matthew Arnold proposed "the renovation of imaginative letters as a secular but nonetheless saving scripture" with a desperate, hopeful urgency, forming "the current which runs steadily, expansively, sometimes turbulently from Carlyle in the 1820s to Hardy in the 1920s. The modern world needed a new testament, and literature was the only mode in which it could be made available."[16]

This vision of literature as a form of unbounded, quasi-sacred creativity existing beyond mundane norms of morality and culture was reinforced by institutional changes in the nineteenth-century literary field. It was in nineteenth-century France that the literary field started to emerge as an independent entity, as writers, reacting against bourgeois philistinism, proclaimed their social autonomy and allegiance to the ideal of "art for art's sake." The artist was neither "the man who works" nor "the man who does nothing" (the aristocrat).

"The artist is the exception," commented Balzac. "He does not follow the rules. He imposes them."[17] "Art for art's sake" asserted a moral neutralism and a new social personality for artists, reinforced by rebellious, Bohemian modes of living and driven by writers' search for distinction and originality.

What makes the positions of French nineteenth-century writers such as Flaubert and Zola particularly relevant to the philosophical origins of the Nobel Prize is their juxtaposition of an "art for art's sake" pure aesthetic with the "art for life's sake" literary form of realism. Just as Nobel appealed for a free-floating, nonnationally specific idealism combined with a literature of benefit to mankind, these writers elided belief in the autonomous aesthetic with social engagement. Flaubert's assertion of autonomy served as precursor to the disengaged engagement of Zola, one of whose principal achievements lay in putting the new institutional autonomy and integrity of the literary field to the service of sociopolitical activism.

> Zola needed to produce a new figure, that of the intellectual, by inventing for the artist a mission of prophetic subversion, inseparably intellectual and political, which had to be able to make everything his adversaries described as the effect of a vulgar or depraved taste appear as an aesthetic, ethical and political stance, and one likely to find militant defenders. Carrying to term the evolution of the literary field towards autonomy, he tries to extend into politics the very values of independence being asserted in the literary field.... The intellectual is constituted as such by intervening in the political field *in the name of autonomy* and of the specific values of a field of cultural production which has attained a high degree of independence with respect to various powers ... the intellectual asserts himself against the specific laws of politics ... as defender of universal principles that are in fact the result of the universalization of the specific principles of his own universe.[18]

The relevance of these historical developments to the Nobel Prize lies in their juxtaposition of a neutral, autonomous aestheticism with an engagement in the social realm; in other words, a literary stance that lays claim to independence while maintaining the right to intervene in society. Zola's establishment of a literature that claimed to intervene in life for art's sake mirrors the neutral stance of "literary integrity" adopted by Nobel judges over the years. It is this modern combination of artistic neutralism and engagement that has so confounded Chinese intellectuals who have yearned for Nobel glory. Chen Sihe, a professor of modern Chinese literature, has remarked:

> A lot of people have criticized Chinese literature for being impure, for containing too much intellectual reflection. But having read many of the Nobel winners,

I thought that most of them did not write pure literature. They made a contribution to the whole of Western culture or society . . . For example in Sartre or Sienkiewicz, there is a lot of political thought. It seems that in the Nobel Prize, Western and Eastern criteria were not too far apart.[19]

Chen has picked up on a key contradiction within Western attitudes toward Chinese literature: reception of modern Chinese literature in the Anglophone West is frequently caught between unspoken and inconsistent beliefs about the sociopolitical role of literature, some of which coincide perfectly well with those traditionally held in China.[20]

The tension between calls for "transcendental literary quality" and literary social intervention is not one faced by Chinese writers alone; it has also been subject to reevaluation in every epoch of Western literary history. But the difference is, defining the correct negotiation of this tension in the modern era has always lain in the hands of Western (i.e., Swedish) writers and critics, and it is against their definitions that Chinese and other non-Western ideas about literature have been measured and, until recent decades, found wanting (or, more often, found to be one to two hundred years behind the West). In the modern era, and in the last two centuries above all, a certain level of historical and cultural amnesia has occurred in the West, in which the sociopolitical nation-building background to literary thought and the autonomous aesthetic has been largely erased. Indeed, when Gustavus III of Sweden founded the Swedish Academy of Arts and Sciences (later to adjudicate the Nobel Prize) in 1784, his inauguration speech revealed a view of literature not merely as "the amusement of a refined and select few, but as a matter of grave political importance, as the surest means of enlightening and ennobling society, of stimulating and sustaining public spirit." Gustavus viewed the Swedish Academy as the proper realm of statesmen, and the first eighteen members included four senators, two bishops, and a state secretary. He proclaimed that to "protect everything which may redound to the welfare of the realm is always my highest object; to contribute to the honor of the Swedish name my dearest desire. . . . With judges such as these, the Swedish language may look forward to a new and glorious era; nor is the duty of protecting her unworthy of those who have already dedicated all their time to the service of the State."[21]

The political and didactic roots of Western literary theory run deep. Plato's belief that the function of poetry was to instruct citizens in moral virtue led to his call to cast subversive poets out of the Republic. Theological thinking dominated medieval theories of literature and authorship, while idealized ethical conventions of form and subject matter held sway over classicism in the seventeenth and eighteenth centuries. It was not until the eighteenth century,

and the advent of Romanticism in particular, that individual aesthetic judgment and the power of emotion came to be prized as universal autonomous
goods. Absorbing the theistic secularism of the Enlightenment, the Romantics
turned emotions and creative aesthetics into a new self-sufficient religion that
led to the nineteenth-century advocacy of "art for art's sake." But Romanticism
took over many of theistic religion's aspirations to the ideal: while in earlier
theistic understandings, art had been primarily the medium for the expression of human ideals, it now became both means and end. Romanticism was,
moreover, closely tied to broader sociopolitical developments, in particular to
the rise of nationalism (an idealizing religion itself). Romantics everywhere
sought to cultivate their national peoples, as in Herder's theorization of the
universal uniqueness of national character and culture. The nation-state, and
its relationship with individual consciousness, thus became the crucial orga-
nizational unit within Romantic schemas of modern aesthetic universalism:
writers gave expression to a universal autonomous aesthetic through articula-
tion of their national culture. Literature came to represent an "effective means
of socializing people into the symbolic and economic values of the bourgeoisie
that beg[an] to represent national values."[22] The implementation of aesthetic
universalism, however, has been constantly hampered by inequalities within
the global system of nation-states.

In the West, views of literature as an independent institution engaging only
autonomously in the sociopolitical world have thus been far from dominant.
They are little more than two centuries old and shot through with contradictions. The state of mind that permits literature's sociopolitical, didactic roots
to be forgotten is in part a result of the "stance of disengaged reason" towards
the world that Charles Taylor sees as inherent in Enlightenment modernity.[23]
One of the hallmarks of this stance is its capacity to foreclose past options
and to ignore superseded philosophical antecedents. The modern epistemic
supremacy of the West (inventor of reason) ensured the victory of this amne-
siac view of literature both in modern cultural production and in institutions
such as the Nobel Prize. Chinese literature, coming from a different historical-
cultural background and coming to modern nationalism later than Western
countries, has thus been dubbed by the West unfashionably and improperly
sociopolitical. Yet even the leveling amnesia of reason has not been able to
completely erase the sociopolitical tendencies of literature in the Western tradition, and this has resulted in inconsistencies of attitude that have clearly
emerged in post-Romantic literature and in the century of Nobel practice.

The link between nationalism and the universal autonomous aesthetic was
reinforced by the relationship that Goethe envisioned between national and
world literatures; this relationship constitutes another important contradic-

tion within Nobel's legacy. The parallel between Goethe's 1827 schema for a world literature and Nobel's vision for a literature prize in which "no consideration whatever shall be given to the nationality of the candidates . . . the most worthy shall receive the prize, whether he be a Scandinavian or not" is an obvious one to draw. Nobel shared with Goethe a modernizing, progressive conviction that world literature could advance human civilization through encouraging mutual understanding, appreciation, and tolerance. For Goethe, as for Nobel, world literature "serves as a link . . . between the nations themselves, for the exchange of ideal values."[24] "The point," wrote Goethe, "is not that nations should think alike, but that they should become aware of each other, and that even where there is no mutual affection, there should be tolerance." For Goethe there was no doubt that the possibility of universality existed; indeed, it was a moral and aesthetic duty of writers. "It is obvious that for a considerable time the efforts of the best writers and authors of aesthetic worth in all nations have been directed to what is common to all mankind."[25] Weimar would serve as the headquarters of world literature for writers from France, England, America, Italy, Scandinavia, Russia, and Poland.

However, Goethe's vision was compromised by the uneasy relationship between national and world literatures and by the unequal global system of transnational exchange. Just as the nation-state formed the basis of membership to the global model envisaged by the 1648 Treaty of Westphalia, the essential constituent parts of Goethe's world literature were national literatures: "the only way towards a general world literature [is] for all nations to learn their relationships each to the other."[26] World literature, as a scholarly discipline, would establish intellectual relations between nations, either by systematic comparison or by historical exposition. Goethe thus smoothly conflated the relations between national and world literatures, envisaging a realm of free exchange — a literary United Nations — in which different national characteristics would not only be mutually accepted and acclaimed, but were indeed a prerequisite to entry. "The sure way to achieve universal tolerance is to leave untouched what is peculiar to each man or group, remembering that all that is best in the world is the property of all mankind."[27] Efforts made to ensure that the Nobel Literature Prize (to a far greater extent than the science prizes) revolves fairly among all nations point to the prize's close links to Goethe's vision of a literary United Nations. (The list of Nobel Science and Economics Prize winners in no way replicates the anxiety to circulate among nations reflected by the statistics for the literature prize. In the Nobel's first one hundred years, for example, 66 physics prizes, 47 chemistry prizes, and 90 medicine prizes went to U.S. scientists; the total of prizes won during this time by scientists working in countries outside the developed West can be counted on the fingers of two hands.[28]) Goethe's literary convictions were fundamental to, and built upon the Romantic philosophy of literature and language: Coleridge, for example, viewed literature as both national and universal, both expressive and formative of civilization, as both representing the national whole and requiring geniuses who would stand above and elevate the lowly plebiscite.[29] The writer, thus, is both the *Volksstimme* (the voice of the people and outward expression of the inner essence of a nation or people) and the artist who towers above the *Volk*. In a similar way, Nobel's literature prize envisioned both an artistic realm that floated free of mankind and would have a salutary effect on mankind. And while he left instructions that national boundaries should be ignored, the literary prize, in practice, has proved to be firmly tied to literary nationalisms.

The cultural centrism shaped by global inequalities inherent in Goethe's vision emerges in revealing conflations such as, "European, that is to say, world literature."[30] Although his *West-Eastern Divan* appeared to remedy such bias, Goethe was more intent on drawing on Eastern "riches" (for example, thirteenth-century Persian poetry) as a "kind of devout longing to be transformed through self-sacrifice, to be purified and born again out of the East, to rise anew as a European. . . . But once the East had fulfilled its mission in extending Goethe's scope, he could return within his European confines. He had become West-Eastern."[31] Goethe envisioned two kinds of roles within world literature: a European community of contemporaries joining together to exchange the particular and the universal, while traffic to the East was unidirectional. "Goethe's conception . . . is permeated by classic Orientalist tropes, in which (an essentialized) difference is projected onto a passive East for the narcissistic benefit of the Western spectator."[32] Goethe saw world literature as, "an intellectual barter, a traffic in ideas between peoples, a literary market to which the nations bring their intellectual treasures for exchange."[33] In this barter, it is the translator who acts as mediator, even prophet. But if Goethe could happily describe world literature as a free market where nations offer their merchandise, it was a market in which the position of non-European, non-Western cultures was dwarfed by the languages and literatures of the giants of imperialism.

Despite Goethe's earlier universalism, furthermore, it was still "the destiny of the German to become the representative of all the citizens of the world."[34] Goethe's project was underpinned by his sense of the historic destiny of German culture, as he considered the German language and culture as the privileged medium of world literature. Combined with his German-centrism, Goethe's use of economic tropes poses a wider range of problems for his utopian vision. Who sets the value on works and types of exchange?

What relationship should writers have with market demands? Where is the market and is there trade exploitation? As Andrew Jones pertinently asks: "Do developing nations supply raw materials to the advanced literary economies of the 'First World'?"[35] For Goethe translation was not a neutral channel of exchange, bringing benefits to both target language and original language; it was conceived as the appropriation of treasures of foreign art and scholarship on Germany's behalf, safekeeping them at the heart of Europe.

Goethe's discussion of translation and world literature reveals a constant tension between universalistic ideals and reverence for national historical mission (in his case, that of Germany). He asserted, on the one hand, his lack of patriotism for anything but the native land of his poetic powers and poetic work, the Good, the Noble, the Beautiful, and claimed that German culture and literature were distinguished, for example, from French by seeking to direct influence inward, as opposed to outward in the French case. On the other hand, his constant lamentations, invoking militaristic metaphors, of the lack of uniformity and unity in German literature were aggressive by implication: "Just as . . . the military strength of a nation grows out of its inner unity, so aesthetic strength is the gradual outcome of a similar unanimity."[36] Goethe intended German literature to become the new fountainhead of European or world literature through its youth and vigor, in contrast to tired French classicism, thus outlining a course of romantic individualism and universal unity in which German literature and language took a leading role.[37]

The Nobel Prize has throughout its history been similarly positioned between its universalistic brief and its location in Sweden. Underneath the apparent initial reluctance of the Swedish Academy to take on its Nobel duties at the turn of the century lay a barely concealed delight at the global prestige and authority that had fallen into its lap. While the Academy's director Carl David af Wirsén spoke in lofty terms of the idealistic benefit the prize money would bring to writers, he also clearly recognized it as Sweden's opportunity to arbitrate world letters. Wirsén composed this little verse for the first Nobel banquet in 1901:

Unwished the task, unsought for, bearing now
So weightily on Swedish backs; it seems
We tremble taking obligation's vow,
Henceforth a world will deem how Sweden deems.[38]

The Nobel Prize has been a global advertisement for Sweden ever since its inception; today, the image of the prize is tied closely to the issue of Sweden's international face. "What do we have in Sweden?" mused a cultural editor of a Swedish newspaper in the late 1990s. "We have Volvo, smorgasbord, Björn

Borg, and the prize. How can the prize not matter? It is the fashion to laugh and say we are above it. But we are not. When the academy seems foolish, we feel foolish, too. And when the prize sinks, so do we."[39] Achieving a reputation in Sweden, through translations and other promotional activities, has often been key to Nobel success. In the race between Sinclair Lewis and Theodore Dreiser for the 1930 prize, Lewis is seen to have gained a critical advantage through his deliberate cultivation of the Swedish public.[40] Gao Xingjian in 2000 doubtless benefited from the patronage of his translator Göran Malmqvist (the Nobel Committee's one sinologist). Malmqvist's Swedish translation of *Lingshan* (Soul mountain), one of the key works mentioned in the prize announcement, was published even before the Chinese original.

The history of the Nobel Prize poses the essential questions of *Weltliteratur*: the clash between world literature as a democratic, universalistic idea and its less-than-perfect application. Goethe's highly attractive ideal notwithstanding, no one, least of all Goethe himself, has proved qualified to carry out this ambitious brief, whose center of gravity has remained located in European, or Western, literature, and in Western ideas of how the individual relates to the nation-state.

The final Nobel contradiction lies in its entrapment of artistic idealism in distinctly materialistic rewards. How are we to reconcile the idea of a freewheeling, autonomous literary field, with the institutionalization and bureaucratization that literary prizes, and the Nobel Institute above all, threaten? The Nobel drags literary idealism into the mire of bourgeois capitalist lucre, the entity against which the nineteenth-century idea of artistic autonomy defined itself — Nobel was, after all, one of the greatest capitalists of his day.

Pierre Bourdieu provides one answer to this conundrum, charting the process by which literary individualism itself becomes institutionalized. In a literary field where the values of indignation, revolt, contempt, and autonomy are celebrated, "all those who mean to assert themselves as fully fledged members of the world of art . . . will feel the need to manifest their independence with respect to external powers, political or economic. Then, and only then, will indifference with respect to power and honors — even the most apparently specific, such as the Académie, or even the Nobel Prize . . . be immediately understood, and even respected, and therefore rewarded."[41] It is the fate of even the most tirelessly avant-garde movement to be institutionalized and out-radicalized by new pretenders: T. S. Eliot brought iconoclastic modernism into the literary establishment within a decade. Bourdieu's sociological study of the literary field makes this point forcefully, highlighting the individualized stance taking that transforms itself into governing practice. This once more invokes tensions inherent in the conceptualization of the Nobel

Prize between visions of an autonomous literature and the social environment in which it exists. The literary field, priding itself on its independence, is as susceptible to cultural and political preconceptions as any social sphere and quickly develops its own set of legitimizing institutions. In the Nobel's century-long history, only Jean-Paul Sartre has refused the prize (in 1964).

During the twentieth century, literary prizes became a crucial tool for legitimizing and raising up works of serious literature. France's Prix Goncourt is an apposite example, offering a mere fifty francs to the winning book but guaranteeing a huge boost to sales. Thus, the means of legitimizing and exalting the chosen work does not contravene the ethos of success in the literary field, where economic tropes are reversed (the less you have to do with financial capital, the more cultural capital you amass). With the Prix Goncourt, a writer can have both. Once a book has received the stamp of seriousness through receiving an accepted and nonlucrative literary prize, sales boom. Literary prizes now permit more writers than ever before to combine cultural and economic capital. Currently in Britain there are probably more literary novelists able to make a living from writing than at any other time in the past century, despite the dominance of popular culture. The Man Booker and other literary prizes have had a large part to play, bringing a cash windfall (the Man Booker Prize was worth £52,250 in 2004), media attention, and a potentially spectacular spike in sales. The Nobel Prize has won its cultural capital perhaps *because* of its monetary value and the difficulty of winning it. It is desirable "as the only distinction by which one can rise above nearly all others."[42] While modern literature is regarded as an independent profession, therefore, it is constantly in the process of becoming variously institutionalized and commercialized.

ALL THESE CONTRADICTORY ideas formed the philosophical and theoretical background to Alfred Nobel's bequest and have continued to influence the practice of awarding the Nobel. Naturalized into a modern identity built around ideas of universalism, freedom, and a rational-romantic assertion of independence in the artistic realm, these concepts unite in the ostensibly neutral nexus of authority that is the Nobel Prize, obscuring the inconsistencies and mutual contradictions between their rational and Romantic, universal and national, independent and bureaucratic components.

In the West, despite the misgivings and criticisms voiced about individual awards, we are fairly happy to accept an institution such as the Nobel Prize at its own valuation, namely that the Nobel Committee is doing its best to keep interest in serious literature alive in a complex and fragmenting global culture. However, in the struggle to create a truly diverse and accountable literary community, the Nobel Prize as an institution of world literature must be questioned and held to account on some of the following issues: What is the relationship between literature of a "world" level and the society in which it is written? Should this literature float independently above society, or be socially engaged? Should it attempt to be universal or particular? Independent and professional, or humanistic? Just as they apply to the Nobel Prize, these same questions have troubled Chinese literature for the past century. Furthermore, what should world literature do as an institution? Who can judge the worthiness of candidates? Who is neutral enough? Can it be an institution? What is the relationship between the institution and those who are incorporated into it? Who legitimizes whom?

The Nobel Prize in Practice

Despite the international repute of the Nobel, criticisms have been voiced. Since its inception, the Nobel Prize for Literature has been periodically lambasted for its choices, omissions, political bias, failure to represent non-Western literatures, or simply on grounds of logic. How can any committee of individuals aspire to judge the "most outstanding work of an idealistic tendency" that has conferred the "greatest benefit to mankind"? The Nobel, perhaps more than any other literary prize, suffers from the imprecision of its criteria. In Britain, the Man Booker Prize is more straightforwardly awarded to the "best" novel of the year written in English, including the Commonwealth but excluding the United States. In France, the aim of the Prix Goncourt (limited to works in French) is to "encourage literature, assure the material well-being of a number of literary figures and strengthen the bonds of fraternity between them."[43] The Nobel, meanwhile, has striven for a century to identify an "idealistic tendency" that has contributed to mankind in general. Should the Nobel Prize then seek out purely professional, technically sophisticated (modernist/postmodernist) writing that denotes some kind of perfection of literary form or advancement on forms of the past? What about socially engaged didactic writing that seeks to achieve a salutary effect on humanity — or popular literature accessible to as much of humanity as possible? Should it pursue difficult, obscure writing, cut loose from coordinates of the real, that can apply to the human condition in its entirety?

"Indeed," Kjell Espmark admits in his study, "the history of the literature prize is in some ways a series of attempts to interpret an imprecisely worded will."[44] A former secretary of the Swedish Academy, Anders Österling advocated only the very broadest of interpretations to Nobel's idealism, claiming that Nobel referred to works of a positive and humanistic tendency. Sture Allén, another former secretary of the Academy, has preferred to attribute to Alfred Nobel the taking of an "independent stand."[45] It is this assertion of broad independence that runs through the Nobel Prize's history, incorporating at the same time the contradictions of its philosophical heritage and historical practice. Regardless of its inconsistencies, the Nobel has laid claim to a neutral, universal realm by dint of its being the only literary prize with a global remit.

Espmark draws a line between two main phases of Nobel practice, falling roughly at the division between the pre- and post-World War II eras. Referring to the latter, he comments: "The Nobel Prize in Literature has gradually become a *literary* prize." It is also this phase that can boast of the most worthy recipients: "What [the Academy] cannot afford is giving Nobel's laurel to a minor talent. Its practice during the last full half-century has . . . largely escaped criticism on that point."[46] Over the last fifty years, therefore, the Nobel Prize has aspired increasingly to being an upholder of pure literary values. This assertion of aesthetic neutrality, however, threatens to obscure the prize's continuing legacy of humanism and social engagement. The Academy has veered between two roles: arbiter of abstract literary achievement, and diplomat in international goodwill and literary politics. Below, I will identify some of the unifying features of Nobel practice, its "neutral aesthetic" that asserts an artistic, humanistic neutrality and independence while passing over inconsistencies and bias.

The History of the Literature Prize: A Synopsis

Espmark identifies the ethos promoted by Wirsén, the Academy's director in the first decade of the prize and a literary conservative, as a classically inspired "lofty and sound idealism." Hostile towards Romantic and modernist strains in literature, Wirsén favored authors such as Sienkiewicz (1905 laureate), whose works were described as having a Goethean "coolness of plasticity." The qualities of purity and objectivity, as incarnated in Goethe, stood in contrast to the tendentiousness of contemporary authors who wrote about "problems," for example Zola, Tolstoy, or Ibsen. Wirsén's "ideal" nevertheless proved to be highly selective about what represented neutrality. Tolstoy was deemed "one-sided," largely due to his denunciation of religion and state. Hardy was rejected on similar grounds, for his characters who "seem to lack all religious and ethical firmness." The committee disqualified James's *A Portrait of a Lady* on the grounds that it was incomprehensible that Isabelle Archer should choose Osmond over the "excellent Lord Warburton."[47]

Wirsén's reign over the Nobel Committee is now viewed as an unfortunate episode in the prize's history, atoned for by an improved later performance. There is an important point of psychological continuity, however, from the prize's first decade through the rest of its history: the assertion of neutralism, a claim to a moral idealism that holds itself above the petty tendentious moralizing of a Tolstoy — even though the prize has been seen as political since its inception. In the furor surrounding the Academy's failure to award the first prize to Tolstoy, the journal *Academy* commented: "Ah, but in all things we must reckon . . . with political interests. . . . Sweden could not afford to offend the Czar, and Tolstoy is not a figure of delight to the Imperial gaze."[48] Twentieth-century Sweden has cultivated an aura of restrained neutrality, which has helped to imbue the prizes with universal authority. Sweden in 1900 was a country of five million people, one tenth the population of Germany, Britain, France, or Austria, and its days as an important military and political power had ended a century earlier. In culture and science, "Sweden exhibited all the symptoms of a small country with large, intimidating neighbors."[49] It is perhaps this quality of being marginal that has engendered more confidence in the Nobel than would be the case for a prize based in France or the United States, nations far more caught up in the middle of European and global transactions.

The following decade (1910–1920) of prizes was initially marked by a broadening of the prize's geographic range, with the 1913 award to the Indian poet Rabindranath Tagore. Prize distribution was subsequently characterized by what has been called "literary neutralism," a declaration of total political impartiality in view of the international tensions that exploded in the First World War. The Swedish Academy desired to take a role in promoting international peace, "to exercise a restraining and counterbalancing influence on the excesses" that nationalism in contemporary literature could so easily generate.[50] In the 1913 award, these two goals — widening geographical distribution and rising above political partisanship — proved handily compatible, since Tagore's prize incorporated a non-Western winner (albeit one from a British colony) into the Nobel fold, giving the prize a more universal scope and avoided favoring a writer from one of the Great Powers. Academy member Verner von Heidenstam wrote: "For the first time, and perhaps also the last time in the foreseeable future, we would have the chance to discover a great name before it has already spent years haunting the newspaper columns." In a private letter, however, Heidenstam's arguments appear more tactical: "What you say about the Indian does not sound so bad. It is necessary in some way to break the routine."[51] The selection of Tagore doubtless strengthened the Nobel Prize's claims to internationalism, but the half-heartedness of the gesture shows through. In official statements, Tagore received the prize "because of his profoundly sensitive, fresh and beautiful verse, by which, with consummate skill, he has made his poetic thought, expressed in his own English works, a part of the literature of the West." It has been further alleged that Tagore's prize was political, with Swedish Crown Prince William prodding the Academy to embarrass the British by awarding the prize to their colonial subject.[52]

Neutralism of varying kinds was pursued throughout the 1920s and 1930s, decades that presented two challenges to the Nobel Committee: the growing stature of modernist writers such as Joyce, Woolf, and Eliot, and the question of taking a stance on politicized (socialist) writers, most notably Maxim Gorky. Kjell Espmark, ever at pains to highlight the historical circumstances behind committee choices, points out that the committee of the 1920s sought the "great style," with Goethe's classicism and "universal appeal" in mind. This translated into the selection of compromise candidates, the omission of Joyce, Woolf, Conrad, and Proust, and the rejection of Eliot until 1948, over two decades after his brand of poetic modernism was first institutionalized in the Western canon. The Nobel Committee took a careful path of moderation that established the prize as a safe, middle-of-the-road organization, reluctant to recognize pioneers from the 1920s until after the Second World War. In Pearl Buck (1938) and Galsworthy (1932), accessibility was prized above all, while difficult modernists were excluded. Other novelist-laureates of these eras now considered second-rate include Pontopiddan and Deledda. The preponderance of novelists emphasized the function of the prize as a neutral, diplomatic instrument.

This stance was extended into the handling of political issues. In pre–Cold War decades, the committee sought a neutrality defined by the non-Communist West. Gorky was rejected for fear of the Nobel name being besmirched with communism, and the first prize to a Russian author went to Ivan Bunin in 1933, an émigré and opponent of the Soviet Union. The award was made despite the committee's reservations that Bunin's writing did not "continue the great tradition of Russian narrative art."[53] Given the misgivings over the artistic merits of Bunin's works, his prize was most certainly politically determined. Scholars of Russian believe that Bunin had for some years been lobbying for a Nobel, playing on anti-Soviet feeling.[54]

The prize took a more literary bent following World War II. Once modernism had been accepted into the literary establishment, it was beckoned into the Nobel roll of honor, with awards to Eliot in 1948, Faulkner in 1949, and Beckett in 1969. Obscure writing was now acclaimed for achieving an idealistic universalism unrestricted by the social reference points of realism. Since this period, the committees have sought refuge in objective technical criteria. "The Prize is in the end not given to an attitude toward life," Espmark has commented, "to a set of cultural roots, or to the substance of a commitment; the Prize has been awarded so as to honor the unique artistic power by which this human experience has been shaped into literature."[55] In some ways, the search for literary pioneers marked a return to the ethos of the Wirsén era, during which the realist fiction of Tolstoy or Zola was regarded with distaste. Artur Lundkvist (one of the foremost spokesmen for the pioneer-seeking school of thought) attacked the choice of John Steinbeck in 1962 as "one of [the Academy's] greatest mistakes," presumably because his works such as *The Grapes of Wrath* are anchored in local social concerns. Lundkvist reasoned that "if attention had been focused on the renewal of narrative fiction, then Steinbeck would at once have been out of the picture in favor of authors like Durrell, Beckett, or Claude Simon."[56] Difficult poets such as Saint-John Perse (1960 laureate), meanwhile, were praised for their "highly individual creations" which at the same time "wished to be an expression of the human . . . and of the eternally creative human spirit." The poet's "isolation and distance" were "a vital condition for ambitious poetry in our age," making Perse "a poet with a universal message to his contemporaries."[57] If previously a literature of "universal interest" had been sought in internationally best-selling authors, postwar committees sought politically opaque universalism in esoteric creations.

After the pioneers of modernism had been recognized, "a pragmatic attitude" took over, focusing on acknowledging authors ("unknown masters") who would be positively helped by the money and kudos that a Nobel Prize brought. Lars Gyllensten remarked in 1984: "It is a matter of finding people who are good and who deserve the prize . . . and for whom the prize can be of benefit to themselves and their work."[58] Gyllensten asserted in 1969 that the "prize must not be a medal for services rendered . . . but rather a kind of investment in — and as such, of course, entailing a degree of risk — the advancement of an oeuvre that still *can* be advanced. And this must be relevant both for the recipient of the prize and . . . for readers and other authors at the frontiers of literature."[59] In the 1930s academician Fredrik Böök criticized the award to Galsworthy, hoping rather to award "a significant and highly individual author who stands somewhat apart from banal world fame and press-inspired popularity."[60] Österling expressed a similar viewpoint in the postwar years. "It would be a justified reaction to this commercialization if in the future the Nobel Prize awards were to favor writers who do not enjoy the benefit of such a market and who, for the sake of it, do not compromise their literary standards."[61] Hesse, winner in 1946, was viewed as a "worthy subject, as one of the last surviving writers of the genuine, romantic, non-commercial type."[62] Committee member Sigfrid Siwertz in 1960 thought that the academy "ought to step outside the dominant cultures and give the prize to someone off the literary beaten track."[63]

Thus, another kind of aesthetic autonomy emerged in prize-giving policy, where considerations of an author's existing fame were set aside, and writers who were less commercial (therefore more independently artistic), who stood "outside the noise of the marketplace,"[64] or who came from "marginal" cultures were targeted instead. Following a pattern set by prizes to Jiménez and Quasimodo in the 1950s, the 1978–1981 prizes (Singer, Elytis, Milosz, and Canetti) can be viewed in the light of this policy. Prizes to Symborska (1996) and Saramago (1998) again brought world attention to two relatively neglected authors. The 1980s saw the prize go to African authors (Soyinka, 1985; Mahfouz, 1988) for the first time. In the first half of the 1990s alone, prizes were given to writers from Mexico (Paz, 1990), Jamaica (Walcott, 1992), and Japan (Oe, 1994). Although this policy has been clearly beneficial to individual authors, it also brought praise for the Nobel Committee, whose mission had became the virtuous promotion of "struggling artists." The championing of lesser-known writers continued to augment the committee's cultural capital from the postwar era throughout the 1970s and 1980s. The Nobel sought to be linked with the names of independent-minded writers who did not write for money. Not only could the Nobel judges assert political neutrality, they were deaf also to the din of commercialism.

> In their concern to situate themselves on a plane above ordinary alternatives . . . they impose an extraordinary discipline on themselves, one which is deliberately assumed against the facile options that their adversaries on all sides permit themselves.[65]

This "extraordinary discipline," observed by Bourdieu in his study of the stance of autonomy within the nineteenth-century French literary field, emerges also in the range of criteria set out by the Nobel judges over the years. The Nobel ethos has moved through aristocratic classicism, neutralism, accessibility, experimentalism, and marginalism, in the interests of asserting an extraordinary discipline of neutrality as arbiters of world letters. Whereas largely before the Second World War, the Nobel Committee sought to legitimize itself through inclusiveness and accessibility, the postwar period witnessed the beginning of a new, more "literary" phase in which the committee asserted allegiance to another kind of artistic universalism: art made universal by its obscurity and by its unpredictable eclecticism. Bourdieu has described the stance of the

CHAPTER TWO

Double Rupture that avant-garde members of an independently constituted literary field assert in order to assure a commanding position: I detest X, but I detest just as much the opposite of X.[66] The double rupture declared by Nobel practice has thus emerged as: we detest those who write for money, but we detest just as much those who write for politics. The final section will be devoted to discussing in detail the role of the committee's political stance, a question that has proved singularly problematic in their efforts to preserve aesthetic neutrality. I will focus on two areas where political considerations have come into clear play: in the selection of Cold War and non-Western winners.

Politics and the Nobel Prize: Cold War Case Studies

Nobel committees have not been disingenuous about the politicization of their prize. Bishop Gottfrid Billing wrote to Wirsén in 1902: "It is true that the awarding of the prize must not become a question of national politics. But it is equally incontrovertible and unavoidable that it has and will have a political aspect."[67] As a prize destined for benefactors of humanity and adjudicated by subjective humans, the politicization of the Nobel has been an inevitability. With this in mind, the Academy has striven to assert a stance of "political integrity" and to assume a position of moral probity concerning that politicization. This standpoint, however, has constantly been qualified by personality and circumstance, and despite assertions of literary professionalism (in particular since the late 1940s), extra-literary criteria have continually come to the fore. The Nobel Committee's definition of "political" has had its own blind spots. Wirsén vetoed a shared prize between Ibsen and Bjørgsen in 1902 on antipolitical principle: "I believe . . . that we are doing not only the wisest thing but also the most just in never using this prize as a political tool or bargaining piece . . . the procedure offends against the impartiality of a literary tribunal."[68] Added to which, of course, Wirsén objected to Ibsen's "negative and enigmatic features" and his use of symbolism, which clashed with Wirsén's own beliefs in the need for ethical correctness in literature. Gorky in 1928 was rejected for fear that a prize "would in the world at large be taken as a mark of approval of Gorky's writings in their entirety and thus provide a dubious advertisement for them."[69] With Gorky, the committee took up its favored stance of neutrality, before five years later blithely making an award to Bunin (importantly symbolic as the first Russian Nobel Prize), situated at the opposite end of the political spectrum.[70]

It was during the Cold War that such political inconsistencies became obvious. The Nobel Committee trod a careful path through the quagmire of Cold War politics, honoring four writers aligned in opposition to the Soviet

Union (Camus, 1957; Pasternak, 1958; Andric, 1961; Solzhenitsyn, 1970), and giving four prizes to Soviet writers or sympathizers (Laxness, 1955; Sartre, 1964; Sholokhov, 1965; Neruda, 1971). This neutral symmetry, however, obscures the intrigues that surrounded these prizes. The 1958 Nobel Prize was one of those that generated the most beneficial publicity. Although Ezra Pound and Alberto Moravia were also considered, it turned into a contest between Pasternak and Sholokhov, two writers ideologically opposed across the straits of communism. The Soviet government aimed to leave little to chance: minutes from Soviet Union Central Committee meetings recorded the petitioning of left-leaning Swedish intellectuals and support of Swedish PEN on behalf of Sholokhov, and against Pasternak in the run-up to the 1958 announcement of Pasternak's award.[71] When Pasternak emerged the winner, he was pressured by the Soviet authorities into declining his prize. Seven years later, Moscow was compensated with Sholokhov's award, although Kjell Espmark emphasizes the fact that the award was fully within the Academy's remit of "political integrity." In his award speech, Academy member Anders Österling focused on Sholokhov's earlier work *Quiet Flows the Don*, whose interpretation of the Cossack revolt took an ambivalent view of the central Soviet authorities and so asserted a more independent stance. "Limiting the award to Sholokhov's 'epic of the Don' was thus eloquent."[72]

The controversy continued, however. Krushchev's claim in his memoirs that it was he who — via a Swedish minister — had advised the Academy to give the prize to Sholokhov provoked a furor in Swedish Academy circles. The Academy responded that there was not the slightest evidence of pressure from Khrushchev in Academy correspondence, or in the minutes, or anywhere else. Lars Gyllensten asserted in 1981 that "for the Swedish Academy . . . avoiding the influence of political powers is axiomatic."[73] In 1984 he reasserted that the academy wished to keep itself immune to all political, diplomatic, or in any other way nonliterary considerations.[74]

While this proclaimed disassociation from politics is true on one level, on another the very assertion of the famed Swedish neutrality has often obscured political assumptions that are billed as neutral and nonideological in contrast to, for example, socialist art. The debates surrounding Pasternak's award played a crucial part in forging the Nobel's international reputation; its world profile rose on the back of the West's stance in the Cold War and built on the intensified aversion to communism that resulted from Soviet intervention in the 1956 Hungarian uprising. By honoring Pasternak, the Nobel Committee was battling on the side of Western intellectual and artistic freedom against communism, stimulating extensive media coverage. A leader article in the *New York Times* declared: "[Pasternak's] plight is a shattering demonstration of the slavery that is the implicit condition of every individual in the power of the totalitarian Communist state. . . . We in the free world—and surely many persons in the Communist world—understand the full meaning and full tragedy of this drama. Pasternak's ordeal serves us well in strengthening our determination that his slavery shall never be ours."[75] The incident awakened a global sense of identity in writers: the British *Times* reported that a group of prominent writers (including Stephen Spender, T. S. Eliot, Somerset Maugham, E. M. Forster, Graham Greene, Bertrand Russell) and International PEN had sent a telegram of protest to the Moscow Writers' Union: "International Pen, very distressed by rumors concerning Pasternak, asks you to protect the poet, maintaining the right of creative freedom. Writers throughout the world are thinking of him fraternally."[76] One commentator remarked in the aftermath that this literature prize had provided a "significant chapter in the development of . . . the 'cold war' . . . one could hardly grudge the journalists their excitement that at long last the USSR had dropped practically its first point in the 'world propaganda' competition with the West."[77]

The media attention intensified over Solzhenitsyn's prize in 1970; the drama this time lasted from the initial eruption of acclaim in the Western media (in contrast with Soviet stoniness) at the announcement of the prize on 10 October 1970 throughout the uncertainty as to whether Solzhenitsyn would attend the ceremony on 10 December. The latter debate drew in the KGB, the Western press, Swedish diplomats, and internationally acclaimed artists such as Rostropovich.[78]

Despite their veneer of neutralist rhetoric, the prizes to Pasternak and Solzhenitsyn are just as political as the opposition expressed by the Soviet authorities. Espmark emphasizes the homage paid to "those great artistic achievements that are characterized by uncompromising 'integrity' in the depiction of the human predicament."[79] This definition of artistic integrity, however, has been elided into the Nobel Prize's "objective" search for artistic excellence, obscuring the fact that sociopolitical circumstance has frequently outbalanced literary achievement. Committee member Artur Lundkvist declared in 1980 that Solzhenitsyn was not "a very big artist . . . . But we helped a man in danger who had important things to say which he was able to say in the world later."[80] His Nobel Prize drew attention to his cause just as much as to his literature. The prize thus emerges as an award for services to humanity rather than for literary production.

Another source of political inconsistency emerges in the respective treatment of Soviet and fascist writers. While pro-Soviet writers have been honored in the cause of achieving neutral balance, judgments of writers with Nazi sympathies have been far harsher. Several of the laureates who were Stalinist defenders had accepted Stalin Prizes: Neruda won a Lenin Peace Prize in 1950 and a Stalin Peace Prize in 1953. "Why," asks Burton Feldman, "was a Stalin Prize acceptable to Nobel judges when a 'Hitler Prize' would not be?"[81] Ezra Pound, considered for a Nobel in the same year that Sholokhov was up against Pasternak, aligned himself with a political regime (fascism) no more destructive of human life than that which Sholokhov, Laxness, Sartre, and Neruda supported. Dag Hammarskjöld explained the committee's objections to Pound (namely, his anti-Semitism) in 1959: "Pound [fell] victim to anti-Semitism . . . such a 'subhuman' reaction ought to exclude the possibility of a prize intended to lay weight on the 'idealistic tendency.'"[82] Artur Lundkvist later declared that "the limited merits" of Pound's work could not atone for his "shameful outpourings of psychopathic hatred and evil."[83] The difference between communist and fascist writers, presumably, lay on a rhetorical level. Lundkvist once commented that the prize "should have an idealistic tendency; it should represent humanism. It cannot be awarded to those who advocate violence."[84] In other words, however destructive of human life communist regimes have been, they at least meant well. Additionally, Nazism during the Second World War remained a recent and particularly painful memory for European intellectuals, whereas Russia had fought and suffered on the side of Western Europe and the United States.

The issue of politicization is forever linked to the question of idealism with which Nobel committees have struggled for one hundred years. Definitions have varied enormously, since the term contains within it the contradictions of its Enlightenment–Romantic heritage. The Nobel Committee has swung uneasily between different definitions of idealism, and its beleaguered other, literary professionalism, over its century of existence. The prize, however, will never be one for sheer literary professionalism or quality alone: compare the laureate for Nadine Gordimer (leading South African activist against apartheid) with the lack thereof for Doris Lessing (also a white African but resident in Europe, less of an activist but arguably equal to or even better than Gordimer as a novelist). Why should Solzhenitsyn win a Nobel and not Nabokov, the acclaimed émigré literary stylist? Why Márquez rather than Borges, the acknowledged pioneer of the Latin American boom generation? Borges lost his chance for a Nobel when he accepted an award from the right-wing dictator General Pinochet, even though his acceptance had little bearing on his political views.

In recent years, Nobel officials have insisted that idealism is a dead issue; only the "best" writing matters. Depiction of the "human predicament," a nicely universalistic aim, won awards for writers such as Beckett (1969) and Cela (1989). Politicization was something the committee clearly aimed to shun in 1989, when the Swedish Academy desisted from openly supporting Salman Rushdie against the Ayatollah's fatwah. Two Academy members publicly resigned as a result. "It was pretty simple," commented the then head of the Swedish PEN chapter, Gabi Gleichmann. "A sovereign nation had condemned a writer to death for expressing his views. And we expected some response from the world's most respected literary authorities. What we got was bureaucracy."[85] The Nobel Committee has oscillated between claims to universalism and neutralism, on the one hand, and specific stance-taking, on the other, just as its philosophical constituents veer between Enlightenment rationality and the autonomous and engaged qualities of Romanticism.

"Marginal" Literatures and the Nobel Prize

A prize with pretensions to global scope will naturally seek to incorporate writers from all over the world. Since the prize's inception, committees have emphasized that it should "circulate in turn between different countries."[86] Just as Goethe theorized national literatures as the base units of world literature, so the Nobel Committee has throughout the prize's history continued to stress the national constituents that make up the prize roll: the press release by the Academy at each year's prize announcement begins by mentioning the nationality of the writer, even before the writer has been named: "The Nobel Prize in Literature for 2000 goes to the Chinese writer Gao Xingjian." Two prize-winners from the same country have never been chosen in close succession, and this consideration has sometimes governed the choices made: for example Yeats was selected over Benavente in 1922, due to the "omissions in the geographical distribution of the Nobel Prize."[87]

If Tagore helped the Nobel Committee "break the routine" of European domination in 1913, since the 1980s it has become something of a mission for the Nobel Committee to prove that the prize is more than an award for European work. Although in 1904 a committee member suggested that "to begin with we work round Europe," a 1922 report spoke of the danger of the Nobel Prize, "which is intended for the richly variegated literature of the whole world," being limited to "a less universal circle."[88] After the Second World War, the prize aspired far more actively to the role of literary United Nations, with awards going to Gabriela Mistral (Chile) in 1945, Yasunari Kawabata (Japan) in 1968, and Patrick White (Australia) in 1973. The bid for global relevance manifestly intensified in the 1980s. In 1982 Academy member Östen Sjöstrand revealed that "the Academy is looking for candidates from small ethnic groups, small languages. You got a very good example of this when Singer got the Nobel Prize."[89] In 1984 Lars Gyllensten, another Academician, said that attention to non-European writers was gradually increasing, with attempts being made "to achieve a global distribution."[90] What is the significance of incorporating non-Western writers into an institution of aspiring global status?

Despite the graciousness of Sweden's gesture towards "small languages," their writers may well harbor reservations on two counts: Firstly, if selected, are they being chosen for their exotic value rather than for their universal literary relevance? Secondly, the imprecise and condescending term "small languages" (indicating, presumably, those languages not yet blessed with a Nobel laureate) lumps together an unruly spectrum of literary cultures, including, potentially, that of China (whose language is spoken by almost one quarter of the world's population, who consider their mother tongue and literary heritage anything but "small"). Moreover, while Scandinavian languages are themselves nothing if not small in numbers of speakers, the remark surely is not meant to include Swedish, one of the crucial linguistic currencies into which literature must be translated to speed Nobel success. These are, again, the central problems of *Weltliteratur*. What is the relationship between the theory of universalistic literary expression and its individual (and especially national) components? Is the channel of exchange uni- or multidirectional? What are the dynamics between the Nobel Prize and its satellite national literatures? The Nobel seems to be heading towards a two-tier system of judgment in which its professed criteria of literary neutralism and universalism are not luxuries permitted to every Nobel laureate. Literature from the Western canon is selected for its "universal" qualities, while non-Western literature is included for its local, refreshingly pluralistic value.

Kjell Espmark notes a distinct change in the Academy's approach to writing from non-European cultures from the 1920s onwards, namely an earnest effort to understand a literary work as it fits into its native milieu rather than judging it from a Swedish cultural viewpoint. From the 1980s, this resolve has been matched by concerted action to enlist the help of experts to overcome the inevitable linguistic and cultural barriers between the committee and these literatures.

> In the case of writers we want to take up and treat fairly it is a matter of trying to acquire some understanding of the traditions and of the literary and cultural milieu out of which they write. A great deal of background reading is needed if one is to grasp something of what a writer from a culture other than one's own feels engaged in and wants to write about. And here, too, we must assume close cooperation between external specialists and those who will in the end reach a decision.[91]

As Österling conceded in 1945, "One must accustom oneself to finding genuineness in foreign dress."[92]

In stark contrast to these publicly declared intentions of the Swedish Academy, Artur Lundkvist in 1977 made the following response to criticisms that the Nobel Prize contained significant omissions concerning non-Western literatures. "The academy is often reproached for thus neglecting the literatures of Asia and Africa and other 'remote' parts. But I doubt if there is so far very much to find there. It is a question of literatures that (with a certain exception, particularly in the case of Japan) as far as can be judged have not achieved that level of development (artistic, psychological, linguistic) that can make them truly significant outside their given context."[93] He enlarged further on this viewpoint in an interview from 1980:

> Lundkvist: There are some good Indian writers, in Hindi for example, but they are not, so far, up to the international standards we must maintain. They [and other non-Western literatures] are primitive cultures, and I do not think somehow they are capable of developing in a global way.
>
> Interviewer: But you conquered literature from a peasant environment.
>
> Lundkvist: That's different; I studied the classics. . . . But there is Japan . . . Japan is a country which has developed a quality in literature comparable to ours, because it is an industrialized, advanced society.
>
> Interviewer: They are westernized, you mean. You are actually imposing western, white, indeed Christian, aesthetic values?[94]

These remarks put Lundkvist's championing of South American literature (Neruda, for example) into context: presumably, its writers were acceptable due to their absorption of the European literary heritage. We should, perhaps, not single out the prejudices of the Nobel Committee alone for criticism. Thomas di Giovanni, a BBC journalist, reiterated in 1982: "Members of the Committee are only too eager to say how much they would like to find writers from places like India and Africa and, thereby, break the stranglehold on literature now held by the superpowers of the West. . . . It is here, in dealing with the lesser-developed countries, that the Academy comes up against the problem of standards — that is, of the out-and-out superiority of writing in the West." Giovanni acclaimed the following remarks by Per Wästberg, former president of International PEN, as clear-sighted: "I think we have to recognise that there are European, westernized literary criteria built on individual excellence, the creation of an individual work. When you come to other continents — totally other cultures — you find other criteria for literature . . . Islam and Iran have a number of writers. They write in a religious, moralist, mythological vein and you cannot extract from their entire work one single volume and say: well, here is a masterpiece."[95]

Kjell Espmark is quick to defend the Nobel ethos as a whole, pointing out that Lundkvist's remarks "are not representative. . . . Further, Lundkvist's statement is incompatible with the modest practice that can be distinguished. The idea of a Western lead that only Japan has to a certain extent managed to close is hardly compatible with Österling's authoritative words on Kawabata. To him, Kawabata represents a cultural consciousness that *vindicates itself* against Western influence."[96] This, however, still poses the question of how these "marginal" literatures relate to the "center" in Sweden. Valued principally for the democratizing aura of exotica they bring to the prize, they are hardly ever allowed to shed their marginal status and be valued as "universally human" like Western literatures. The relationship echoes that between Goethe and Eastern literatures, cozily ensconced together on Goethe's *West-Eastern Divan*. As Goethe hoped to be transformed by Eastern riches, so the Nobel Prize is strengthened by acknowledging what its committee views as the potted essences of national literatures, which are subsequently tied to being narrowly representative. Those literatures that are seen as achieving a broader significance can do so only in terms of their degree of Westernization.

Compare the following two groups of Nobel citations:

1. "for the depth of spirit and the art with which he has described the life of Finnish peasants and the nature of Finland in their reciprocal relations"
   "for the lyricism inspired by the power of feeling which has made the name of this poet the symbol of the Latin American world"
   "for his remarkable lyric oeuvre, which so deeply inspires a sense of the culture of the Hellenic world"
   "an eminent representative of modern Latin American literature"
   "for his narrative art which expresses with refined feeling the special qualities of the Japanese soul"
   "spokesman for Arabic prose"
2. "for his observation, imagination and descriptive art"
   "for his comprehensive and artistically significant writings, in which human problems and conditions have been presented with a fearless love of truth and keen psychological insight"
   "for his outstanding, pioneering contribution to present-day poetry"
   "his vigorous mastery with its influence on style in contemporary story-telling"
   "for his important literary production, which with clear-sighted earnestness illuminates the problems of the human conscience in our times"

"for his description of the human condition"

"who with poetic force creates an imagined world, where life and myth
   condense to form a disconcerting picture of the human predicament
   today."

"for an oeuvre of universal validity, bitter insights and linguistic
   ingenuity"[97]

The first group applies to writers of marginal or non-Western literatures, and are clearly identified as such by the nationalist tag that is attached to each. The second group applies to Western laureates, apart from the last two citations for Kenzaburo Oe and Gao Xingjian respectively, two writers who have perhaps reached a level of development sufficiently Westernized to make them truly significant outside their given context. It is worth noting that Oe is viewed as one of the most Westernized writers of his generation, a maverick loner among the Japanese; Gao lives and works in France, and incorporates influences from modern French literature in his drama and acceptable dissidence in his fiction. News of their prizes was stonily received by the literary establishments in their respective native countries.

The Nobel Committee's ambivalent acceptance of writers from marginal literatures means that writers of non-Western literatures have to do either of two things: achieve a "universal" level of development (as defined by the Nobel Committee) or earn their exotic keep as representative of their neglected corner of the literary world. The message from Japan's two laureates comes across clearly: either express "the special qualities of the Japanese soul" (Kawabata) or produce a "picture of the human predicament" (Oe). The Greek poet Kostis Palamas did not meet these criteria and thus slipped through the Nobel net in 1930: "If . . . we are going to give a Nobel Prize to an exotic author," judged academician Henrik Schück, "we ought at least to have convinced ourselves that it is original and national."[98] In 1929 the committee expressed a wish "to greet with satisfaction the opportunity, through the medium of the Nobel Prize, to draw attention to the great and vigorous literature of the South American language area." Unfortunately, Venezuela's Rufion Blanco Fombona failed to win approval as "a sufficiently important author to fill the place of a representative of his culture."[99]

Furthermore, whatever its intentions, the Nobel Committee's plan to validate itself globally by incorporating "small languages" has at least partly backfired in terms of its resulting reputation among the writers of "big languages." At the start of the 1980s it began acquiring a reputation for tokenism. The desire to include marginal literatures, di Giovanni commented in 1982, "goes a long way to explain the choices that have puzzled so many over the last four years. Singer, a Polish-born Jew, a nationalized American, who writes in Yiddish; Odysseus Elytis, a Greek; Czeslaw Milosz, a Lithuanian-born Pole . . . Elias Canetti, a Bulgarian-born British national of Sephardic origin who writes in German . . . a clear pattern emerges."[100] Incorporation of these "marginal" figures into the literary mainstream can either be accomplished only through Nobel approval, or can never take place, as Western journalists and critics such as di Giovanni refuse to be fooled by the Nobel's attempts at authentication — once local marginalia, such commentators steadfastly believe, always local marginalia. Highlighting this conviction, British media reactions to Gao Xingjian's prize in 2000 focused on the sociopolitical issues behind the award, rather than trying to fill in ignorance about the literary oeuvre that had been honored. For those writing in a mainstream language in a mainstream literary scene (especially English), there are now bigger, or more relevant fish to fry than the Nobel Prize (although no one, doubtless, would refuse the million-dollar Nobel question). When asked in 2000 whether he would like a Nobel Prize, Gore Vidal replied dismissively that it was a "prize for the literature of small countries."[101] "The ideal candidate for a Nobel Prize today would be a lesbian from Asia," remarked Mats Gellerfelt, one of Sweden's leading literary critics, in 1998.[102] It is most unfashionable actually to *worry* about winning a Nobel: a semi-serious hope for a Dutch prize expressed in a review of Gao Xingjian's *Soul Mountain* was edited out before it appeared in a Dutch newspaper in October 2000.[103]

Writers of nonmainstream, non-European languages are locked in a no-win situation vis-à-vis the Nobel Prize: appreciative of the money and publicity it brings, they nevertheless have to deal with the uncertain slur of tokenism that comes with the Nobel, a symbol of the system known as world literature that everyone still thinks is based rightfully in the West. Toni Morrison, in 1993 the first African American to win the prize, has commented:

> If a white male wins it, they would not say it's political. So I can't take the criticism seriously. I know and you know that if an African American wins it, or somebody from a Third World country wins it — somebody who is not from America, the center of the universe — they say it's political. "Political" is a real word, and it has real meaning. But it is a term here that is sly and suggests something not superior. When it is used this way, it is a racist term.[104]

IN SPITE OR REGARDLESS OF the above, the Nobel Prize continues to provoke its annual one-day media splash, living on in our subconscious as a basically good, or at least not fundamentally wrong-headed idea. This glosses over the bizarre amalgam of philosophies and ideas behind it, the questions its history poses concerning the uses of literature, and also the responsibility it still holds towards nurturing and governing world literature. The Nobel Prize has come to represent a modern global literary standard, in the process blurring modern ideas of literary universalism and autonomy with exhortations that literature should improve and engage with society and nation. Throughout the prize's history, and particularly in the post-World War II period, assertions of autonomy and literary professionalism have not only concealed politically and culturally determined sources of inconsistency and prejudice, but have also established a two-tier set of criteria for mainstream (liberal, Western) and nonmainstream literatures (generally non-Western or written in non-Western languages). Universalism and independence of specific social context have become naturalized, privileged literary attributes of the developed Western nations, while "marginal" literatures are largely valued (if at all) for their local, sociopolitical value.

Current general indifference on the part of Western readers and writers as to how the Nobel conducts itself obscures the fact that the Nobel Prize has been a source of anxiety to many Western nations in the past. At the turn of the nineteenth century, England — then still near the pinnacle of imperial self-confidence — was showing exactly the same symptoms of a Nobel Complex as did the Chinese in the 1980s and 1990s. Following an exchange of letters in British broadsheet newspapers bemoaning the fact that — unlike French writers — English writers had not been nominated for the new Nobel Prize in a systematic way, a Nobel Committee was formed to manage nominations. Presumably, this anxiety did not subside until Kipling won the prize in 1907. This historical amnesia in the West concerning the national, social, and political roots of literature is embedded in the current concept of world literature, in which Western standards occupy a neutral, universalistic middle ground, incorporating the margins either as satellites to further legitimize Western-centrism or as the exception that proves the rule for "less developed," local literatures.

It is easy to point out the limitations of the Nobel Prize, its flawed record, and the dubious credibility of the judgments of the Swedish Academy. It is equally easy to feel puzzled, even impatient, at China's anxiety and impatience to win. This, however, would mean overlooking the role the prize plays in global culture, a structure whose center of gravity remains in the West and which therefore continues to reflect the imbalance of economic and cultural capital. It is the Nobel Prize's ambiguous power to confer economic and cultural capital in the hazy but confidently modern realm of world literature that makes it such a revealing index of the insecurity and ambivalence a nation like China has felt over the last century concerning its position in the global order. As a contradictory symbol of modernity, the Nobel continues to exercise fascination over those cultures and literatures that consider themselves outside the mainstream of the modern, global community. Gaining recognition from a canon-making body such as the Nobel Prize, however, is accompanied by all kinds of compromises and anxieties. It is to these that we turn in our consideration of China in the following chapters.

CHAPTER THREE

Ideas of Authorship and the
Nobel Prize in China, 1900–1976

The history of the Nobel Prize for Literature coincides with a tumultuous and formative period in the development of modern
Chinese writing and culture: the collapse of the sinocentric Confucian worldview, the clash with Western modernity and the
emergence of the modern concept of authorship. True, China has not spent
the entire century agonizing over the Nobel Prize—that would wait until the
1980s, when Chinese interest in the prize reached the intensity of a complex.
Yet the fact that the Nobel Prize has tapped such a reservoir of disquiet in
modern Chinese letters makes little sense without consideration of conflicting
ideas about authorship that emerged in the twentieth century: the struggles
of many Chinese writers to measure up to a modern, international, and theoretically autonomous standard of writing while striving for national salvation
have created enormous tensions within the practice of authorship. During a
century in which the forging of a national culture and literature that would
enable China to compete with the West has been so central, Chinese encounters with the Nobel Literature Prize before 1976 illuminate representative dilemmas in the modern Chinese literary identity.

In *Sources of the Self,* Charles Taylor draws attention to the fundamental
importance in the modern era of individual identity, "our sense of what underlies our own dignity . . . what makes our lives meaningful or fulfilling."[1]
The self-articulating, self-determining capabilities of the individual have
taken on a preeminent importance in modern artistic production, thanks
largely to the Romantic emphasis on the primacy of self-expression; Western
literature bears the direct imprint of this modern quest for identity. Emphasis
on the individual turned Western literature inward in the eighteenth century,
and a clear line of influence can be perceived between Rousseau's (1712–1778)
Confessions and the inner worlds of Joyce's (1882–1941) *Ulysses.* The rise of

individualism led to a focus on the subject with a concomitant separation of self and world, subject and object.

Although Taylor's frame of reference is largely limited to Western sources on the self and identity, and much of his reasoning is drawn from the sense of morality historically based in Judeo-Christian theism, inasmuch as Taylor is probing the modern condition, his observations about the primacy of individual identity are highly relevant to problems faced by Chinese literary intellectuals in the twentieth century. Chinese dilemmas around the literary self have been rendered even more contentious by their historical background. The traumatic encounter with imperialism, which made participation in the international system through nation building into the dominant model of modernity in China, pushed writers to express a new kind of individual consciousness in their writing that juxtaposed individualism and autonomy, collectivism and nation building, internationalism and universalism. The perceived need for a new kind of consciousness echoes the call to "awaken" that, John Fitzgerald shows, has been immensely powerful in modern Chinese nation-building discourse. This "awakening" was not only to the imperative of nationhood, but also to a concomitant host of "universal ideals of enlightenment, progress, and science, to the autonomy of the individual and 'self-realization.'"[2]

In literary terms, this translated into an embrace of the autonomous aesthetic, associated notably with the May Fourth promotion of a realist literature inspired by Western models and written by enlightened individuals — the literary equivalent of the modern forces of science and democracy. But while this idea of the autonomous aesthetic (art for art's sake) in literature has been enormously influential in China at various moments in the twentieth century, it has been most importantly prized, paradoxically, for its actively transformative functions — the capacity to liberate the Chinese from tradition and forge a national culture that would establish China as an equal player on the global stage. The principle of literary autonomy — learned from the (imperialist) West, in order to compete with the West — has been invoked in modern China as a means to preserve the nation. Needless to say, these great and contradictory expectations of the autonomous aesthetic and of its executor, the professional writer, have often proved challenging.

Competing with the idea of the modern self were traditional Confucian views of self and mind, aspects of which have persisted in the modern Chinese intellectual identity. Chinese philosophy, while emphasizing the social basis of individual behavior, did not lack the concept of a transcendent self, yet fundamental differences between Western and Chinese cosmology meant that the Chinese preoccupation with mind did not lead inevitably to the egoism associated with Western Romanticism. For the Chinese, self-awareness meant sensitivity to the external world, especially the social world of human relations; Heaven and man were a unity, held together by the primacy of ritual (*li*). Traditional Chinese narrative does not show the same interest as Western literature in representing, through language, the mind cut off from the external world. These residual habits of thought, Kirk Denton believes, underlay the radically new narrative orientation of Chinese modernity.

> In both literary theory and practice, modern writers were unconsciously working out, with new discursive tools borrowed from the West, a predicament about the self's relationship to the world and its role in social transformation that had ties to tradition. With the appropriation of Western liberal humanist models of self by intellectuals in the late Qing and May Fourth periods, the neo-Confucian promise of mind's linkage to the outer world was broken, although the desire for such a linkage continued. The traditional tension surrounding the linkage was enhanced in the process of borrowing from the West and became an epistemological problem that . . . lies at the heart of Chinese modernity.[3]

In hoping to achieve national recognition in the form of a literary prize such as the Nobel, modern Chinese writers have needed to aspire to aesthetic individualism *and* nationalist collectivism; to be the voice of their people that addresses a world audience. The intense interest in an external source of valuation such as the Nobel Prize raises key questions in modern Chinese literature and culture: what is the relationship between intellectuals and national identity, and between the individual author and his social function within the nation, particularly against the backdrop of Western stimuli and traditional expectations?

Literary intellectuals placed a weighty task on the shoulders of Chinese literature in the modern era. Not only was the new literature, through the genre of realism, aimed at achieving social transformation, it also became the passport to China's place in the international community. "From the beginning, the Chinese translation of the term, *shijie wenxue* (world literature), has assumed the enormous burden of explaining and justifying China's membership in the modern international community," asserts Lydia Liu. "May Fourth writers turned to European literature largely with the intention of learning how to produce a national canon worthy of being accepted by world literature and being valued by the West." However, as Liu goes on to point out,

> It would be inaccurate, if not downright absurd, to conclude that modern Chinese writers are merely infatuated with the dream of seeking a legitimate place

for themselves in world literature. The Chinese translation of the notions of national literature and world literature must be considered along with a whole set of other competing theories and discourses — many of which are also imported from the outside — about what literature is and how it should function in modern Chinese society. These competing positions include the familiar theory of "art for art's sake," *rensheng pai* (humanist theory), *pingmin wenxue* (plebeian literature), class literature, and proletarian literature, among others.[4]

Liu's comments draw attention to the way in which modern Chinese literary identity has been situated between several overlapping areas of concern: the aesthetic (art for art's sake vs. socially transformative or utilitarian), the national (China vs. the West, or political vs. cultural), the philosophical (Confucian vs. individualist), the historical (tradition vs. modernity), the question of audience (elite vs. mass), and so on. Liu also has valuable insights into the dislocation within twentieth-century Chinese literary discourse between the frequently nationalistic view of literature sponsored by dominant male intellectuals, and the representations of certain female writers, such as Xiao Hong (1911–1942).[5] These dilemmas of identity run right through China's twentieth-century literature, from Liang Qichao to the literary critic and theorist Hu Feng (1902–1985), the chief object of the first major purge of intellectuals after the 1949 Communist revolution, and beyond, rendering clear-cut, binary interpretations of literary identity largely untenable. For example, the opposition between the writer and authority that has become the stereotypical Western view of relations between artists and party in socialist regimes does not entirely fit the modern Chinese intellectual experience. It is facile, Denton believes, "to view the gradual marginalization of subjectivism . . . that came to a head with the Anti-Hu Feng campaign as simply imposed by the party on a resistant group of writers and critics struggling heroically to maintain allegiance to the individualist values of the May Fourth."[6] Instead, Denton has identified twin strains of "romantic individualism and revolutionary collectivism" that constitute a fundamental source of tension for modern Chinese literary intellectuals. Key texts from modern Chinese literature are obsessed with the crisis of both the national and the individual Chinese self, held to be deficient at a local and international level.

The questions of identity at the heart of China's Nobel Complex are thus central to the broader trajectory of modern Chinese literary identity. The demands (often imposed or readily accepted by literati themselves) that writers should be both Chinese and international, both autonomous and engaged, both cultural elites and builders of national consciousness continued to exert contradictory pressures on many writers and their attitudes to audience and subject matter for much of the twentieth century. The quest for a new individual subjectivity, the forging of a national identity and the desire for equality with the West all make up the sources of the modern Chinese literary self.

Late Qing–May Fourth:
The Birth of the Modern Chinese Author

Two significant developments changed the Chinese outlook on literature from the late Qing onwards. The first was the impact of new external influences: writers' creative energies were no longer held within indigenously defined limits but had begun to be shaped by the cross-cultural exposures effected by nineteenth-century Western colonialism. The second was the development of authorship into an independent profession. Audiences and the literary market grew rapidly with the late Qing fiction boom: two thousand or more works of fiction were written and circulated between 1898 and 1911, published through at least four channels (periodical newspapers, tabloids, fiction magazines, and books), with 170 presses catering to a potential audience of two to four million readers.[7] The growth of the Treaty Ports was principally responsible for this development, since it created a community of readers whose tastes had spread to many parts of China by the end of the nineteenth century and a new professional function for literati.

Writers of this new hybrid literature found themselves caught between often contradictory roles, asserting the need both to learn from Western models of modernity and foster national consciousness. The demands of nationalism in turn required that literature, traditionally more of a straightforward elite activity, now had to focus on cultivating all the people as constituents of the new nation. These demands immediately presented writers with several dilemmas. Firstly, who were "the people" and what kind of culture would draw them in? Secondly, what relationship should be struck with the cultural past, which both accounted for China's national uniqueness and for its historical predicament at the turn of the century? Thirdly, what relationship should be struck with the West, given that it had introduced the positively valued paradigm of national and universal modernity, yet was at the same time an aggressor undermining the foundations of Chinese culture? Set against all this, what role remained for the autonomous literary creator?

The thinking of Liang Qichao, the essayist and theorist who envisioned a new Chinese identity, perhaps epitomizes these tensions. In his numerous writings, Liang defined the "new citizen" (*xin min*) as a free, active, self-conscious, and creative member of the nation (as opposed to a slave of imperialism). Yet group membership remained fully half of Liang's theorization of the individual. In his article "Shuo qun" (On the group), he wrote: "Men must not be slaves to other men, but they must be slaves to their groups."[8] Liang also imagined a China thrown onto the great stage of world history, participation in which was possible only as a nation-state. However, it was equally clear to Liang that "world history" was not a neutral concept. "The Westerners are so self-important that they always believe they have possession of the whole world. Because of this complacency, a story of an Aryan race that migrated westward to either prosper or wither away is very often erroneously entitled 'History of the World.'"[9]

Literature was quickly incorporated into Liang's model for Chinese modernity. As he cast around for instructive examples from strong Western nations, he concluded that "political fiction" was a genre that had "done wonders in Japan and the West as a vehicle of social reform and intellectual enlightenment."[10] While bemoaning the current state of fiction in China, he commented that in Western countries "a newly published book could often influence and change the views and arguments of the whole nation. Indeed, political novels should be given the highest credit for being instrumental in the steady progress made in the political sphere in America, England, Germany, France, Austria, Italy, and Japan."[11] Fiction, due both to its prominence in the West and to its popularity among the mass readership, underwent an awkward transformation. Traditionally scorned by the Chinese scholarly elite, it was rapidly promoted up the literary hierarchy as an instrument of national salvation. "If one intends to renovate the people of a nation," Liang enthused, "one must first renovate its fiction."[12] Fiction became in many ways the defining genre of modern Chinese literature, yet even among its most enthusiastic early intellectual advocates, it retained the unsavory aura of a traditional popular literary form or an ideologically ambivalent foreign import. Fiction served at best a utilitarian purpose, tying in with traditional Confucian intellectual notions of public service.

David Wang has argued that there were other possibilities for late Qing literary production, in which the excesses of late Qing fiction — denounced by Liang Qichao as a backward and corrupting influence on the nation's youth — signaled a unique revitalizing of Chinese literature from within, rather than from foreign stimuli alone. Exaggeration of traditional tropes and devices broadened the scope of genres such as the courtesan, detective, and exposé novel and manifested an experimental daring that far exceeded that of the May Fourth reformers. Wang's approach to Chinese literary modernity poses new questions about its provenance and direction, releasing Chinese literature and authorship from their subordinate position vis-à-vis the West. Firstly, he grants traditional Chinese forms their own internal cultural momentum and the capacity to develop towards modernism rather than to atrophy. Secondly, the anti-utilitarian excesses of late Qing fiction give "obsession with China" a sardonic, almost postmodern twist, countering the gravely didactic, politicized literature advocated by Liang Qichao. Wang describes a literature whose modernist decadence heralds the arrival of a new era and presents an intriguing alternative direction in which Chinese literature might have developed, had it not been for the May Fourth movement.[13]

If the idea of the professional writer arose in the late Qing, the May Fourth movement, initially an anti-imperialist protest, gave such a career choice moral kudos, established new Europeanized literary forms and, by 1921, installed the vernacular as the "national language."[14] May Fourth ideas about literature shared two crucial aspects with the late Qing: first, both promoted the development of literary activity into a self-constituting field, independent of the imperial bureaucracy, which until 1905 had provided the official rationale for the study and writing of poetry; and second, the May Fourth movement also emphasized foreign knowledge and literatures as integral to the new-style education that formed a common background for many of the participants. The stimulus and threat of Western influence coexisted with the accruing of prestige to an elite group whose rather more traditional raison d'être consisted of worrying about the fate of the Chinese people through intensive discussion of the literature-mediated relationship between intellectuals and the masses. Authorial autonomy and individualism were enrolled in the service of social engagement; new Western genres and ideas were adapted to traditional Chinese purposes in the pursuit of national modernity. The most obvious instance of this was the hope invested in the "science" of Western literary realism — its potential to enable the writer to represent the people "objectively" and to sway society to its new responsibilities. China, as a modern nation, needed a national literature and "this literature would henceforth not be artistic and feudal, but social and international."[15]

Questions of selfhood illuminate the tensions between individual and collective, national identities in May Fourth intellectuals. "A strong, autonomous self," observes Kirk Denton, "was needed in the struggle to break with tradition, but the demands of resistance to imperialism required a national unity that could easily subordinate self to a collective will."[16] The unavoidable question of the nation-state surfaced in the writings of many May Fourth intellectuals in a way that was in constant tension with the unprecedented florescence of discussions of the individual. The assertion of *geren* (the individual) and *zijue* (self-consciousness) became linked to the higher goals of national regeneration and national unity, as individualism was beset by the opposing discourses of romantic individualism and revolutionary collectivism. As reformers called for literary autonomy and innovation, asserting that "literature is literature," they reexpressed an "obsession with China." "Revolutionized literature itself is compellingly associated with the rise of 'China' in the modern era," comments Rey Chow. "Looming over 'autonomy'-as-liberation is thus the preoccupation with the 'continuity' of Chinese culture."[17]

Theorization of the new May Fourth poetry illustrates these overlapping areas of concern. John Crespi terms nationalism "the missing problematic" in the study of modern Chinese poetry, identifying in the critical and poetic writings of prominent intellectuals such as Hu Shi (1891–1962) the conceptualization of modern poetic reform that would become the vehicle for a new national consciousness. Hu came "to make the connection between poetic form, the literary representation of 'reality,' and 'the people' as national subject," thus constructing "a situation in which poets can legitimately and with epistemological authority connect their literary discourse with a popular national subjectivity."[18] Hu envisioned a poetry in which the antimodern, antipopulist shackles of form would be broken, allowing the pure national essence of internal poetic content to stand out, clad only in the simple formal garments of realism. Poetry-writing intellectuals of the late 1910s and early 1920s (culminating in the "commoner poetry movement" of 1921–1922) theorized the release of poetry from the externals of form and its return to the domain of "truth" and "reality" located in a popular national subject; this movement identifying folk song and "commoner" poetry as the site of a nationally authentic poetic *vox populi*. These efforts to link poetry to a popular national subject reveal how deeply nationalist ideologies had permeated Chinese poetic discourse by the early 1920s.[19] These episodes, moreover, showcase attempts to mediate the tensions between elite and popular forms that would reemerge throughout the century, during the populist cultural campaigns of the War of Resistance (1937–1945), the Great Leap Forward (1958–1960) and in the controversies over audience and style that underpinned discussions of the Nobel Prize in the 1980s and 1990s.

These tensions between individualism and collectivism in the forging of a national cultural identity also intersected with the desire for international parity combined with misgivings about the degree to which international recognition was rooted in imperialist, Western systems of valuation. May Fourth writers on the one hand took pride in their cosmopolitanism and in the extent to which their work was influenced by foreign models (a pride that laid itself open to satire in Leo Lee's account of the May Fourth, *The Romantic Generation of Modern Chinese Writers*).[20] On the other hand, they were firmly committed to a project of national literary reform that would rescue the Chinese nation from its degeneracy. Two Nobel encounters of the 1920s bring into sharp relief tensions surrounding the estate of the professional writer and Western influences: intellectual reactions to the 1924 visit to China by Rabindranath Tagore (1861–1941); and Lu Xun's refusal to be nominated for the Nobel Prize in 1927.

Tagore and Chinese Intellectuals

Against the backdrop of May Fourth cosmopolitanism, the news of Tagore's visit caused great excitement in China's cities. The journal press of the 1920s and 1930s, open to news from abroad, was well aware of the prestige attached to Nobel Prize winners and, as the first Asian to win the prize, Tagore was a particularly significant figure. Not only that, he seemed also to fit the paradigm of "writer as cultural spokesman" that was so central to the self-image of May Fourth elites. *Xiaoshuo yuebao* (Short Story Monthly) produced two Tagore issues in 1923. The details of Tagore's message to China, however, were less universally acclaimed by Chinese nationalists, despite the enthusiasm of liberals such as Liang Qichao and Xu Zhimo (1896–1931).[21] When Tagore arrived in Beijing, his lectures on the need to preserve Chinese traditions and Eastern spiritual civilization, and on the dangers of material, industrial civilization were not well received by nationalists and leftist intellectuals. A group of Beijing reformist agitators expressed their disappointment thus:

> We have suffered much from the ancient Chinese civilizations. . . . Dr. Tagore would have nationality and politics abolished, replacing them with the consolation of one's soul. . . . We cannot but oppose Dr. Tagore, who upholds these things which would shorten the life of our nation.[22]

Traditionalists such as Gu Hongming refused to accept the pan-Asian identity Tagore preached; indeed, Gu asserted, Indian not Western civilization was responsible for China's current predicament: "It was Buddhism, a product of the Oriental civilization of India, which after the Han dynasty nearly destroyed the true ancient Chinese civilization . . . if we Chinese want really to make progress, instead of reviving, we must get rid of this Oriental civilization."[23]

Chinese writers and intellectuals, keen both to catch up on the Western model of modernity and to gain international recognition for China's new culture, found in Tagore evidence of the contradictions inherent in such an undertaking. Chinese intellectuals had imagined Tagore to be an ideal example of how to export Asian culture in exchange for international cultural capital and recognition, and a model for promoting the role of literary intellectuals in cultural transformation. But Tagore's Asian revivalism was, to a degree, an undertaking compromised by the Western gaze. (Tagore's global fame, it should be recalled, sprang largely from his winning of a Nobel Prize for work written in English.) Tagore's encouragement in carrying out lecture tours in East Asia came principally from the West, where intellectuals and writers such as Thomas Mann (1875–1955) and W. B. Yeats (1865–1939) saw him as representative of a unified, spiritual Eastern culture. Predisposed to view himself as a global ambassador for "Eastern civilization," Tagore subscribed to the Western essentialization of the Orient into "a natural unity," as Martin Buber termed it.[24]

Thus, while Asian cultures aspired to take their places in the international community, they found themselves in peril of being fossilized by an essentializing West. Anxious to attain the material modernity of the West, Chinese intellectuals saw in Tagore a representative of an Eastern culture valued by the West only for its backwardness, for its strangulating past. Moreover, Gu Hongming's reaction demonstrates another key feature of China's modern cultural identity: despite feelings of inferiority toward the West, the Chinese considered themselves more culturally advanced than other Asian countries. Though temporarily abased before the West, China was its potential equal, its civilizational other. This combination of inferiority and uncertainty concerning Western recognition was echoed by Lu Xun's refusal of the Nobel nomination in 1927.

Lu Xun and the Nobel Prize

Lu Xun's life, oeuvre, and legacy embody the contradictions that have dogged the modern Chinese literary self. In his thought and literary work, he moved between patriotism and pessimism, between an elitist belief in heroic literary intellectuals who would lead a feudal China to rebirth (as exemplified by his Romantic, enlightened Madman) and skepticism about the possibility of national, collective reform through revolution (witness the despair of *Ah Q zheng zhuan* [The true story of Ah Q]), between his leftist prorevolutionary activism and visions of patriotic self-sacrifice, in which his intellectual efforts to save the Chinese nation and people would consume and destroy him. Although the literary form he most favored during his lifetime was the high-brow essay (*zawen*) and although his last years were spent in frequent conflict with the League of Left-wing Writers, Lu Xun was posthumously sanctified as a hero of the Communist cultural revolution. Selectively focusing on Lu Xun's self-distrusting, procollectivist tendencies, Mao Zedong approvingly quoted in his 1942 "Talks at the Yan'an Conference on Literature and Art" — which was to become party orthodoxy on the role of the writer in the Communist Revolution — Lu Xun's professed desire to serve the masses "like a willing ox."[25]

It is thus appropriate, in an examination of the dynamics between the Chinese authorial identity and the Nobel Prize, that Lu Xun should be among the first Chinese names linked with the prize. On a visit to China in 1927, the Swedish explorer and member of the Swedish Academy Sven Hedin allegedly suggested to Liu Bannong, a professor at Beijing University, that Lu Xun should be proposed for a laureateship. Lu Xun's reaction is quoted below:

> Concerning the Nobel riches, Liang Qichao isn't suitable and neither am I. There's still hard work to be done before this money can be won. There are so many writers in the world better than I, yet they are unable to win. Think about *Little John*, which I translated; how could I, rather than this writer, win?
>
> What gives me an unfair advantage is the fact that I am Chinese and helped by the word "China" . . . it would be laughable. I feel China doesn't yet have anyone who can win the Nobel Prize, in fact, and Sweden had best take no notice of us, best not give it to anyone [of us]. If the yellow-skinned people were given preferential consideration, it would only encourage the egotism of the Chinese, convincing them they really were equal to the great foreign writers. The result would be terrible.
>
> Everything before me is still black, there's fatigue and dejection; I don't know how much more I can write. If I won this thing and stopped writing, I would be doing people a disservice; if I continued writing [after winning], perhaps it would just be Hanlin literature, totally worthless. Carrying on as of old, obscure and impoverished, is the best way.[26]

Four reasons within Lu Xun's refusal summarize the archetypal dilemmas of modern Chinese writers when faced with the Nobel Prize. Firstly, his denigration of modern Chinese literature expresses his sense of national inferiority. Lu Xun famously advised writers not to read Chinese literature or criticism, only foreign writings; he was a practitioner of "hard translation," designed to introduce Western grammar into Chinese writing.[27] Secondly, Lu Xun's rejection of foreign tokenism towards China indicated, on the one hand, a fundamental doubt concerning the West's ability to judge Chinese achievements, and on the other, a desire to distinguish his identity as an individual author from that as member of a national collective. What good would there be, he asked, in honoring him and his writing simply for being "Chinese"? International fame for a "marginal" culture such as China's, he recognized, always brings with it a sense of tokenism, the burden of being recognized as merely representative rather than for literary quality. The burden of representing China, however, was one that May Fourth literati, Lu Xun included, found both appealing and appalling. Lu Xun's works are shot through both with the intellectual's disdain for, and feelings of guilt, responsibility, and moral inferiority before the benighted masses. Lu Xun both advocated intellectual activism and harbored a deep pessimism over the fate of the intellectual in the national revolution to come.

Thirdly, Lu Xun's doubts about his ability to continue writing illuminated the uncertain position occupied by the estate of creative writing and the autonomous literary aesthetic in the sociopolitical environment of twentieth-century China. In the course of Chinese political and cultural reforms, the independence of the Romantic creator ran headlong into conflict with the social role of the collective revolutionary. In 1927, in response to the deteriorating political situation, Lu Xun renounced the writing of fiction and poetry, restricting himself to argumentative essays.

A fourth reason for rejecting nomination was Lu Xun's aversion to the political, national, collective uses to which he could be put as a Nobel winner by the ruling government (this is indicated by his denunciation of "Hanlin" — the imperial academy, or government — literature). "A universally circulated explanation for Lu Xun's refusal to be nominated is his hatred for the GMD regime," Chen Chunsheng recently asserted. "Lu Xun accepting nomination for the Nobel Prize would have added luster to a newly established reactionary regime, something for which Lu Xun, transformed from democrat to communist, would have had the greatest contempt. . . . He didn't want to write 'Hanlin literature,' to wear the halo of glory for rulers he hated so deeply."[28]

A fifth, speculative, reason has been suggested by other Chinese scholars. Nomination alone would not guarantee Lu Xun the prize, and as a proud man would he have been willing to risk letting it be known that his candidacy had failed? Hedin had unknowingly committed a tactical error in dispatching Liu Bannong to convey the message to Lu Xun. Liu had come to be distrusted by Lu Xun when he sided with Zhou Zuoren (1885–1967), Lu Xun's brother, after the two had quarreled. Even though Liu sent his student Tai Jingnong as an intermediary, the association of the news with Liu lingered. Then, as now, the Chinese literary scene was a complex mix of personalities, occupied by writers pursuing a multiplicity of social, public, and personal aims. My discussion below of China's post-Mao Nobel Complex, with its mix of hurt national pride and authorial ego jostling, will present in greater detail the complexities of this field.

The whole Lu Xun incident foreshadows the feverish, highly speculative debate on the Nobel that took place within post-Mao literary circles. In 2000 Gao Jianping, a Chinese historian of aesthetics, again raised the question of Lu Xun's nomination, which had by then become a national myth that chimed with all the feelings of defiance and inferiority associated with the Nobel Complex.

I once discussed this matter with a scholar of the affairs of the Swedish Academy who... immediately intoned solemnly: "This didn't happen!" The Swedish Academy had wanted to find candidates from outside Europe, and it just so happened that Sven Hedin was going to China, so they got him to make enquiries about well-known authors in China. Hedin mentioned this when he met Liu Bannong and Liu Bannong suggested a few Chinese writers, including Lu Xun. No one has any way of knowing whether Hedin brought this letter over or what the Swedish Academy thought about it. . . . No one knows whether Tai Jingnong relayed [Lu Xun's full response] to Liu Bannong, whether Liu Bannong conveyed this to Hedin, or whether this was finally conveyed in full to the Swedish Academy. Lu Xun's letter is very short and its meaning is far from complex, yet it later became a matter of public concern in China, dragged into all kinds of irrelevant issues: what kind of a person Sven Hedin was, how Lu Xun saw through the secret plots of imperialism and so on.[29]

These are the sorts of rumors and speculations that have long characterized debates around the Nobel Prize, and the insecurity and desire for recognition that lie at the base of them. Although no one knows what actually happened, the Lu Xun incident—like the Nobel Complex itself—has taken on a life of its own, even generating a museum relic. When the display at the Lu Xun Museum at Fuchengmen in Beijing was revised in the mid-1990s (a mature stage in China's Nobel Complex), Lu Xun's reply to Tai Jingnong was reproduced and hung on a wall, perhaps to show that the father of modern Chinese literature came close to a Nobel Prize, or perhaps to indicate that if Lu Xun deemed the Nobel unsuitable, it is unsuitable for any Chinese writer.

The 1930s and the Cosmopolitan Revolution

During the 1930s, questions of Chinese identity and audience became increasingly urgent following the growing threat of Japanese encroachments into China, the collapse of the 1927 revolution, and the perceived failure of the May Fourth movement to reach its target, the masses—due to its excessive Westernization and elitism. At the same time, China's literary scene became internationalized as practically never before, as Shanghai with its sophisticated print culture developed further as an urban environment. Translations and even first editions of the latest works by Joyce and Eliot appeared promptly in Shanghai bookshops. The lack of a truly effective central government permitted a diverse literary scene in which Marxism, nationalism, and cosmopolitanism each fought their corner. Novelist and essayist Shen Congwen's most productive period and the modernist experiments of the neoperceptionist (*xin ganjue pai*) writers coincided with divisions between Lu Xun and the theorists of the League of Left-wing Writers. (Shen's biography is itself a revealing barometer of how one writer perceived transformations of the politico-literary climate of the 1930s after the Communist takeover in 1949. A prolific novelist and essayist of the 1920s to 1940s celebrated for his portraits of West Hunan, Shen renounced writing fiction after 1949 for a career as a historian of Chinese artifacts.)

Leftist politics brought crucial changes to discussions of authorial identity and selfhood in literary production. As members of the Creation and Sun societies, the most vocal occupants of the literary field, underwent conversion to Marxism in the late 1920s, the concepts of revolution, history and the people became even more crucial to intellectuals struggling to grasp the teleology of modernity. May Fourth representations of intellectuals and the people began to give way to idealized portrayals of the masses as the source of national historical transformation. While Chinese Marxists struggled uneasily to find a place for intellectuals in national revolution, the category of the masses evolved into an all-enveloping concept that posed a threat to intellectual subjectivity and identity.[30] Leftist intellectuals sought union with the masses, but at the price of submitting to a collective authority such as the CCP. Writers did not engage in this without ambivalence, and even Mao Zedong found himself caught between contradictory views of "the people" as a blank, ignorant mass to be interpreted by the intellectual, and as the motive force of history.[31] The debate concerning the role of the writer remained implicated in Romantic discourses of individual creative genius, now even further glorified by a process of self-transcendence that would permit the expression of the collective other.

Both Western and Chinese literary intellectuals faced the onset of mass culture and mass literacy with apprehension. Given the dominant discourse of national crisis, Chinese intellectuals felt they could not afford to disparage the existence of the masses, yet at the same time they could not abandon the idea that they were society's leaders by dint of their education and creativity. Western writers such as D. H. Lawrence (1885–1930), however, felt no such compunction about belittling mass culture. In *The Intellectuals and the Masses*, John Carey makes an intriguing point about the question of intelligibility and modern artistic elitism. "The early twentieth century saw a determined effort, on the part of the European intelligentsia, to exclude the masses from culture. . . . Irrationality and obscurity were cultivated . . . the placing of art beyond the reach of the mass was certainly deliberate at times."[32] Although, unlike their European counterparts, Chinese writers focused on producing a literature "of the common people," questions of literary intelligibility and elitism remained hard to resolve. Western influences (stylistic, thematic, formal, grammatical), viewed as modern, progressive, and democratic in the May Fourth era, came by the late 1920s to be increasingly condemned for their incomprehensibility, even while writers were unwilling to abandon their elitist cultural cosmopolitanism.[33]

Central to the modern (late Qing/May Fourth) concept of *wenxue* (literature) was both a Western model of vernacular literature and the need for that literature to be accessible to the Chinese masses. May Fourth literary reformers, in their rejection of all things outwardly Chinese and traditional, made their task more difficult by not only censuring conventional popular literary forms but also the familiar, old-style vernacular in which they were written. Despite the rhetoric of "commoner literature," May Fourth intellectuals set out to replace the traditional vernacular with a Europeanized one, which, through incorporation of grammatical structures and neologisms from Western languages, was largely incomprehensible or at least unappealing to readers who had not received a predominantly Western-style education. This legacy of elitism — associated with the modern progressive advocacy of Western forms, the pursuit of cosmopolitanism, the independence of literature, and the primacy of individual subjectivity and creativity — remained a source of tension in Chinese literary culture up to and beyond debates about the Nobel Prize in the 1980s and 1990s.[34]

Despite this fresh impetus towards "massification" and away from the elitism of Western forms among the sloganeers of the 1920s and 1930s, there were also writers who struggled against political tendentiousness in literature and who were interested less in the provenance of foreign literary influences than in the modernist effects they produced. The neoperceptionists were a group of experimental writers based in 1930s Shanghai ("the three-mile foreign mall") who made free use of foreign, modern, and traditional influences in their attempts to capture in print the conditions of modern experience. Direct access was possible not only to foreign books, but also to their authors, as a steady stream of literary visitors flowed through the city, including Nobel laureate G. B. Shaw, Noël Coward, and W. H. Auden. *Les Contemporains*, the foreign title of *Xiandai zazhi*, reflected the self-image of its neoperceptionist editor, Shi Zhecun (1905–), and his contributors: they wished to be "contemporaries" with their European counterparts.[35] They were also determined to avoid political partisanship. As Shi wrote in the first issue, "Articles will be chosen for publication in accordance only with the subjective criterion of the editor himself. This criterion, of course, refers to the inherent quality of the literary work itself."[36] This apolitical stance was partly enforced by the repressive tactics in use at the time by the right-wing GMD, but also partly in order to differentiate *Xiandai zazhi* from the sloganeering cliques on the left.

The impression of a new degree of international self-confidence in the estate of 1930s Chinese literature is reinforced by an act of canonization that took place in 1936: the publication of the *Zhongguo xin wenxue daxi* (The compendium of modern Chinese literature), a commercial project edited by Zhao Jiabi. Setting out to preserve key May Fourth texts that he was afraid would otherwise fall into oblivion, Zhao united literary figures across a broad political spectrum — names such as Lu Xun, Zhou Zuoren, and Yu Dafu (1896–1945) — in compiling and editing the multivolume work. This project suggests a new sense of confidence in this youthful Chinese literature; writers and editors considered the literary production of the last twenty years worthy of marshalling into a Western-style canon. In his "Introduction" to the compendium, Cai Yuanpei (1868–1940) used coordinates from Western literary history, in particular the European Renaissance, to plot the hoped-for progress of modern Chinese literature and to appeal for a Chinese Raphael and Shakespeare. "In a sense," writes Lydia Liu, "the *Compendium* was a self-colonizing project in which the West served as the ultimate source of authority in terms of which one had to renegotiate what was meaningful in Chinese literature."[37] Despite the negative, disempowering implications of such an endeavor from a contemporary postcolonial perspective, it still poses interesting questions about the meaning of agency and the difference between colonization and self-colonization. The fact that Zhao Jiabi started planning in 1937 a sister compendium that would anthologize great works of foreign literature indicates "a growing confidence . . . in the status of modern Chinese literature as one of many worthy national literatures. . . . In the making of the sister anthology, the unspoken word suggests that, taken together, these two anthologies would make a statement about modern Chinese literature and its relation to world literature."[38] The compendia represented a psychological step forward towards candidacy for world literature.

Chinese Intellectuals Debate Pearl Buck

These literary issues of the 1930s — representation of the masses, the correct literary stance towards revolution, cosmopolitanism, and the quest for international recognition — found a point of intersection in the discussions concerning the American writer Pearl Buck (1892–1973), whose descriptions of the Chinese peasantry in the late 1920s and 1930s made her an author of international best-sellers (such as *The Good Earth*, 1931) and earned her a Hollywood blockbuster, a Pulitzer Prize, the Nobel Literature Prize in 1938 and lifelong renown as a China expert.[39]

Buck's fame was not limited to the West; members of the Chinese literary field were also struck by her runaway success. In 1998 the Chinese critic He Xianglin recalled: "In the 1930s–1940s, there was an American authoress of whom practically all intellectuals of the time would have known: the 1938 winner of the Nobel Prize, Pearl Buck."[40] *The Good Earth* was translated into Chinese in 1932 as *Dadi* (The great earth) and her other books on China published in the 1930s and 1940s also appeared in Chinese translation, several in multiple versions. *The Good Earth* alone has eight different translations published by eight different companies, one of which put out twelve different editions between 1933 and 1949. "No other book by any foreigner has ever achieved such popularity in China," commented Liu Haiping.[41] Writers who commented on Pearl Buck's work include Lu Xun, Zhao Jiabi, Hu Feng, Ba Jin, and Lin Yutang (the last was nominated by Buck for the Nobel Prize in 1945).

The attention given to Pearl Buck is suggestive of the curiosity aroused in Chinese critics and writers regarding her attainment of cultural capital in the West through depiction of China. Many expressed outright pleasure at having foreign attention directed onto Chinese subject matter. In 1992, at the height of Nobel envy in post-Mao China, Zou Zhenhuan wrote, "*The Good Earth* by American writer Pearl Buck won the Nobel Literature Prize. This meant that the treasury of Nobel Prize-winning works includes works containing Chinese subject matter, describing the fate of Chinese peasants and reflecting Chinese rural life."[42] However, a more skeptical view had been expressed in the 1930s and 1940s by writers such as Lu Xun and Hu Feng. "Firstly, how has this female writer, who has lived in China for twenty or thirty years, observed rural China?" asked Hu Feng. "In her writing, what kind of truthful reflection has been given of the peasant's fate and of the conditions that produce this fate? Secondly, has this book achieved such astounding success among European and American readers because of its artistic quality or for other reasons?"[43] Zou countered his earlier comment: "Of course, compared with the works of Lu Xun, Mao Dun, Ba Jin, Shen Congwen and others that portray rural Chinese society, *The Good Earth* cannot avoid seeming rather superficial."[44]

There is nothing new about representations of China by and in the West. Jonathan Spence's recent survey of "sightings" of China by Westerners takes in missionaries, travelers, poets, writers, and diplomats from Marco Polo in the 1270s through to Borges, Calvino, and Jean Lévi in the late twentieth century.[45] "China" remains a highly saleable subject today: novels written by Westerners about China are published and reviewed, and memoirs in the style of Jung

Chang's hugely successful *Wild Swans* continue to come out.[46] However, despite the longevity of this phenomenon, Western representations of China in the modern era have taken on a significance entirely different from those produced in premodern periods, due to the transformed relationship between China and the (Western) world. Before the nineteenth century, China's confident perception of itself as the Middle Kingdom obviated anxiety concerning its international face. Moreover, Enlightenment philosophers such as Leibniz acclaimed Chinese civilization as a source of progressive religious toleration. To Voltaire, Chinese society offered proof of the relativity of morality and nullified arguments on the need for Christian institutions in imposing moral systems.[47] But for modern Chinese intellectuals, achieving international recognition and parity with Western nations has been key in their desire to measure up as a modern global culture.

Representation of "China" on the modern global stage therefore emerges as a highly sensitive issue — even more so when the spokesperson is a foreigner. While commentators were initially intrigued and pleased at the success in the West of Chinese material under Pearl Buck's pen, this quickly gave way to ambivalence concerning China's face in the world and the discursive right of Chinese writers themselves to draw attention to China's situation. Such issues of cultural sovereignty and selfhood — the fear of Westerners learning about China from "inauthentic sources" — resounded in debates over the Nobel Prize up to 2000. The question, meanwhile, of what constitutes an "authentic" source has been fiercely debated and strongly politicized.

Pearl Buck probably knew China's countryside better than most foreign observers: she grew up a missionary's daughter in Nanjing, then accompanied her husband John Lossing Buck, a missionary and agronomist, around villages on the North China plains, acting as interpreter while her husband carried out agricultural surveys. *The Good Earth* glorified the diligence of the peasant farmers, whose greatest enemy was not imperialism or class oppression, but natural disaster.[48] The novel relates the story of Wang Lung and his wife O-Lan as they try to live on the land and produce descendants. Forced to abandon the land for the city during a severe drought, they live by begging before being caught up in a riot on a rich household, during which Wang Lung and O-Lan both chance upon fortunes. They return to the land and with their newfound riches Wang Lung becomes the biggest local landowner. With wealth comes decadence, however: he buys a concubine to give him the sexual pleasure that stolid O-Lan never could. Having been prepared for lives away from the fields (one is sent to school, one trains as a merchant), Wang Lung's sons plot to abandon and sell the land after his death.

The Good Earth is a paean to the antimodern forces of traditional ways.

When the weather allows, Wang Lung and O-Lan are in perfect harmony with the earth they inhabit, farming by hand with crude implements. O-Lan is an earth mother whose bodily fluids seem part of the land. Working in the fields until the last stages of pregnancy, she squats to give birth on the land, her blood soaking the ground, then picks up her hoe again once she has finished. Buck's characters are the pure practitioners of a holistic way of life, whereby humanity and nature are connected, unsullied by contemporary outside influences. The most troublesome social problem for Wang Lung is a blackmailing bandit "uncle," a relic of Chinese tradition, rather than some comprador landlord, a modern symbol of class oppression. It is worth remembering, however, that all these local Chinese elements were exotic to a foreign audience. With the introduction of Wang Lung's concubine, the "imagined realms of Oriental sensuality and excess that many readers were waiting for" is additionally brought into play.[49]

Yet Buck is not so easily categorized as an Orientalizer (in Said's understanding of the term). When *The Good Earth* was first received in the United States, literary journals such as the *New York Times Book Review* asserted that the novel offered no "mystery or exoticism," no racial stereotypes that could be branded "Oriental," while the *Saturday Review of Literature* assured readers that "the China of fantasy so often exploited" in fiction was absent.[50] Buck's work, as seen above, was not without its exotic elements, but its exoticizing emphasis was on the city and its sites of "Oriental" decadence. In *The Good Earth*, the farm is familiar ground, while the city is foreign, distant, and dangerous.

It was this emphasis that made the Pearl Buck phenomenon so relevant to Chinese writers and intellectuals of the 1930s. Pearl Buck, it seemed, had realized many of their most dearly held aspirations. She had won the international literary acclaim that the cosmopolitan May Fourth generation still desired, through the deployment of authentically Chinese material, just at the time when reformist Chinese intellectuals were moving from urban intellectualism to rural proletarianism. Her focus on the Chinese peasantry coincided with debates by Chinese writers around mass literature and the portrayal of the peasant masses. Buck's positive emphasis on the natural countryside over the corrupting city foreshadowed interpretations that became widespread following the triumph of the leftist viewpoint during the War of Resistance against Japan. Buck, however, went one stage beyond prioritizing the rural and the Chinese over the urban and the cosmopolitan: she had also resolved the contradiction between producing mass literature and winning the international recognition for which Chinese writers yearned.

The rub, of course, was that Pearl Buck was a foreigner, and reception of her work by Chinese writers and intellectuals was dominated by evaluations of her moral right to Chinese subject matter and the accuracy with which she portrayed it. The sensitivities of such reactions highlighted the close links between literary realism and nationalist pride in the minds of modern Chinese literary intellectuals. Lu Xun dismissed her work in a letter from 1933:

> It is always best that Chinese people write about matters Chinese, that is the only way to see the truth. Even though Mrs. Buck . . . claims she views China as her motherland, her works ultimately reflect only the standpoint of an American woman missionary brought up in China . . . what she knows of China is no more than superficial. The truth is only produced when we set about writing it ourselves.[51]

Other writers acknowledged that Buck's portrayal of China went deeper than the average stereotypes produced by Westerners. "The reason why many people who write Chinese fiction fail," Zhao Jiabi remarked, "and why Mrs. Buck's *The Good Earth* can win world praise — even in China — is because the former only sketch the outside of Chinese people, while Mrs. Buck has got hold of a part of the Chinese soul."[52] Zhao also commented approvingly on evidence of Buck's knowledge of traditional Chinese literature, which turned on its head the one-way exchange between Western and Chinese literatures of the previous decade. "Most of the book uses a simple style, very similar to old-style Chinese fiction. Today, when writers of China's new fiction are imitating the complex and inverted style of the West, the fact that Mrs. Buck is instead learning from the straightforward, simple writing of old Chinese fiction really is food for thought."[53]

Yet despite praise for Buck's relative success in portraying Chinese lives, even favorable critics closely scrutinized Buck's work for its "truthfulness." One of the most scathing Chinese attacks on Buck came from Jiang Kanghu, a professor at McGill University. He criticized her unhealthy emphasis on sex and inaccuracies in her depictions of how Chinese peasants drink their tea. Neither, he asserted, do Chinese eat moon cakes for New Year or have black faces and white hair. He summarized his criticisms thus: "I find that Mrs. Buck's novels represent a particular aspect of the dark side of Chinese people's lives."[54] As this developed into a battle over Chinese authenticity, Yang Changxi rejoined: "The lives of ordinary Chinese experienced by Mrs. Buck, who has lived in China since childhood, will be more truthful and accurate than the view of Jiang Kanghu, who has long been resident overseas."[55]

Other critics responded to Buck's choice of rural subject matter. *The Good Earth* was first serialized in translation in the magazine *Dongfang zazhi* (The

Orient), placed alongside Peng Zijun's descriptions of Shanghai urban life. Yi Xian's preface compared the significance of the two.

> China is a country made up of over three hundred million suffering peasants and China's core lies in the countryside, not the city . . . there are still hardly any long works in China that can represent a region and the actual life and thoughts of peasants. Now we are introducing Mrs. Buck's *The Good Earth* to fill in this gap . . . Mrs. Buck's choosing to describe these pitiful peasants will perhaps seem disgusting to those readers long resident in the cities and with a strong bourgeois consciousness. However, I believe that China's fate lies entirely with these suffering peasants, and if we wish China to attain salvation, we must first of all know them properly. The peasants that Mrs. Buck has represented in her work . . . are largely truthfully written . . . I think that if we're not afraid of facing the truth, it should give us grounds for deep thought.[56]

But the question of what constituted the "true" Chinese peasant proved to be a major stumbling block in the reception of Buck's work in China. The peasant masses had become an abstract political category in Chinese literary discourse of the 1920s and 1930s, defined as possessing specific (anti-imperialist, antifeudalist, revolutionary) forms of consciousness. In 1927, while *The Good Earth* was being written, the forces of revolution, watched by Mao Zedong, were remaking the goals of modern China. "In a very short time, in China's central, southern and northern provinces, several hundred million peasants will rise like a mighty storm, like a hurricane, a force so violent that no power, however great, will be able to hold it back. They will smash all the trammels that bind them and rush forward along the road to liberation. They will sweep all the imperialists, warlords, corrupt officials, local bullies and evil gentry into their graves."[57]

Use of the term "peasant" in teleological Enlightenment histories is associated with feudalism, the official designated precursor of progressive modernity. The word "peasant," significantly, does not appear in *The Good Earth* once; Buck's protagonists are "farmers." In this way, Charles Hayford believes, the novel "implicitly questions and resists Progressive assumptions . . . Buck's implied historical placement of the Chinese farm economy, nationalism and revolution, and the Chinese family system all go against the conventional understandings of missionaries, Marxists, and liberals who wanted to uplift and civilize China."[58]

Buck's hostile stance towards nationalist revolution and the inevitable March of History earned her the enmity of the CCP, who refused her a visa for a final visit to China in 1972. In 1932 Buck explicitly attacked revolution as destructive anarchy,[59] and *The Good Earth* fails to draw any Marxist conclusions about Wang Lung's problems or the historical condition of the Chinese countryside.[60] Wang Lung is the "phlegmatic farmer happily mired in the eternal Good Earth [what Karl Marx called the 'idiocy of rural life']. In the city, a young agitator passes out political leaflets; Wang . . . stuffs it into his shoe to fill a hole. He blames the weather, not the landlord, for his troubles. Where Mao sees a revolutionary hurricane, Buck describes a looting mob as emitting a 'tigerish howl.'"[61] For Wang Lung, the good life results not from social revolution but from a bout of lucky pillaging, and mother nature is his greatest source of oppression.

Buck's lack of revolutionary consciousness did not go unnoticed among Chinese commentators. The harshest criticism came from the left-wing critic Hu Feng, who probed the degree to which Buck had produced a "truthful reflection" of China. Her subjective position as an enlightened Christian, he thought, prevented her from understanding the Chinese countryside and society in three ways. Firstly, "the author is very vague about the structures of the rural economy." Secondly, she is blind to the social causes of the fate of peasants, blaming only natural conditions and chance. In describing relations between Wang Lung and his estate manager Chin, "the cruel relations between landlord and tenant are totally invisible." Furthermore, "[t]here is absolutely no shadow of the imperialism that has sucked the blood dry out of the Chinese countryside. . . . Once she has wiped this away, Wang Lung can't have much significance as a realistic person." Thirdly, "not only is there no accurate understanding here of the Chinese race's struggle for liberation over the last few decades, there isn't even any reflection of such phenomena . . . the author has no actual understanding of or sympathy for China's liberation movement." Buck's claims to realism (and hence to represent Chinese experience) were thus undermined by her political shortcomings. "Even if you can see the poverty and ignorance of things, if you can't find their roots then you won't be able to avoid errors and distortions of understanding and you won't be able to achieve truth in artistic creation."[62] Similar accusations intensified throughout the 1950s and 1960s, when Buck was accused of standing in the "vanguard of United States imperialist cultural aggression."[63]

When Pearl Buck won the Nobel Prize, Chinese reactions expressed surprise and suspicion. Si Masheng in 1939 commented: "There's nothing remarkable about Pearl Buck's fiction; her description of matters Chinese, in particular, are quite simply absurdly superficial. Chinese peasant life as described in *The Good Earth* is 'selling the heads of savages to Westerners'; when we read it ourselves we see a lot of flaws. But it seems that because she's a Westerner, this amount of knowledge is sufficient for her to win the admiration of readers. The reason why she can achieve a 'sensation in American publishing,' 'make a fortune from her pen,' even win the Nobel Prize, is most probably because of this." Ba Jin was similarly unimpressed by her award: "I simply have no good feeling towards Pearl Buck. . . . Even after she's won the Nobel Prize, she's still the old Pearl Buck."[64]

Yan'an and Literature of National Resistance

During the Anti-Japanese War, when the struggle for national survival became more pressing than ever before, contradictions that had emerged in earlier decades were still being worked out within the leftist literary community. The unified strategy of "facing the people" did little to lessen the fitful interplay between at least three ideological tendencies: the vulgar Marxism of rank and file CCP; the traditional worldview of the Chinese common people; and the artistic ideology of literary youth and some Chinese writers, who combined attachment to literary cosmopolitanism, belief in "literary greatness" and iconoclastic views on Chinese tradition.[65] The CCP, aided by the May Fourth writers who migrated to communism, quickly developed its own policies of cultural mobilization. Among their ranks an open power struggle played out over the balance to be struck between popularization and elevation, and internationalism and national forms.

Elevation (associated with intellectual elitism, artistic quality, and foreign forms) remained an acceptable goal up until 1942. Even an orthodox literary ideologue such as Zhou Yang (1908–1989) would only advocate the temporary use of old popular forms "so that the toiling masses will be able to draw near to genuine great art one step at a time."[66] The early years at Yan'an (the late 1930s) were a period of relative artistic freedom; consequently, the majority of literary production was too Europeanized to appeal to the peasant masses the CCP needed to mobilize. Maoists attempted to render more palatable the idea of using old traditional forms by terming them "New Forms"; advocates of these "new" national forms were themselves far from inward-looking. Chen Boda (1904–1985), for example, in his defense of national forms, still asserted that the ultimate aim was the creation of "works of art of a world standard."[67] Zhou Yang, in a slighting theorization of mass literature, left writers with the option of working either for mass or for "higher" audiences.[68] In 1940–1941, literary education and composition still emphasized foreign works and style, while the May Fourth author Ding Ling (1904–1986) and other famous writers published essays in *Liberation Daily* pleading for artistic autonomy. Though writers subscribed to the view that the masses were their source of inspiration, the dynamics of this "union with the people" still made authors such as Ding Ling uncomfortable.

> Today's process of massification does not mean that we are transformed into something the same as the common people, nor something that follows them. It is under our influence and leadership that the masses will be organized, take the path of resistance, and build the nation.[69]

Despite her ambivalence, the draw of nation building and the urge to "go to the people" still run strong in Ding Ling's comments; writers desired a "correct" path that would define literature's role in achieving the social and political transformation of a nation under siege. Mao's "Talks at the Yan'an Conference on Literature and Art" in 1942 finally provided specific answers to questions that had been posed since the late Qing about the relationship between literary intellectuals and the masses in the nation-building process.

From the 1920s onwards, the question of the writer's role in the revolution to come had become paramount in the minds of politically conscious writers. On the one hand, writers urged revolution to achieve cultural transformation and gain China international standing; on the other, it was far from clear what role intellectuals and literature could play in the revolution, particularly since the May Fourth rejection of tradition had left writers without the support of the past and dependent on newly introduced Western theories of little relevance to the lives of the masses. Mao's 1942 contribution lay in pitching the cultural struggle at the same level as the national, military one. He asserted that literature must serve the hundreds of thousands of laboring people; if this was utilitarianism, it was at least a utilitarianism where 90 percent of the masses benefited. The leftist emphasis on literary nationalism and utilitarianism was echoed on the political right. Also in 1942, the GMD cultural theorist Zhang Daofan (1896–1968) in his article "Women suo xuyao de wenyi zhengce" (The literary policy we need) elaborated a set of strictures on the links between art and politics based in Sun Yat-sen's Three Principles of the People, but bearing a striking similarity to Maoist ideas.[70]

Yet controversies over individual creativity did not end in 1942. "Mao's Talks," by urging writers to subordinate themselves to the masses and to learn their language, resolved the problem of how to bridge the gap between intellectuals and masses — cause of the sense of anguish and guilt evident in much of Lu Xun's fiction. Yet this required a down-leveling of literature and self-devaluation on the part of writers themselves. The tensions between intellectuals and the party that resulted from this collectivist self-belittlement would not be so easily eliminated post-1949, despite the brutality of measures adopted to deal with early opponents of massification such as Wang Shiwei (1900–1948).[71] These contradictions were dramatized even in the life and works of the paradigmatic "peasant writer" Zhao Shuli (1906–1970), whom one Mainland critic has identified as "not a peasant, not a folk artist, but an intellectual who had been influenced by the May Fourth new culture movement."[72]

Moreover, Mao's main focus in the Talks was on popularization and political stance, leaving questions of creative method and the use of foreign forms open to future debate. And despite the participation of the Yan'an writers in the 1942 Rectification Movement that flanked the Talks, the immediate scope of the movement outside Yan'an was limited, even among leftists. The leftist intellectual Hu Feng, based in GMD-held Chongqing, was able to express dissatisfaction with the new party literary policy. He continued to uphold his theory of the subjective spirit of the writer of critical realism, cause of tensions between him and party ideologues from the mid-1930s that would culminate in the anti-Hu Feng Campaign of 1954. Battles over authorial subjectivity, literary identity and foreign influences continued to be fought well into the 1950s.

Qian Zhongshu's "Inspiration"

The general adoption of Mao's vision in the 1940s was by no means inevitable, particularly after the cessation of war with Japan in 1945 removed the immediate sense of national crisis and with it the most powerful motivation for politicization of literature. Throughout the war itself, a group of writers that Edward Gunn has termed "Anti-romantics" were active in occupied Shanghai, including Zhang Ailing, Qian Zhongshu, one of the most cosmopolitan figures of modern Chinese literature, and his wife Yang Jiang (1911–), all of whom remained detached from the patriotic discourse of both GMD propaganda and the Yan'an writers. Gunn defines these writers by what they rejected: "their work was a form of anti-romanticism: unreforming and de-idealized; the emotions of characters viewed ironically rather than exploited for themselves; transcendence either a dream or a work of art, but not a reality."[73] Anti-romantic scepticism thus cut through the "romantic individualism and revolutionary collectivism" that dominated debates about authorial identity elsewhere. The anti-romantic writers were united in their preoccupation with the theme of self-delusion, in which both individual ambitions and social institutions — including literature — were based. "Literature must perish," declared Qian Zhongshu,

> but there is no harm in encouraging writers — encouraging them not to be writers. . . . As for most writers, to speak frankly, there is little love for literature and little excellence. . . . All men of learning are filled with a sense of their

importance and prestige. They are self-satisfied, heaping praise on the special discipline they study with 120 percent conviction. Only writers are filled with self-doubts, make placating smiles and feel endless shame. Even if they happen to run off at the mouth about patriotic literature, the weapon of propaganda, and so on, it's like beating on a waterlogged drum; there's just no resonance to it.[74]

One of the most entertaining if barbed depictions of the modern Chinese literary scene, and of the various facets of China's Nobel Complex (forty years before its maturation), was Qian Zhongshu's 1944 story "Linggan" (Inspiration).[75] Qian's targets are multiple: the figure of the writer, Chinese literary nationalism, foreign literary authorities and, above all, the puffed-up aspirations of the modern Chinese literary identity. The story's "hero" is China's most famous and popular writer (left unnamed), whose writings are translated into Esperanto in order to win the Nobel Prize. However, not only is the Esperanto incomprehensible to members of the Nobel Committee, it is mistaken by a Swedish sinologist for romanized Chinese. He protests that he cannot explain its meaning, since his specialization is in Chinese pronunciation, not in interpreting its meaning. The author's failure to win the prize then provokes a media storm in China. After satirizing the Nobel Prize and the Chinese literary scene, the story plunges further into the surreal: the author dies of rage and humiliation and gets his comeuppance in the afterlife from all the characters in his books he has "murdered" through his deathly prose. In the end, the Head of Underworld, Inc. decides that he will be punished by being reincarnated as inspiration for a young writer who has been sitting in front of a blank sheet of paper for three years. Just at this moment, the young writer decides that if he "wanted to write a maiden work, he should take himself off to find a maiden," and is in coitus with his landlord's daughter when the writer arrives under ghostly escort (p. 149). Amidst all the thrashing of limbs, the writer mistakenly enters the ear of the maiden rather than the young man, resulting in aural insemination. The couple marry and the young man renounces writing for shopkeeping to support his family.

Qian's main target for ridicule is the vanity of the literary scene. Introducing his writer, he tells us this is an author "of great repute, but we don't actually know what he is called — though not because he lacks fame, or his fame is in ruins, or because he is anonymous, or nameless. The reason is very simple: his fame is too resonant, so earthshaking that we can't hear his name clearly. For example, you only need write on an envelope 'France's greatest poet' and the postman will naturally deliver it to Hugo. . . . This writer of ours is even more famous, not only do you not need to write his name, you don't even need to know it, as it is totally buried in his reputation" (p. 128). Qian also satirizes the lofty discussions of audience and of cultural tradition by modern literary intellectuals: "We Chinese, as befits a nation with an ancient literary heritage, do not speak about the material side so much, but instead we take the intellectual level of middle-school students as the standard for literary works" (p. 128). Aiming at high school students is this writer's secret of success, since only they are willing to spend money on books and magazines. University students have literary ambitions themselves; university professors only write prefaces for other people's books; those even more senior only have time to stick inscriptions on the covers of other people's books that have been respectfully presented to them. The next step in this writer's progress is achieving official acknowledgment for services rendered to humanity. After his "nationally recognized genius" is translated by government decree into Esperanto, an admirer exclaims in a newspaper: "It's entirely right that the government should do this! . . . there are so many characters in his books, if they were all counted up they could colonize a desert island. Wars are currently bringing about a decline in population — it's right to promote the glory of reproduction. He should get a national government prize" (p. 129).

The portrayal of the arbiters of the Nobel Prize in Sweden is no less scathing. These "mouldy old curios" repeatedly wipe their half-moon pince-nez but are still unable to make out the Esperanto. The Swedish sinologist who proclaims the Esperanto to be romanized Chinese is thought to be a satirical portrayal of Bernard Karlgren, who, although not himself a member of the Swedish Academy, advised the committee on Chinese works and whose expertise lay in the phonological reconstruction of ancient Chinese.[76] "Dear experts," he replies to his colleagues' demands that he translate what he has identified as Chinese, "the value of scholarship lies in specialization. My predecessor spent his life specializing in Chinese punctuation, and for the last forty years I have been researching the phonetic sounds of Chinese. What you ask concerns the meaning of Chinese writing, and that does not fit the scope of my research. I dare not make any arbitrary assertions over whether Chinese has any meaning before I have definite proof of the matter" (p. 130). Finding this entirely laudable, his colleagues dismiss the writer's works.

The carnivalesque debate in Chinese newspapers that follows this humiliation prefigures public debate on the Nobel Prize during the 1980s and 1990s. One newspaper curses the Nobel Prize Committee for having "forgotten their roots: old Nobel made his fortune in dynamite, and China was the first nation in the world to invent gunpowder, so the prize money should have originally been given to Chinese people anyway." A second celebrates an Ah Q-style spiritual victory, "comforting this writer with congratulations, saying he'd always been a successful writer but now he qualified as a wronged genius, a great artist ignored and treated unfairly: 'being successful and wronged are contradictorily opposed — actually having them both is a rare and enviable stroke of fortune!'" A third takes a farcically nationalist stance:

> Borrowing foreign money is not a harmful policy, but it is humiliating to be given a foreign prize. . . . We should establish a literature prize ourselves to boycott the Nobel Prize, to avoid losing sovereignty in artistic criticism. The basic condition for this prize is that only writing in one of China's dialects can be considered . . . these will include the English spoken in Shanghai and Hong Kong, the Japanese spoken in Qingdao, and the Russian spoken in Harbin. With this prize, the Nobel Prize won't seem so unique. European and American writers will naturally work hard to write in Chinese, trying to win our prize, and China's five thousand years of culture will hence penetrate deep into the West (pp. 131–132).

The newspaper debate mocks China's sense of cultural nationalism: the belief that China and its unique ancient culture should be recognized by the world; the Ah Q-ism of failure; and the inability to admit the hybrid nature of modern Chinese culture contrasted with the unwillingness to concede rhetorical sovereignty. Finally, the absurd measures suggested for resolving Nobel aspirations anticipated debate in the 1980s and 1990s, when the winning of a Nobel Prize became a policy issue. Neither does Qian miss a chance to mock the scholarly world. On his deathbed, the writer's last words are: "In times to come . . . I don't want to have a collected works . . . because . . . ." Debates about this enigmatic sentence were split between two viewpoints, and "the controversy between these two groups became the most interesting episode in modern Chinese literary history" (p. 133). Meanwhile, the narrator follows the dead writer into his study, where he ponders the afterlife, for which he has high hopes. "It was only right and proper that Heaven should soon send a representative to welcome and receive someone like him who had made such great contributions to society and culture" (p. 133).

Suddenly, the pressure of his massive oeuvre on the bookshelves in the room causes the floor to give way underneath him. His excessive writings drag him down to hell, where both he and his books tumble into the office of the director of the underworld, who tells him that a lot of people want to settle accounts with him. The bizarre episode in which the characters in his books confront the author in the afterlife can be read as a comment on the politics of subjectivity and the relations between the author and the masses. Instead of benefiting the People by turning them into literary subject matter (the key justification for realism during the May Fourth and beyond), this writer draws fame and cultural capital entirely for himself from his portrayal of subaltern protagonists. Our writer even refuses to recognize his suffering progeny: "'You've got the wrong person! I don't know a single one of you, not a single one.' 'We know you!' 'Of course people I don't know at all know me, that's what it is to be famous'" (p. 142). He is also confronted by his best friend, a businessman, for whom he recently wrote a birthday eulogy. It turns out that his deadening prose consigned even his friend to the underworld. "On hearing his crimes enumerated, an unhappy thought suddenly struck root in the author's heart, like some hard, indigestible object in his stomach. Just before his death, he had written an autobiography which he had originally planned to publish after receiving the Nobel Prize. According to what the capitalist had said, his writing stripped characters of life, so he himself hadn't died of anger; the cause of death, he feared, was that autobiography" (p. 147).

This death-by-writing is an ironic inversion of the high-flown claims made for literature since the late Qing and May Fourth eras. Chen Duxiu (1879–1942) declared that China's new society would be "sincere, progressive, activist, free, egalitarian, creative, beautiful, good, peaceful, cooperative, industrious, prosperous for all," and literature was to play an important role in this transformation.[77] From Hu Shi's attraction to Ibsen and other Western realists because of their relevance to everyday life, through Zhou Zuoren's appeal for a "humane literature" (ren de wenxue), to Mao's exhortations for writers to learn from the lives of the people, literature in twentieth-century China has carried the enormous moral responsibility of being "lifelike," or of being even larger than life, of reviving Chinese society from the stranglehold of tradition and imperialism. Qian Zhongshu punctures these literary visions. The literary world is depicted as one of suffocating phoniness, in thrall to the forces of cultural nationalism and an inferiority complex. Our writer begs that his punishment for literary wrongs be mitigated to reincarnation as a writer, but he promises to restrict himself to translating or to historical dramas where all the characters are already dead. Alternatively, he could adapt Shakespeare: "This colleague of an earlier generation sent me a message in a dream, saying that the characters in his plays are too long-lived and that living all these centuries has made them impatient, they want a quick death, so he asked me to have mercy and give them a painless end" (p. 148). This is an ironic response to Chen Duxiu's 1917 plea: "Pray, where is our Chinese Hugo, Zola, Goethe, Hauptmann, Dickens or Wilde?"[78] Rather than succeeding these literary masters, Qian's eminent representative of Chinese literature offers to put to death Shakespeare's immortal creations. The target of Qian's satire is perhaps personal: his fictional writer's ruminations on post-death experiences could be a sardonic reference to the prose poem "Si hou" (After death) by Lu Xun, the paradigmatic modern intellectual, and an active, sometimes vituperative player in the literary field.[79]

Qian Zhongshu's "Linggan" turns the business of writing into a circus in which everyone is complicit: undiscerning readers; egotistical and image-conscious writers; critics and scholars; and journalists and politicians, the inflators of national egos. The last tableau with which Qian leaves us is of the child produced by the misdirection of the writer's inspiration and cause of his father's abandonment of a literary career. "It was said that the child laughed all its life, and when he saw his father his laughter took on a more victorious tone. Relatives all declared this child was destined to be merry. Right now, we can't tell whether or not he will become a writer when he grows up" (p. 150). The final product of all this literary intrigue is a triumphant laughter, mocking the pomposity of overblown literary discourse. In his exploration of fictional realism in modern Chinese literature, David Wang cites Lao She's impulses towards the carnivalesque as an integral part of his original contribution to realism. Rather than label Lao She a straightforward, humanist realist, Wang argues that "laughter is the means by which Lao She questions the cultural/moral codes that sanction the concept of the real in his society."[80] By a similar principle but a different technique, Qian Zhongshu subverts "obsession with China" and the seriousness attached to modern Chinese writing, pointing out the absurdities of the literary field.

Literary Identity in the 1950s and 1960s

Once in power, a central purpose of the CCP cultural leadership was to carry to fruition the logic of Mao's 1942 Talks: the universalization of a popular national culture in tune with the party's reading of truth and reality. Assertions by writers of their individual creativity led to persecution, and the Great Leap Forward witnessed a push for literary amateurism, replacing the professional writer with mass authorship.[81] Although the Maoist era witnessed efforts to professionalize and institutionalize literary writing—such as the establishment of the Writers' Association (Zuojia xiehui) in the early 1950s—a strong radical current of Maoist thought sought to erase the very category of "author."[82] As the 1957–1958 antirightist drive ended, Mao's culture tsar Zhou Yang commented, "Our ultimate goal . . . is to obliterate the boundary between mental labor and physical labor."[83] Guo Moruo (1892–1978) further specified that "cultural work must be led by amateurs who have mastered Marxism-Leninism."[84] Although during the Great Leap Forward years of 1958–1959, the laboring masses were exhorted to produce countless poems, professional literary output dwindled dramatically under Mao. An average of eight novels were published every year between 1949 and 1966; this figure fell even lower during the Cultural Revolution years (1966–1976), when millions of intellectuals—including writers and critics—were banished from the cities to the countryside.[85]

Following the triumph of Chinese Marxism, Western influences and value systems were, with a few exceptions (Ezra Pound's anticapitalist canto "With usura" for example), regarded as capitalist and bourgeois. Yet the internationalist orientation of Chinese modernity survived the nationalist renaissance symbolized by the founding of the People's Republic, and Maoist China remained eager to gain recognition from other international sources of authority (such as the Stalin Prize, which Ding Ling won in 1951 for *The Sun Shines over the Sanggan River*).[86] Mao Zedong and the party leadership replaced one universal modernizing schema, the Western one, with others: up to 1956 the Soviet model; subsequently, the vision of anticolonial solidarity among "third-world" Asian and African states, prefigured by the spirit of the 1955 Bandung Conference.[87] Even though an antiforeign nationalism appears to be at the heart of Mao's sinification of Marxism and the Cultural Revolution promoted an apparent repudiation of all foreign influences, Maoist ideology and Cultural Revolution extremism pinned many of their claims to legitimacy on portraying China as an outward-looking leader among third-world countries, destined to liberate the rest of the suffering capitalist world. Under Mao, socialist China believed it had stood up to be counted in the global network of national cultures as a leading representative of communist ideology. The latent internationalism of the Maoist regime can also be seen in the PRC's entry into the United Nations in 1971, by the occasion of President Nixon's visit in 1972, and by the gradual rapprochement between China and the United States that this initiated.[88]

The cosmopolitan legacy of early twentieth-century Chinese literature also left an admiration for the modern West that could not be easily erased, and neither the idea of the author as expressive self nor pro-Western tendencies succumbed completely in this period. Despite the injunction that "literature should serve politics," despite the monotony of much artistic production, and despite the vision of a China united behind a program of national modernization that conflated society, culture, and the ruling ideology, and that rejected external influences, the years 1949–1966 still saw varied discussion of the function of literature and the arts. There are two ironies in this. Firstly, these debates were often initiated by the CCP itself, anxious at the paucity of literary output. Secondly, it was the May Fourth revolutionary writers who most openly expressed opposition to the party line in intellectual and literary thought. Many of the debates concerned style and creativity, often played out in terms of sinicization versus Westernization. Even though the West was an ideological category inimical to Communist China and to which writers would not consider direct address (as Boris Pasternak did, by implication, in sending *Dr Zhivago* out of the USSR for publication first in Italy), Western ideas were cited by writers to justify the need for independent artistic aims. Once more, and in even the most unpropitious political circumstances, this rhetorical regard for the West demonstrates the complex interaction between modernity, nationalism, and individual authorial identity in twentieth-century China.

The responses of the writers Ding Ling, Feng Xuefeng (1906–1976), and Hu Feng, all standard bearers both for May Fourth cosmopolitanism and for political revolution, provide apposite examples of the contradictory reactions of May Fourth figures to the new intellectual environment of the 1950s and of the clashes that resulted, in which party antiforeignism was frequently elided into anti-intellectualism. On the one hand, Ding Ling was a model of orthodoxy, welcoming the use of folk forms and the prioritizing of political interests above the personal. On the other, disturbed by the question of professional standards versus party standards, she urged other writers to share her ambition to "write a good book." She also admitted that she liked "to hear people tell her she is highly cultured" and loved to "talk of foreign places, use difficult phrases and quote famous people."[89] Feng Xuefeng hoped that China was "gradually approaching the time when we will produce our own Dante."[90] The survival of intellectual pro-Western yearnings in the pursuit of artistic independence and international recognition in this hostile political environment augured the eruption of China's post-Mao Nobel Complex.

Among the most prominent and complex cases of resistance to PRC literary policy, Hu Feng had presented his ideas in his report of 1954 to the CCP Central Committee, which subsequently unleashed a campaign of persecution against him and his supporters. His report praised empirical literary creation over party policy and asserted the importance of the writer's subjective spirit in portraying objective reality. Hu Feng's criticisms were also tinged with regard for the West: he attacked the use of popular forms as a retreat from the May Fourth spirit of internationalism and invoked Western realist masters such as Balzac and Tolstoy, while criticizing the understanding of them held by party officials.[91] (From the time of the 1938–1939 "national forms" debates, Hu had allied himself with the cosmopolitan May Fourth heritage, considering traditional forms to be inseparable from backward feudal consciousness.) Yet the complexity of Hu Feng's advocacy about the role of the writer in socialist society went far beyond simple Westernization vs. sinification, liberalism vs.

Marxism, or elitism vs. popularization. Ambiguously positioned between the coordinates of international modernity, Marxist orthodoxy, and autonomous subjective expression, Hu's ideas expressed many of the uncertainties that had long surrounded modern Chinese authorship.

Hu Feng had developed since the 1930s a theory of an active, or acting, subject both inseparable from and shaping the spirit of the age; it moved with history, rather than being crushed by it. After 1942 Hu advocated the "subjective fighting spirit" in order to attack party anti-intellectual formulism. The subjective spirit, as he saw it, needed to absorb, embody, and subdue its object, while in grasping the object's social significance the writer's spirit would also, in turn, be forged. Although life must be studied, the struggle between subject and object was paramount in the creative process, for the writer to develop his/her self through the conditions of history. Hu Feng extolled the writer's "imagination," "genius," "intuition," and "passion" as the means of "forging" into art "impressions taken from life."[92]

Hu cannot be straightforwardly categorized as either anticommunist, pro-Western, or antitraditional. As a Marxist, he defended his ideas from being labeled bourgeois or humanist by upholding the interrelation between society and subjectivity. Hu's lack of interest in mimesis and linguistic representation, and his emphasis on subjective involvement with the world, distinguished his theories from Western ideas of realism. Hu Feng thus reflected the discomfort felt by literary intellectuals since the May Fourth era with respect to the idea of the Romantic autonomous self, detached from the objective world. This discomfort derived at least in part from the central importance of holistic philosophy to premodern Chinese culture. The dilemma for literary intellectuals of the 1930s onward, and which was embodied in the writings of Hu Feng's disciple Lu Ling (1921–1994), was how to assert *and* transcend the self in order to participate in the historical movement of the world. Hu offered a way out for the bourgeois writer in an era of mass revolutionary literature:

> The bourgeois writer may experience the social reality of other classes, embody that experience through a process of interiorization, and thus be able to write about the "subaltern" sincerely, truthfully, and without distortion. . . . Although he is limited by historical and ideological forces, the writer has "passion" and "genius" with which to both reflect the reality of social life and re-create the world.[93]

This solution, however, was deemed deeply subversive by party authorities, who condemned Lu Ling's works as promoting individualism and attacking the collectivism of the working class. Caught between the march of history and society, the authoritarianism of a socially transformative CCP literary policy whose roots lay in intellectual advocacy of May Fourth ideals, the unhinged freedom of the Western Romantic self (another part of the contradictory May Fourth heritage), and the constraints of tradition, Hu and his ideas fell within a familiar range of conflicts experienced by modern Chinese literati. The questions he raised about subjectivity and selfhood, the balance between theory, practice, foreign influences, national relevance, universal literary worth, and epochal specificity, and the dislocation between intellectual and mass audiences continued to preoccupy literary intellectuals after 1976.

TWO OF LITERARY China's fundamental aims in the twentieth century were to forge its own identity and situate itself within a global framework. To this end, literary intellectuals endlessly imported, imitated, reformed, rejected, and experimented, and every available cultural form and register was implicated in the search for national modernity. A gap between audiences for high and low, popular and elite forms is to be expected in any reading community. For much of the twentieth century, however, this divergence was often barely acknowledged and regarded as unhealthy by those in the business of reading and writing professionally. Chinese authors were caught between aspiring, on the one hand, to globally dominant Western models and to independence from the past; and on the other, to maintaining the traditional holistic vision that united literature and society, to playing a central role in China's national renovation, to mobilizing the masses, and to subordinating themselves to history and society. To increase the confusion, many writers seemed to do the former in order to achieve the latter.

In the first few decades of its existence, the Nobel Prize figured in a series of encounters that presaged its status as a focus of anxiety among Chinese writers and literary intellectuals of the 1980s and 1990s. The episodes involving Tagore, Lu Xun, Pearl Buck, and Qian Zhongshu illustrate the burdens of expectation and ambivalence that have dominated Chinese discussions of their modern literature. Post-Mao debates around the Nobel Prize would throw these uncertainties into further relief, indicating that issues of national and aesthetic identity, and audience remained as vexed as ever over the last two decades of the century.

China's Search for a Nobel Prize
in Literature, 1979–2000

C hina's Nobel Complex owes its genesis to the collapse of the Mao- ist model of internationalism at the end of the 1970s and the re- establishment of the Western-oriented vision of international modernity that had flourished in the first half of the twentieth century. The Chinese search for a Nobel gathered so much momentum in the post-Mao era largely because it centered around one of the key sociocultural questions of the twentieth century: the position of Chinese intellectuals in an era of transnational exchange. Yet the peculiar intensity of post-Mao Nobel anxiety was also heavily determined by its historical context — the repudia- tion of the Cultural Revolution's rural proletarianism and the return of intel- lectuals to public life after 1979. Widespread preoccupation with a symbol of elite culture such as the Nobel Prize signaled the reassertion by intellectuals (in particular, writers, critics, and Writers' Association literary bureaucrats) of their central role in representing the nation at home and abroad. The win- ning of a Nobel *Literature* Prize above all (more than a Nobel Prize in science or economics) was desired within both literary, and wider media and cultural circles to affirm China as a powerful, modern, international civilization at the end of the century.

But even as literary intellectuals stepped forward to be global ambassa- dors for Chinese modernity after decades of persecution and marginalization under Mao, the association between intellectuals and the nation-state, and the idea of equivalence between Chinese national identity and international standing, began to come apart. Yearnings for the aesthetic universalism im- plied in the desire that Chinese literature "march towards the world" (clarion call of China's Nobel Prize campaign in the 1980s) were complicated by the underlying awareness that "the world" was, in fact, equivalent to the West. This revived the familiar conundrum of Chinese modernity: How can China become an equal participant in a global system that is far from universal and autonomous, that is at once rooted in the West (as represented by the Nobel Prize) and in cultural nationalisms?[1] Literature, moreover, turned out to be a highly inappropriate candidate for the role of "representative of the nation." Despite the powerful hold the ideal of world literature has had on the modern imagination, literature, an elite linguistic art form dependent on translation to achieve global dissemination, is the cultural form least suited to the collectivist purposes of nationalism and internationalism. Members of China's official literary scene (in particular, those with bureaucratic positions in organizations such as the Writers' Association), more independent Chinese writers and critics, and the Nobel Committee consistently diverged in their opinions on what kind of literature should represent China internationally. While Chinese officialdom argued for politically orthodox candidates, the Nobel judges preferred the avant-garde heterodoxy of artistically dissident experimental writers. Bei Dao and other practicioners of "Misty poetry" (*menglong shi*), the first literary movement of the late and post-Cultural Revolution period to break significantly and publicly with socialist realism, were widely favored in the West but condemned by staunchly socialist critics at home for their work's level of abstraction and its Western influences.[2] China has won success in practically every cultural field — film, sports, music (none of which is so dependent upon translation to reach international audiences) — *except* literature, the most privileged sphere of cultural endeavor throughout much of Chinese history has not been similarly recognized. And yet it is in literature that some of China's greatest hopes for winning international recognition have been invested.

The Nobel Complex is, of course, deeply embedded in modern Chinese nationalism and its links to literary identity, in the perception that China, as a nation with a long cultural tradition and millions of writers and readers, has a right to a Nobel Prize. It also illuminates the other side of Chinese nationalism: the sense of inferiority and impulse towards self-criticism at apparently falling short of the global standard. The complex is a curious phantom syndrome that no one will admit to personally, for anyone shamelessly self-interested enough to do so will not be counted part of "serious" literature. It has been a source of recrimination between writers, critics, literary bureaucrats, politicians, and even foreign sinologists, all of whom have suspected the others of harboring the complex; all have blamed each other for failing to raise the quality of modern Chinese literature and thus resolve the syndrome. The term "Nobel Complex" in fact covers two sources of national and global angst: Firstly, what is so wrong with Chinese writers that they cannot win the world literature championship? Secondly, what is so wrong with Chinese writers that they are obsessed with this prize — and the money and fame it brings? The Nobel Complex is a self-perpetuating discourse, generating ever more diagnoses of the sickness at the heart of Chinese literature, and by extension of China itself.

This deeply held sense of insecurity returns us to Xueping Zhong's interpretation of modern (male) Chinese intellectual nationalism, with its marginality complex and relentless desire to gain credibility in modern global culture. Yet this desire is doomed to frustration, due to the tug-of-war between marginal and central, and national and international aspirations, to tensions between intellectuals and the nation-state, and to the conviction that China is both unique *and* needing recognition of the fact from the West. Zhong's observations are grounded in the historical context of the 1980s, a decade in which intellectual voices began to reemerge after years of Maoist repression, lamenting past weaknesses and "feminization" at the hands of the state while celebrating the figure of the marginal male destined for a return to the center of national and international prestige. Zhong reads the search for *zhong* (Chineseness) that came to a head in the roots-seeking movement (*xungen pai*) as suggestive of the potency of Chinese culture as a whole. Chinese culture "becomes a totality (again) that can find itself only when recognized as a powerful . . . culture and nation, especially in relation to the West."[3]

Attitudes towards the Nobel Literature Prize — a high-profile focus for intellectuals' national and international aspirations — thus illuminate the changing sociopolitical profile of literature and literary intellectuals in post-Mao China. The writer Li Feng (1968–) made a direct link between 1980s preoccupation with the Nobel and the resurgence of the male intellectual self-image:

> The 1980s was a golden age. . . . Writers were excited because of the enormous difference with the 1970s. The status of writers was very high and they had lots of female fans. It was a decade of male authors. . . . Interest in the Nobel Prize in the 1980s reflected this: this golden age, the readers, the women, all produced a kind of crazy hope.[4]

But male literary intellectuals' new sense of relevance to the national modernizing project was almost immediately challenged. After a brief, relatively liberal period in the early 1980s, during which a new literary generation committed to high levels of artistic freedom and experimentation began to win some influence in the mainstream literary scene, the Anti-Spiritual Pollution campaign of 1983 brought a jolting return to stringent political control and to attacks by conservative officialdom on writers and artists.[5] With the divergence between the socialist nation-state and creative writing thus restated, it soon became apparent both inside and outside China that the works most likely to win the Nobel Literature Prize would not be works promoted by the Chinese state. Nor were the cultural artifacts most valued by the Mainland intellectual community inevitably those prized within the international community. For Chinese writers, meanwhile, the Nobel had become not only a means of winning international recognition for China's national literature, but also a symbol of artistic freedom and resistance, standing for a universal literary community beyond the political frustrations and uncertainties of creative life in socialist China. Officials for their part desired that a writer who represented socialist literary orthodoxy win a Nobel Literature Prize for the "face" it would bring them and the regime that employed them. More independent writers and critics, however, desired a Nobel both to reassert their right to represent the Chinese nation to the world after years of being marginalized by the Maoist regime and to distinguish themselves outside the confines of a state authority discredited by the isolationist excesses of the Cultural Revolution. Particularly in the 1980s Chinese writers, stifled by an unpredictable regime that still oscillated between reform and censorship, saw winning a Nobel Literature Prize as a route to international audiences and financial rewards that otherwise remained far out of reach.

In the 1990s, when the Nobel question was dislodged from its prominence among official concerns and literary intellectuals retreated back to the margins, displaced by the market economy, the Nobel Complex itself became a thing of the market, a subject for media hype. The impassioned invocation of the complex, the insistence that China needed to win a Nobel, indicated a desperate effort on the part of critics to make literature newsworthy once more in a decade when it had lost its "sensational effect."[6] For some writers, this return to the margins made them yearn ever more for recognition within a "universal" world literature. Yet Chinese views of the Nobel Prize also changed, as literary intellectuals felt increasingly uncertain about the aims and values cherished in the 1980s. Their cold-shouldering by the state's ideological apparatus, by the West, and by the Nobel Committee only intensified the sense of bemusement and resentment.

In short, the Nobel Complex points out the high and largely unrealizable hopes invested in the transformative power of the autonomous aesthetic in the making of modern China. However contradictory their hopes may appear, there can be little doubt of post-Mao Chinese writers' belief in universal aesthetic ideals; indeed, their regard for such values is often quite possibly more fervent than that of writers in the West, since they have had extensive personal experience of the suffocating inverse of literary autonomy. Much post-Mao literary history describes the unease felt by Chinese literary intellectuals resulting from their conflicting desire both for the depoliticization of literature and for a redefinition of literature's sociopolitical role in a national and a global context.

The hopes and insecurities that both Chinese intellectuals and politicians have projected onto the Nobel can be loosely termed "Occidentalism." According to Chen Xiaomei, "The Chinese government uses the essentialization of the West as a means for supporting a nationalism that effects the internal suppression of its own people."[7] Among groups of the intelligentsia with diverse and often contradictory interests, however, this Occidentalism can be employed "as a powerful anti-official discourse using the Western Other as a metaphor for a political liberation against ideological oppression within a totalitarian society."[8] Chen's analysis also encapsulates many of the issues tied up with the Nobel Prize, as both an external Western system of evaluation and a dream of glory juggled between China's officialdom, intellectuals, and the writing and reading communities. Her remarks provide a reminder of the complexities of the Chinese literary and intellectual scene, whose diverse participants move between official and nonofficial, establishment and avant-garde, public and private, and national and individual identities, a fact that is amply illustrated by the development of the Nobel Complex. Throughout its history in contemporary China, the complex has oscillated between being a quest for official political prestige, a bulwark against Maoist isolationism, a beacon of pure literature, a source of money and prestige, and a mark of imperialist hegemony.[9]

The national imagination of China, with its constituency of 1.3 billion, moves in multiple directions and the Nobel Prize has been a focus of competing collective, nationalist, and individual desires. In this era of transnational exchange, whom should China's literature be for? How can Chinese writers as individuals best position themselves between the state (the political embodiment of the nation), the millions of Chinese who make up the nation, and the (Western, bourgeois, liberal) global audience whose gaze—imagined or real—has played a crucial role in the creation of a modern Chinese consciousness?

Debates around the Nobel Literature Prize: A Synopsis

Open discussion of the Nobel Prize in China became possible again in 1979, after official condemnation of the Cultural Revolution and extreme anti-Western leftism. At the Fourth Congress of Writers and Artists in 1979, attention focused on literary quality and the need for foreign influences. New questions were posed: why had no great writers emerged since 1949, and why were post-Liberation works of established writers inferior to those written earlier? Calls were made for the implementation of wide-ranging educational policy and for an end to isolationism.[10] In a 1978 article entitled "Absorb the Synthetic Essence of Foreign Arts," Xu Chi asserted: "To build our strong, modernized socialist country and raise dramatically the scientific and cultural level of the entire Chinese race, there is no way we can refuse to inherit and learn from the ancients and from foreigners."[11] As a further gesture towards bourgeois literary values, new prizes in the arts were founded that year.[12] Artistic universalism was also making a comeback: "Much of the world's treasury of literature and art and scientific inventions has already become a part of human civilization," wrote Huang Qingyun in 1981, "it's useless to create divisions or obstructions."[13]

The Nobel Prize for Literature was identified as a convenient representative canon of the modern foreign arts and coverage of its winners began to appear in journals from 1979 onwards, with brief introductions to writers such as Singer and Elytis (laureates in 1978 and 1979, respectively).[14] In 1981, Zhejiang People's Publishing House brought out a selection of Nobel Prize winners' works (*Nuobeier wenxue jiangjin huodezhe zuojia zuopin xuan*); further collections followed over the next two decades, with an immediate effect on writers. The novelist Yu Hua (b. 1960), for example, became a voracious reader of foreign literature from the start of the 1980s:

> The Nobel Prize had a big impact on me because a lot of great writers of the twentieth century were translated into Chinese due to their having won the Nobel Prize. So I've always loved the Nobel Prize, I've always thought it was a great literary prize. . . . I chose what I read of twentieth-century literature on the grounds of whether it had won the Nobel Prize or not. The first Kawabata I read was from the Zhejiang selection of Nobel Prize–winning works.[15]

China's new internationalist aspirations ensured that its absence from the Nobel roster would become a contentious policy issue by the mid-1980s. Yao Jian advanced a manifesto in 1982 for "increasing the propagation of our national culture to foreign countries": "Our country's literature is an astounding jewel in the treasury of world literature, it should become one of the commonly enjoyed riches of humanity." Under "the correct guidance of the Party and the flag of Marxism-Leninism and Mao Zedong thought, our foreign literature workers will diligently apply the policy of putting 'the foreign to Chinese use, the ancient to contemporary use' . . . using the powerful weapon of literature to encourage and unite our whole people, working hard in the struggle to keep extending our country's exchange and cooperation with every culture in the world!"[16] Mu Jun's 1983 overview of Nobel Prize winners, "The elite of the twentieth century," raised the issue of China's failure to win Nobel laurels: "The fact that Mr. Lu Xun never entered the list of prize winners in no way reduces his reputation, but great writers should get world acknowledgement."[17]

CHAPTER FOUR

A dynamic internationalism was apparent in the veteran novelist Ba Jin's speech before the 1984 meeting of the Writers' Association: "We . . . yearn to soon produce a contemporary Li Bai, Du Fu . . . to produce China's Dante, Shakespeare, Goethe, Tolstoy. . . . Sports and music have already won global laurels, why shouldn't our literature also stand at the forefront of world literature?"[18] Some of the most famous slogans of the 1980s invoke these aspirations: Chinese literature must "march towards the world," letting "China link up with the world" (*Zhongguo yu shijie jiegui*). These slogans had been appearing since at least 1981, but they are most often associated with the mid-decade intellectual-dominated "culture fever" (*wenhua re*).[19] Furthermore, from the mid-1980s onwards, the "world" as symbolized by the Nobel Prize and a host of other international prizes that *Renmin ribao* (People's Daily) claimed China had won in 1988, seemed to be beckoning China in.[20] The awarding of the Nobel Literature Prize to Gabriel García Márquez in 1982 and to Wole Soyinka in 1986 appeared to signal a new era of inclusiveness for the Nobel and the institution of world literature that it represented. Since the early 1980s, articles had appeared in Chinese journals explaining the mechanics of the prize and its nomination procedure.[21] Ba Jin, as head of the Writers' Association, was invited to nominate candidates for the prize in 1984.[22]

The presence of Göran Malmqvist, a newly elected member and the first sinologist at the Swedish Academy, at a major international Shanghai conference on contemporary Chinese literature organized by the Writers' Association in November 1986 (the Jinshan Conference) clearly foregrounded China's concern with the Nobel Prize. Both in his speech and in reported interviews, Malmqvist focused on the lack of good translations as the crucial barrier between China and a Nobel Prize, mentioning Shen Congwen and Misty Poets such as Bei Dao and Yang Lian (b. 1955) as his own translation projects. Extensive coverage ensued in the official press (especially *Renmin ribao* and *Wenyi bao* [Literary Gazette]), in addition to cultural periodicals, in which the conference was described largely as a think-tank for debating the problem of Chinese literature "marching towards the world" and winning a Nobel Prize.[23] Geremie Barmé recorded the encouragement that Malmqvist's comments gave to writers. "News of his visit spread like wildfire among Mainland writers who yearn for international praise and recognition."[24]

An intriguing perspective on the genesis of the Nobel Complex in 1980s China, and on the role played by Göran Malmqvist, is provided by the scholar and translator Bonnie McDougall. She traces the first links between Chinese writers and the Nobel Prize to an early 1980s publishing and publicizing initiative orchestrated by Western translators (herself included) of Bei Dao's poetry. In 1983, the targeting of avant-garde authors such as Bei Dao by the

Anti-Spiritual Pollution campaign pushed admirers of his work to generate as much international publicity for it as possible, first of all through publication of translations but also through direct overtures to the Western diplomatic community in Beijing, including the Swedish embassy.[25] Göran Malmqvist responded enthusiastically to Bei Dao's poems and agreed to act as his translator, winning Bei Dao a public profile in Sweden. When Malmqvist was elected to the Swedish Academy in 1985, rumors concerning Bei Dao and the Nobel Prize rapidly began to circulate, particularly after Malmqvist invited Bei Dao and his fellow avant-garde poet Gu Cheng (1956–1993) to visit Sweden, and following his praise of these poets at the Jinshan Conference. The anxiety of the Chinese Writers' Association about the connections between a formerly underground writer such as Bei Dao and the Nobel Prize, McDougall believes, led them to produce their own candidates and delegations to Sweden. "I don't think there was much official interest in the Nobel Prize until the Swedish connection with Bei Dao emerged," remembered McDougall.[26]

Suspicions among Chinese critics (and some writers) that certain figures in the literary world were writing *for* the Nobel Prize during the 1980s focused also on the representatives of the roots-seeking movement of mid-decade, influenced by Márquez, whose 1982 Nobel Prize and international success had an enormous effect on Chinese literary circles. Márquez represented a novelist from a developing country who had beaten writers from developed countries at their own Nobel game, and whose most famous work, *One Hundred Years of Solitude*, catered to all constituencies by combining authentic national characteristics with the universally acclaimed modernist technique of magical realism, invented in economically backward Latin America. *One Hundred Years of Solitude* was first published in Chinese in the journal *Shijie wenxue* (World Literature) in December 1982, provoking an overwhelming response from Chinese writers and critics, who sought to distill all possible lessons from this "successful 'march towards the world,'" as Zhu Jingdong phrased it in 1988.[27] Admiration for Latin American literature grew to such proportions towards the close of the decade that it was actually satirized in Wang Meng's (1934–) 1988 novella *Qiuxing qiyu ji* (Strange adventures of a soccer star).[28] The novelist Qiu Huadong (1969–), a student in the 1980s, related how he and other would-be writers at his university used to "get together with friends to practice writing in the style of Borges, to see who could imitate him most accurately."[29]

There were, however, some reservations. In 1987, Feng Yidai reported Mao Dun's cold reaction to the news that he had been nominated for the Nobel Prize in the early 1980s: "If it were a prize for Asians, would they have only given it to Tagore and Kawabata in seventy years?" Having recounted the prize's biases, Feng went on to protest: "And why should Chinese literature become an ornament for the Nobel Prize, all for the sake of winning?"[30] Another article, "The Prejudice of the Nobel Prize and the establishment of the Chinese Literature Prize," attempted to refocus attention on the domestic literary scene. After lamenting the inability of the Mao Dun Prize to attract international attention due to its meager purse, the author called for a new prize for works by Taiwanese, Hong Kong, Macao, and overseas Chinese writers to rival the Nobel. Somewhat ironically, the Chinese Literature Prize mentioned in the article's title was apparently established by the Writers' Association "to help Chinese writers contend for the Nobel Prize."[31]

Interest in the Nobel Prize otherwise showed no signs of abating. Another member of the Swedish Academy, Kjell Espmark, visited China in 1987, and his lecture at Beijing University on "The Nobel Literature Prize: Changes and Developments in the Criteria" was fully reported in *Wenyi bao*.[32] "Chinese writers, please come in!" ran the title of a front-page *Wenyi bao* article reporting the personal attention lavished on the Writers' Association party visiting Sweden by worthies such as the mayor of Stockholm and, most importantly, Göran Malmqvist.[33] A 1987 Writers' Association delegation to Stockholm presented Ba Jin and the orthodox poet Ai Qing (1910–1996) as candidates.[34] A 1988 Friendship Association meeting was held in Shenzhen for Guangdong, Hong Kong, and Macao writers, at which the establishment of a world organization and prize for Chinese writers was discussed, to "break open the path to international fame. . . . The reason why Chinese literature hadn't yet won a Nobel Prize became a hot topic at the meeting."[35]

By the start of the 1990s, a shift in official attitudes had taken place, due largely to the events of 4 June 1989. Intellectuals and writers were forced out of their role as spokesmen for the nation, the works of prominent writers were banned, censorship of pro-Western publications was reinforced, and Chinese citizens "were reminded of their history of oppression by foreigners that began with the Opium War of 1839."[36] Western media attention on a new, prominent group of literati exiles after 1989 undermined officialdom's dream of socialist Chinese literature marching towards universal global acclaim. Jin Jianfan, secretary of the Writers' Association in 2000, protested the use of an international PEN meeting as a platform for Bei Dao to discuss his petition for the release of the prominent dissident Wei Jingsheng.[37] In 1990 an article in *Renmin ribao* entitled "Marching towards the World and the 'Foreign Complex'" criticized the way "some comrades in the 1980s followed the cultural lead of the West, or even only the Nobel Prize, viewing this as the necessary path of the march towards the world."[38] Instead, the need for preserving "national characteristics" received renewed emphasis: "Under the direction of Marxism, we must create a new culture with socialist characteristics that both inherits fine national traditions and fully embodies the spirit of the age, rooted in our nation and facing the world."[39] The discovery by Chinese critics of postcolonialism encouraged further protest at the West and Western systems of evaluation, providing the basis for a new understanding of China's relationship with such institutions as the Nobel Prize. The introduction of postmodern and postcolonial theories by scholars such as Zhang Yiwu coincided with the crackdown on liberalism and the rise of a new official patriotism in 1990s China. In the academic vacuum following 1989, when research on foreign literature and theory was severely restricted, such approaches constituted a relatively safe academic path, echoing, to a certain degree, anti-Western nationalist orthodoxy.[40]

Nevertheless, it is questionable to what degree these changes fundamentally affected the Chinese Nobel industry. Coverage of prizewinners and translation of their works persisted, as did publication of articles discussing China's lack of a prize. Articles about the prize continued to be written as policy statements, seriously and systematically probing its history to rationalize China's failure to win. As other non-Western writers won the prize (the Mexican Octavio Paz in 1990, the South African Nadine Gordimer in 1991, Kenzaburo Oe in 1994) and yet Chinese literature remained ignored, the hopeful internationalist ideals of the 1980s (Chinese literature should "march towards the world"; the more national, the more global, *yue shi minzu de, yue shi shijie de*) seemed increasingly elusive.

There was a growing opinion that New Era (*xin shiqi*, the Chinese term for the post-Mao period) society and literature had already passed their teething stage, and it was now time for China's achievements to receive due recognition. In an account of intellectual nationalism in the 1990s, Suisheng Zhao describes the psychological development of the Nobel Prize syndrome as "first hopeful, then disappointed, and finally angry and presumptuous."[41] "Many countries and peoples see their writers winning the [Nobel] Prize as a sign of having marched towards the world," wrote Zhang Quan in 1992. "Therefore, as China's international position becomes ever more important . . . it's very natural that the problem of why the Nobel Literature Prize has never come to China should have become the hot topic of many conferences, journals, and books, and attract widespread attention abroad among Chinese scholars, writers, and the judges of the Nobel Prize."[42] Official support for the Nobel Prize campaign, however, had disappeared after the 1980s, since the only writers mentioned in connection with the prize were exiles (Bei Dao) or took little part in the official literary system (Mo Yan [1956–]).

Commentators in the journal *Dushu* (Reading) were among the first to express public skepticism about the Nobel Prize in the second half of the 1990s.

Zi Zhongjun prophesied that whenever "out of some consideration or other they choose a Chinese person, the Chinese literary world won't know whether to laugh or cry."[43] If in the 1980s the Nobel Prize represented the pinnacle of world literature, greater familiarity with the workings of global culture in the 1990s disillusioned some writers, leading to suspicions that the prize was not a pure meritocracy and that chances of winning were influenced by networking and translating politics. "Tell the Nobel Prize to go away!" He Song asserted in 1998 in the pages of *Dajia* (Expert), criticizing the journal's "Nobel Complex."[44] As newspapers became caught up in the Nobel hype of the 1990s, cynicism sometimes took over from anxiety. The furor over news of the Taiwanese author and presidential candidate Li Ao's nomination in early 2000 finally provoked wry bitterness in *Zhonghua dushu bao* (China Reading Times). "[T]his isn't a farce of unrequited love performed by our countrymen, we haven't performed anything at all. . . . We're only concerned onlookers, watching to see how the Nobel Prize Committee will perform!"[45]

Other writers, meanwhile, turned their attention to more pressing domestic matters: the position of the writer in a burgeoning market economy, for example. Those interested in financial rewards were better off courting mass audiences in China than hoping for a windfall from Sweden. Those yearning for international fame focused on trying to persuade the director Zhang Yimou (1950–) to turn their works into films.

The ongoing rumble of the Nobel Complex, therefore, often seemed more than anything else a publicity stunt by critics to make literature headline news again. However, even as the century drew to a close, and despite the emergence of anarchic elements in the Chinese literary scene in the shape of "free writers" (*ziyou zuojia*) declaring themselves immune to anxiety about external sources of authority, least of all the Nobel Prize, critics continued sighing about "the glorious dream of contemporary Chinese literature" — to win a Nobel Prize.[46] In 1997 the prominent postcolonial and postmodern critic Zhang Yiwu admitted, "the Nobel Prize is an unavoidable topic as far as the Chinese literary world is concerned."[47] In 1999 the Taiwanese journal *Lianhe wenxue* (Unitas) ran a long article by the noted critic Liu Zaifu on "A Nobel Century and the Absence of a Chinese Writer," while *Mingbao yuekan* (Mingbao Monthly) in Hong Kong devoted its November issue entirely to the subject of the Nobel Prize.[48]

The Nobel Complex may have publicly disappeared from official agendas during the 1990s, but few doubted it still rankled among writers, critics, and officialdom. It was, however, always an attributed disorder; no one would admit personally to being a sufferer, and well-known writers such as Han Shaogong (1953–) and Mo Yan asserted indifference.[49] Yet suspicions at the end of the decade still ran high that writers had been, or were now writing for the Nobel Prize, or at least for foreigners. According to the poet Xi Chuan (1963–), the novelist Su Tong (1963–) joked that he had won the Nobel Prize three times. "Why does he mention the Nobel Prize in the first place? He must be thinking about it himself."[50] The controversy over Gao Xingjian's 2000 Nobel affirmed that the complex remained a fixture of the Chinese literary scene at the start of the new millennium.

The 1980s: Intellectual Euphoria

Three million intellectuals returned to public life in 1979, and it is no coincidence that the prominent public phase of China's Nobel Complex occurred in the ensuing decade of "high culture fever." 1979 ushered in a new state ideology for plotting Chinese modernity that based its claims to legitimacy on denunciation of the Cultural Revolution. As the principal victims of the Cultural Revolution, intellectuals, the representatives of elite culture, assumed their place in this new modernizing schema as advocates of modern enlightenment, freedom, democracy, and internationalism. This heroic rhetoric overlay, the cultural critic Dai Jinhua believes, a collusion between elite culture and ruling ideology. "Modernization, democracy, and freedom were used in this discursive situation to construct a kind of utopian futuristic vision . . . a panacea that presented the Cultural Revolution as its inverse. . . . A new, latent cultural hegemony, or common social understanding came into being, namely that only socialist modernization could save China."[51] One collective consciousness (intellectual, pro-international) was taking over from another (proletarian, ultraleftist), still under the aegis of the socialist state. Writers, all of a sudden, enjoyed a status close to celebrity. Social and cultural debate culminated in a mid-decade "Culture Fever" celebrated in countless conferences and journals and fostering an epochal spirit that reveled in "revalorizing intellectualism and disdaining the populace."[52]

Interest in the Nobel Prize and its development into a policy issue in the 1980s were therefore deeply entangled in the heroic self-image of advocates of elite culture and their implication in China's ruling ideology. Ba Jin's appeal at the 1984 Writers' Association meeting for a literature of international stature signaled that the literary community was very much reinstated as standard bearer in China's progress towards full participation in modern global culture. The desire of the mass of intellectuals to succeed in this mission coincided neatly with government ambitions.

Edward Friedman characterizes changes in the construction of Chinese national identity from Mao to Deng as a shift from a (northern-based) antiforeign Maoist model to a (southern-based) open model. The nationalism that emerged under Deng Xiaoping (1904–1997) was identified with the market-oriented activities of southerners, with whom lay the promise of a reformed and prosperous China. In the interests of promoting openness, beginning in the 1970s scholars revised the entire historical teleology linked with the Maoist model of anti-imperialist nationalism, abandoning the idea of a unified (Han) origin for the Chinese people in favor of a multilinear view which emphasized the "importance of foreign contacts in the development of Chinese civilization and culture and the relative impact of non-Han peoples on Han."[53] The source of the nation's backwardness lay in its lack of openness to the world, rather than in external imperialism. Chinese isolationism had culminated in the suffocating atmosphere under Mao, which was blamed for the failure to produce a great literature and a Nobel Prize winner after 1949. Calls by politicians, critics, and writers for Chinese literature to internationalize its outlook were thus all implicated in a newly open and heterogeneous vision for national identity, aimed at discrediting Maoism and promoting Deng's modernizing vision. "This slogan ['march toward the world'] was fashionable in the 1980s," recalled the radical critic Li Tuo, "but . . . it was, pretty much, official-speak. . . . Some good writers embraced it, but in fact they also unconsciously embraced official discourse . . . those who didn't approve were a minority."[54] "There were a lot of political elements concealed within this 'march towards the world,'" the writer Feng Jicai (1942–) commented. "It was part of wanting the world to acknowledge China, just as the United Nations had acknowledged China."[55]

Literary histories were brought into line with the quest for a Nobel Prize, accounting for past failures to win in order to reflect greater glory onto Deng Xiaoping's New Era and its policies, which were advertised as being progressive beyond anything known in China before. "Real, full-blown 'marching towards the world' only took place after the eleventh meeting of the third party plenum," wrote Chen Liao in 1986. "This . . . is unprecedented in our nation's literary history."[56] "Since the reforms and opening up, after China shook off its leftist influence and opened its great doors to the world, literature also began to flourish," declared Jian Jinsong in 1988. Because, according to the new orthodoxy, China's modernization only truly started to accelerate in 1979, assessment of the recent past—the Cultural Revolution in particular—had to corroborate this vision, accounting for the lack of great works in the New Era. "For historical or other reasons, the level of cultural education of a lot of Chinese writers is not high," Jian added soberly.[57]

This enthusiasm for the Nobel Prize expressed the combination of confidence and fragility that made up the early post-Mao construction of Chinese national identity: confidence that Maoism represented a blind alley for China, but fragility following the disintegration of a worldview. Mao had proclaimed the People's Republic the upstanding leader of progressive third-world nations, giving China, Dai Jinhua comments, "a position equal to that of the Soviet Union and the United States. In fact, China was a real leader. They were just two countries, but we were leaders of Asia and Africa."[58] As the Maoist model was discredited in favor of Deng Xiaoping's open-door policy, however, China's self-image partially collapsed. "In the transition between the 1970s and 1980s, China experienced another 'world encounter.' This . . . smashed in one blow the image of Socialist China as the center of world revolution . . . . China, it seemed, began to accept its own Western-centric 'backward reality' in world history, began to acknowledge its marginal position in the (Western-centric) world."[59]

This shift in consciousness led to a resurgence of anxious universalism and renewed faith in literature's capacity to mediate between these new national and international identities, as Chen Liao spelled out in 1986.

> In the past, it was very fashionable to believe that it was fine for Chinese literature only to have Chinese readers, that not having world readers wasn't important. . . . This kind of view is actually very one-sided. . . . We can't be satisfied with Chinese readers, we have to fight for world readers. The arts serve the people: "the people" here is not limited to Chinese people, but encompasses the people of the whole world. Serving the people of China and the people of the world are one and the same thing.[60]

The Nobel Prize for literature, according to Mu Jun in 1983, celebrated humankind's universal path from savagery to civilization. Mu characterized prizewinners as demonstrating a combination of idealism, love of the motherland, glorification of literary tradition, and exploration of human truths throughout modernity.[61] The juxtaposition of patriotism and universalism in this analysis highlights the straightforward unity imagined in some quarters between national and international, official and intellectual identities as expressed through literature.

Yet even as some intellectuals and writers proclaimed their return to the center, many retained a dissenting consciousness that conflicted with officialdom's desire for progress and glory. Since his speech at the Jinshan Conference in 1986, Göran Malmqvist has always made it clear he was interested in representatives of underground, avant-garde or nonofficial literature (including an author such as Shen Congwen, who stopped writing after 1949) rather than high-ranking members of the socialist literary establishment such as Ba

Jin or Ai Qing. "It was mostly officials, like those in the Writers' Association, that worried about the Nobel Prize," remembered Li Tuo.

> They particularly hoped that Ba Jin or Ai Qing, the best official writers, would win it, and they made a lot of effort to help Ba Jin win the prize. Then when it looked like Shen Congwen might win, they got very anxious. But what really worried them was after the avant-garde and roots-seeking writers emerged, Goran Malmqvist paid attention to them, not to official writers.[62]

Li's comments are reinforced by Bonnie McDougall's insights into the genesis of the official Nobel Complex as a *defensive* reaction on the part of the Writers' Association against Malmqvist's interest in nonestablishment poets such as Bei Dao and Gu Cheng. McDougall's observations further illustrate the tensions between nonestablishment writers and the notion of a centralized, national identity. She testifies to a strong rejection of "China" — as defined by the Party-state — among Chinese writers and artists in her circle of acquaintances in the 1980s.

> Everyone I knew was disgusted with China, with the government, with Chinese life. I would be approached all the time by people asking me to translate their poems, to get them invitations abroad. . . . I don't think that the radical writers saw themselves as presenting a political alternative. Their writing was politicized, but they were presenting art as an autonomous entity. Their personal concerns show quite strongly that they wanted to get out of China, and so many of that group left China with no intention of returning. If you're really patriotic, you don't leave your country.[63]

Instead, she sees some writers' desire for the Nobel Prize in the 1980s as stemming from personal, and not from political and nationalistic motives: "They were after the individual glory associated with the prize, the freedom of movement it would bring, the money." This individualized response to the possibility of a Nobel Prize, she believes, holds true also for the Writers' Association. "I'd be more cynical about their motives for promoting their own candidates. If these bureaucrats had won this glory for one of their writers, it would have given their own careers a great boost and enhanced the power and glory of their own organization. There was a collective sense that writers wanted a higher position in society. They weren't chasing this or any other prize because of their pride in China."[64]

At the same time, however, intellectual professions of disgust with China often overlay a worrying consciousness (*youhuan yishi*) about the state of Chinese society that also translated into a form of nationalistic feeling. In

Perry Link's interviews with Chinese intellectuals at the end of the 1980s, for example, his interlocutors frequently combined denunciations of China in its present state with a sense of deep, patriotic anxiety about how the nation might raise itself out of its current predicament.[65] It is these apparent contradictions and tensions (again, reminiscent of Zhong Xueping's remarks on the intellectual marginality complex) that make the links between intellectuals, nationalism, and the Nobel Complex so complex and intriguing.

The Nobel Complex has repeatedly illuminated clashes between diverging visions of the national imagined community, on the one hand, and individual writers, on the other. In the 1980s memories of the Cultural Revolution — kept fresh thanks to periodic political campaigns against (or between factions of) intellectuals (Anti-Spiritual Pollution in 1983, Anti-Bourgeois Liberalization in 1987 for example) — coexisted with the campaign for the Nobel Prize: writers had to both struggle to win international plaudits for the nation as creative workers and guard against accusations of bourgeois liberalization. In 1986 some in official circles felt that Nobel Fever was escalating out of control and serving as a rallying point for politically heterodox literary forces, and the propaganda department circulated a general notice to tone down and redirect the coverage of this and other international prizes.[66]

While the development of the search for a Nobel Prize into a policy issue highlighted intellectuals' reassertion of their centrality to the new national modernization program, it thus also denoted fundamental mistrust among certain groupings of the nationalist blueprint associated with Maoist state ideology. Some literary intellectuals, of course, were still eager to remain central to the state establishment and its modernization program.[67] Many, however, no longer wanted Chinese literature to be locked within the boundaries of the national unit ruled by the Party-state, and sought solidarity and equality within world literature.[68] Moreover, to Chinese writers of the 1980s, the Nobel Prize offered a ladder to the international community beyond the nation-state: in the 1980s, writers depended almost entirely on the official Writers' Association for opportunities for travel abroad; winning a Nobel Prize represented an alternative nongovernmental route to the outside world.

But where, precisely, was "the world" and its corresponding global culture towards which intellectuals desired to advance? The writer Liu Xinwu in 1987 asserted that "the implication of 'marching towards the world' is in fact winning a Nobel Prize, it isn't a question of marching towards Nepal, the Arab Emirates. . . . The best thing would be to immediately approach Western Europe, Sweden, the Swedish Academy, Göran Malmqvist, the Swedish sinologist who has most power over the Nobel Prize, his bookshelves at home."[69] Chen Xiaoming described this attitude bluntly: "China's is a great national culture . . . it isn't willing to be other, it wants to be equal. It doesn't want to be alternative, or backward. China looks down on Pakistan, India, Southeast Asia."[70] Despite the enormous impact of Márquez's Nobel Prize in 1982, there was no comparable rush to draw lessons from Africa's first Nobel laureate, Soyinka, although in many ways this was a more meaningful gesture towards non-Western literatures (three South American writers had already received the Nobel before Márquez). This is indicative of post-Mao Chinese disdain for the cultures of most developing countries, in particular African culture.[71]

Despite China's current backwardness, intellectuals preoccupied with the Nobel Prize implied that their destiny was to be recognized as part of "world civilization," namely, the first-world club. This precisely recapitulated the dynamics of the marginality complex in modern Chinese nationalism, where Chinese intellectuals both perceive themselves as backward or marginal, *and* desire to attain the central universal position owed to China as a great national civilization. This pride in China's former glories fuels the sense of self-disgust that Chinese culture has been allowed to decline so drastically in the modern era; it also underlies the desire for recognition from the West that that decline has indeed been reversed.

Yet Chinese thinkers have been continually frustrated in their attempts to reposition themselves. Intellectuals who asserted that China should "march towards the world" confidently believed that they should be recognized by the West. But by subscribing to only one mode of modernity (that of the advanced, developed West), they denigrated other systems (notably those of third-world countries, which to all intents and purposes China was and still largely is), and maneuvered themselves into a servile position in which modernity will never lose its ambivalent taint of Westernization. "We know nothing of Africa," commented Chen Sihe in 2000,

> We know some Latin American writers because they were communist or won the Nobel Prize, like Neruda. In India, there's no one but Tagore. The Nobel Prize is still the standard. . . . What do we know of Arab culture, of Iraq? We knew plenty about writers from Poland, Bulgaria, Romania in the 1920s. Now, no one does . . . only French, English, German count. . . . It's quite terrifying the way we inevitably take our criteria from the West.[72]

However, this imbalance cannot be resolved simply by Chinese writers and scholars shifting their cultural paradigms, since there is a powerful economic dimension to China's dilemma; the economic might of the West has generated cultural influence that is hard to ignore. Although many Chinese intellectuals have not been unaware that anxiety to secure the Nobel Prize risks capitulation to Western literary values, the money and prestige that modern Chinese literature would stand to gain have remained a strong attraction, especially since the politics of international translation and publishing play such a central role in breaking into the world market. As apparent as the bias of this "international" cultural system was to many Chinese even in the 1980s, the material advantages of participation — prize money, a boost to sales, funding opportunities abroad — could not be easily dismissed by writers eager to leave behind the isolation of Maoism.[73]

These sources of ambivalence were always implicit in the search for the Nobel Prize, but they were rarely openly acknowledged. For much of the decade, concepts such as "the world" and world literature were idealized as neutral signifiers of a modernity in which each country's national characteristics would be welcomed and accepted. Indeed, promotion of national characteristics was regarded in 1980s China as the surest way of gaining entrance to this global canon and as such was enthusiastically debated in literary circles. "In the 1980s," remembered Dai Jinhua, "everyone believed in 'marching toward the world,' endlessly debating about national traditions and the world, about how the more national you were, the more global. It was laughable. The relations between China and the world weren't seen as difficult or problematic; there was no properly deep appreciation of the problem."[74] It was the roots-seeking movement that both enacted, and placed these relations in question.

Occidentalist Orientalism among the Roots Seekers

The roots-seeking manifesto was the literary embodiment of the utopian plan to export Chinese literature to the world. Based on uniquely Chinese material (the historical rural "roots" of Chinese culture), it aimed to achieve world recognition by following the example of South American literature.[75] The root-seekers were thus implicated in official discourse on China's global literary ambitions and in the construction of a new open-door model of national identity. Yet they also marked one of the earliest decisive breaks with Maoist social realist rulings on language and form, thus demonstrating the potentially emancipatory function of aesthetics within the post-Mao national literary identity.

The root-seekers were squarely situated within the mid-decade debate over the "correct" path for Chinese literary modernity, a discussion that reverberated between various binary oppositions — realism vs. modernism, China vs. the West — and that was deeply implicated in the construction of new national identities in literature and in the search for a Nobel Prize.[76] From May Fourth until the 1980s, the hallmark style of Chinese literary modernism had been realism, favored by May Fourth intellectuals for its seeming capacity to represent people and nation. With the advent of Mao's ambition to forge one classless culture for China, the pressure on Chinese writers to portray their audience of hundreds of millions of workers, peasants, and soldiers grew ever greater. But when China's doors reopened around 1979, the debate over Chinese literary modernity started anew, based in part in hopes of producing Nobel Prize–winning literature. Winning the prize, it was felt, represented an important step towards inclusion in an ill-defined but modern "world literature" for various interested parties: for the nation-state, with its desire to win recognition as a strong, modern international power; and for writers and intellectuals, who wished both to gain recognition for China by winning international plaudits and also to maintain an open China that would never repeat the isolating repression of Maoist anti-intellectualism. Yet how could the interests of these very different audiences — the global and the local, the intellectuals and the masses (whoever *they* were) — be reconciled in a literature that could win a Nobel?

A craze for studying Western modernism and experimental literature banned under Mao took hold in the 1980s. "For many years," Li Tuo remembered, "a great number of young writers and readers . . . seriously believed that the only way out for Chinese literature lay in the study of Western modernism."[77] Writers such as Yu Hua readily acknowledge foreign influences during this period: "All our generation was pretty much the same: we all chose foreign literature, for historical reasons. During the Cultural Revolution, there were no foreign books we could read, then suddenly lots were available. . . . This foreign literature was really powerful. A lot more powerful than our own modern literature."[78] Yet despite their widespread popularity, deployment of foreign styles still inspired official resistance, culminating in the 1983 Anti-Spiritual Pollution campaign. Works that reproduced these influences were denounced above all for the way in which they cut themselves off from the Chinese masses: Misty poetry, for example, was condemned for its "obscurity," for its rejection of the idea of the writer serving the socialist collective. "Poetry that cannot be understood, accepted, and appreciated by the masses," wrote one orthodox critic, "is either bad or not poetry at all."[79]

Adherents of fictional realism had also been discomforted by the importation of Western modernism; the hostile reaction of realist writer Liu Xinwu to Gao Xingjian's pioneering pamphlet "Xiandai xiaoshuo jiqiao chutan" (A preliminary inquiry into the techniques of modern fiction) is a case in point, as is Liu's defensive forecast that "critical realism" would represent the "mainstream" of Chinese literature for some time.[80] In the literary and cultural ferment of the 1980s, burgeoning hopes for a Nobel Prize overlay disputes concerning the national politics of content, form, and literary representation. Liu Xinwu argued that Westerners had only started to be interested in contemporary Chinese literature since Deng Xiaoping's economic and social reforms, and therefore it was works that reflected the social, political, and economic reality of China that would win international acclaim. "[W]riters who hope to attain international recognition should not abandon such works in favor of the 'literary' works which have 'abolished meaning' that they think Westerners prefer."[81] The realism/modernism debate as it related to the Nobel Prize hung on the question of whom New Era literature was for: Westerners who could, it was believed, readily understand these modernist forms, or the Chinese who, it was decreed by the socialist literary establishment, preferred and could only understand homegrown realism? At the same time, intellectual voices were staking their own claims to represent and speak directly to the collective Chinese readership via new experimental forms taken from the West. Using Western literary techniques and manifesting a distinctly nonsocialist aesthetic individualism, Misty Poets wanted to emancipate literature from the political dictat of stifling Maoist control and return it to the individual reader and viewer, achieving widespread popularity in the process. In 1989 a quotation from Bei Dao's poetry was placed on prominent display by prodemocracy demonstrators in Tian'anmen Square.[82]

A way out of this contested domain was sought in the creation of a more homespun Chinese modernism.[83] The phrase "the more national, the more global," current in the literary discussions of the mid-1980s, conjured up for both writers and politicians a congenial means of reconciling their internationalist ambitions with long-held convictions about Chinese literature representing the collective. They believed that the path to achieving global success and parity lay in nurturing China's national characteristics rather than losing itself in imitation of the West. This was theorized as a smooth, easily legislated process:

> Because if Chinese literature wants to have a dialogue with the world, if it wants to enter the world's cultural "United Nations," then just as it must first have its own nationality to enter the political United Nations, it must be permeated with a vivid consciousness of Chinese national culture . . . in our contemporary literary scene, not only are some young writers "relying on Western fiction to produce Chinese fiction," but there is also some biased literary criticism that "binds the hands and feet" of Chinese national cultural works . . . with Western discursive and critical terms. . . . Only by courageously digesting Western culture while stressing the absorption of nourishment from national culture can our literary writing and criticism beat with a pulse unique to the Chinese nation, and advance powerfully towards the world.[84]

In 1986 Chen Liao announced that no inevitable barrier existed between the literature of socialist and capitalist countries:

> In recent years a "Chinese-style modernist literature" has finally emerged. It uses modernist forms . . . but represents the psychology of people in a socialist society . . . and so has already attracted interest in Western modernist literary circles. . . . The reforms our country is now implementing are of global importance. If our New Era literature can describe the formidably complex nature of the reforms and four modernizations . . . and maintain a high level of national culture, then it will certainly win even more readers in the world and will successfully serve the people of China and the world. Thus, writers of the New Era should harbor this kind of lofty aspiration, to become not only Chinese writers but world writers.[85]

Li Yukun in 1987 concluded that the "national" and "global" facets of art are "not only not opposed; 'national' characteristics are indeed an essential prerequisite" for art "marching towards the world."[86]

There was, however, a strange subtext to this reassertion of national Chinese values in the mid-1980s. From the start of the decade, Western influences had been held suspect on the grounds that they were foreign, bourgeois, and obscurantist. Yet advocacy of more "Chinese" subject matter took as its stimulus the appraising gaze of the West, since the "world" recognition the Chinese sought had to come from the developed West. Chinese writers had to write about China because that was what foreigners wanted to read. "[T]he more national, the more global: literature of the New Era must have national characteristics," insisted Chen Liao. "Foreign readers like works that help them get to know contemporary China, works with Chinese characteristics. . . . The modernist literary world in the West is interested in Chinese modernist literature, but they mostly see it as a branch of modernism, they don't hold it in high regard at all."[87] In their search for a Nobel Prize and theorization of roots-seeking literature, Chinese writers and literary intellectuals found themselves participating in a debate about their own Chineseness that could not exist without reference to the gaze of the foreigner.

The roots-seeking manifesto—represented by Han Shaogong's 1985 essay "The Roots of Literature"—was the Chinese version of the South American strategy for winning Western recognition. Han's essay called for a Chinese nativist revival. "Where has the colorful culture of Chu gone?" he asked, calling to mind the post-Mao model of national identity analyzed by Edward Friedman, in which the ancient state of Chu, situated in the southern half of contemporary China, is a vital source of modern Chinese culture. "Literature has roots," Han asserted, "literature's roots should be deeply planted in the ground of national cultural traditions."[88] He cited examples from Western literature (or literature recognized by the West) to back up his arguments: "American black humor owes a debt to American humorous legends, Latin American magical realism is linked to the fairy stories, parables, and legends of Latin America. Another Nobel Prize winner, the Greek poet Elysis, is even more obviously connected to the heritage of Greek myths and legends" (p. 5). Han appealed for a revival of national self-confidence and a shift away from adulation of all things foreign. The justification for this, however, derived from a Western source:

> The Western historian Toynbee invested great hopes in Eastern civilization. He believed Western Christian civilization was already in decline, but ancient, slumbering Eastern civilization, facing the "challenge" of foreign civilization, would "reemerge" after retreat, to illuminate the whole globe. For the time being we shouldn't worry whether Toynbee's remarks are true or are speculative; what is significant is that many Western scholars had similar ideas . . . . There is a story that when Zhang Daqian went to study painting from Picasso, Picasso said, "What are you doing in Paris? What art is there in Paris? Only in your east, in Africa, is there art." . . . Is all this accidental or providential? (p. 5)

Han Shaogong's was not a lone voice: another roots-seeking writer, Zheng Yi, had chimed in with similar criticism of the damaging "cultural rupture" (*wenhua duanlie*) caused by twentieth-century China's antitraditionalism. "In these last ten or so years we could, in terms of social life, certainly produce works that meet the highest world standards. But deficiencies in the national cultural education of an entire generation of writers still make it hard for us to top those standards."[89] Latin American writers, observes the scholar Catherine Yeh, had "not only shown a way to use traditional culture in order to create a distinct literary style," but also "offered proof to young Chinese writers that being economically backward does not prevent a nation from producing first-class literature."[90]

The reasoning of the Roots Seekers was therefore shot through with contradictions. Writers were being exhorted to dig deep into China's traditions to produce a literature that would be judged on an international level. The rationale for excavating Chinese antiquity derived from the esteem in which Westerners held ancient Chinese culture. Although Chinese writers followed an example from outside the Western mainstream by revering authors like Márquez, the distinction was largely a rhetorical one: instead of learning from the West how to succeed in the West, Chinese writers looked to other third-world countries for strategies for success. As a further irony, local (marginal minority) cultures were invoked to shore up the Han (orthodox majority) culture identified with official goals. Han Shaogong wrote of culture's native "roots": "All this is like the gigantic, diffuse and tumultuously boiling deep layers of the great earth, hidden underneath and supporting the crust of the surface, which is our orthodox culture" (p. 4). Cultivation of local roots would "reforge" the national self in its progress towards modernization (p. 5). Additionally, the tone of roots-seeking commentators who advocated the formula "the more national, the more global" was more clearly reminiscent of a policy directive than of an appeal for a creative revival: if we write X (national culture), we will achieve Y (global recognition and a Nobel Prize).

In short, the Roots Seekers proposed a literature that expressed all the tensions inherent in both its long-term and immediate historical provenance: Chinese intellectuals' obsession with their marginality within the nation and the world, their desire to return to the center by asserting a strong, independent literary identity and to regain control over a national essence that could take its proper place in the world. Xueping Zhong notes in male Chinese writers of the 1980s, and roots-seeking authors in particular, a preoccupation with, and celebration of marginal male intellectuals, often expressed through fantasies of sexual and physical potency. Marginal figures were reestablished as heroes, as romantic selves fragmented and decentered, but still capable of self-strengthening and returning to the center of an orderly world. (Their authors, Zhong notes, appear to identify strongly with these heroes, who are often semi-autobiographical portraits.) Han Shaogong's antihero Bingzai in the roots-seeking novella *Bababa* (Dadada) is an allegorical instance of the marginality complex. Born in a remote, even primeval backwater, the idiot Bingzai represents all that is marginal in Chinese culture. Throughout the course of the story, however, Bingzai becomes less and less abject, and is finally worshipped following his miraculous survival of an apocalyptic disaster. Bingzai, Zhong concludes, represents the return of the repressed intellectual to express truth through his own alternative aesthetic language.[91]

Zhong theorizes the "search for roots" as implicated in an intellectual marginality complex that invests heavily in the search for a strong Chinese identity and aims at constructing a modern cultural identity designed to compete with that of the West, indeed that can only become complete when recognized by the West. The search for roots "shifts away from questioning and challenging the existing sociocultural structures (as a politically oppositional move) and hence toward an obsession with the essence — roots — of Chinese culture . . . . This literature's tendency to mystify the past and cultural roots eventually becomes less of a showcase for the diversity in Chinese culture . . . than for one single cultural identity," with extra emphasis placed on its present-day "potency."[92] This search for Chineseness becomes once more the fundamental struggle of modern China: coming to terms with the West and the sense of Chinese national weakness that the modern encounter with the West has engendered. The Chinese intellectual manifesto, as revealed by the search for roots, reveals a consciousness of marginality, but rather than accepting the oppositional possibilities this marginality provides, such writers feel an impetus to relocate the center in a "true" Chinese identity currently at the margins. Their implication in the drive to "march towards the world" and win a Nobel Prize expresses the "need for conviction of China's equivalence to the West" that Levenson found embedded in every modern Chinese theory of Chinese culture.[93]

Stimulating as Zhong's arguments are, they perhaps do not give full due to the movement's complexity, nor to the inevitable slippage between corporate expression of purpose and the actual works produced. Firstly, her portrayal of the Roots Seekers as a unified movement with a corporate, legislated sense of purpose needs to be questioned, and a line should be drawn between official/intellectual identities and critics/writers. In fact, the Roots Seekers were a highly disparate group, each with his or her own reasons for investing in nativist traditions. Han Shaogong now argues that the role of group theorist was imposed upon him by others: "Everyone always talks about 'The Roots of Literature,'" he observed. "But I also wrote lots of other articles, 'The Leaves of Literature' for example. No one ever talks about them."[94] Critics such as Chen Xiaoming and Chen Sihe, meanwhile, believe that there was nothing particularly orchestrated about the Roots Seekers' use of local subject matter; it was a question of having no alternative. These writers had all been classified as "educated youths" and thus had spent their formative years in rural areas. When they returned to the cities at the end of the Cultural Revolution, an inevitable feeling of awkwardness resulted as politics shifted from Maoist peasant mobilization to urban-oriented modernization. While modernist literature of the 1980s emphasized urban consciousness in the writings of Liu Suola (1955–) and others, the returnees had no comparable experience to draw on and inevitably turned back to rural subject matter.[95]

Additionally, language and technique interlock in roots-seeking literature in a way that cannot always be clearly attributed to the politics of foreign influence or national identity. The question of literary aesthetics, Susan Daruvala finds in her study of Zhou Zuoren, is a fruitful way of escaping the normative pressures of the nationalist discourse that has dogged discussion of modern Chinese literature and culture, and of fashioning other kinds of identities in relation to the nation-state. Zhou Zuoren evolved a system of aesthetics whose concern with locality and *fengtu* (social customs and natural conditions) coexisted with a view of Chinese modernity that dissented from the dominant May Fourth intellectual nation-building paradigm, indeed which made the intellectual and political establishment so uncomfortable that he has been continually excluded from the mainstream literary canon in the Mainland. Turning from politics to culture, Zhou suggested the primacy of aesthetic categories such as *quwei* and *bense*: "A writer's work was to be valued to the extent that it evoked the true 'flavor' [*quwei*] of the human and natural worlds, and that depended on his or her ability to perceive and convey it through imagery. *Bense* referred to the ability to develop and impart one's own independent insights and depended on sensitivity to language."[96] A second strand of Zhou's approach lay in his making the locality, rather than the nation, a crucial part of a writer's identity. Zhou's emphasis on the aesthetic effects evoked through locality and by language privileged a more relaxed, tolerant sense of national identity. Departing from nationalistic May Fourth rulings on aesthetics, style, and language, a more open-ended reading of human and aesthetic relations emerges in Zhou's vision of a modern literary sensibility that combined foreign influences and Chinese aesthetic categories without essentializing the national tradition. These aesthetic categories provide philosophical leverage for breaking out of the normative nationalist mode of linking writer and world. An inherent flexibility can be contained within modern Chinese writers' aesthetic yearnings that often clashes painfully with the more cut-and-dried, exclusionary aims of nation(-state) building.

It thus becomes significant that many of the roots-seeking writers were preoccupied particularly with questions of language and with creating and re-creating expressive techniques such as the use of imagery that point "the writer to a more stringent, thoughtful use of language and the reader to new ways of seeing."[97] Rather than an essentialization of tradition, this movement represented a strong statement of rebellion against Maoist normalization of literary language and form, a turning point in the development of post-Mao literary aesthetics. Ah Cheng's (1949–) 1984 novella *Qiwang* (The chess king) made an immediate impact within the literary scene; its relaxed storytelling style was far more evocative of the premodern vernacular than the Europeanized vernacular associated with the Maoist era. Roots-seeking literature bucked modern political controls by making free use of traditional literary forms, for example, the jottings (*biji*) form, in Jia Pingwa's (1953–) collection of Shangzhou stories, *Shangzhou xilie*. Image making, a crucial part of traditional Chinese lyrical aesthetics, was consciously revived by these writers. "It is through reviving the image in modern fiction as a traditional form of aesthetic consciousness," wrote Li Tuo of the Roots Seekers, "that they are attempting to establish a kind of fiction writing that is a Chinese style full of modern consciousness."[98] Airbrushed Maoist narratives were bypassed by a new emphasis on the materiality of bodily needs and the influence of cultural tradition, as in *Qiwang*'s dual focus on food and chess.

Just as David Wang disagrees with evaluations of Shen Congwen's writing as rural romanticism, preferring the more ambivalent expression "imaginary nostalgia," the Roots Seekers did not sentimentalize their impressions of the countryside from the distance of the mid-1980s.[99] At a time when Communist Chinese society was, as ever, being instructed to look forward rather than reflect on the past, the conscious use of literary sources that predated the founding of the CCP and the exploration of the irrational, backward forces of the rural past diverged no little way from the "positive, healthy, and inspiring" qualities that still constituted official criteria for cultural production. As Dai Jinhua has commented: "The narrative of 'marching towards the world' implied development, globalization, historical progress, the way in which we should advance. Roots-seeking literature expressed a feeling of doubt, a feeling that we were entering on a process and that this process wasn't necessarily a joyful one."[100] Roots-seeking writers were torn between two types of distinctly modern consciousness: on the one hand, the widespread desire for China and its literature to join the modern civilized world; and on the other, the unavoidable sense of psychological and aesthetic conflict that emerged with the realization that to do so meant cutting themselves off from their past and their traditions. Theorized as necessarily native and traditional in order to be enjoyed by a modern global readership, the individual aesthetic subject inscribed in roots-seeking literature is continuously struggling against both the orthodox definition of tradition and the demands of an imagined global modernity.

Performing China, Act I

As the Misty Poets and the Roots Seekers were challenging the tidy notion of a modern Chinese literary identity that expressed modernizing socialist ideals, the equivalence drawn between domestic Chinese and international criteria was also disintegrating. It had originally been expected that China's "march towards the world" would be a process in which plaudits in China were echoed by plaudits abroad: that which was validated nationally would be further validated internationally. A 1985 article about Jiang Zilong (an orthodox writer on Dengist reforms, b. 1941) and his prodigious leap to international fame clearly illustrates this assumption. While on a writers' delegation visit to the United States, the article recounts, Jiang Zilong walked into a bookshop and was amazed to find his works on sale there. "Jiang Zilong is the representative of the new generation of Chinese writers. The attention paid to Jiang Zilong has coincided with the astounding speed at which contemporary Chinese literature has 'marched towards the world' in recent years."[101] Jiang Zilong's success abroad was due, apparently, to both the speedy dissemination of his works within China and abroad, and also to the way his works "reflect the ups and downs of China's reforms . . . [these works] possess an irresistible attraction for foreign scholars and readers . . . we can surmise that as time goes on and our national reforms gradually intensify, Jiang Zilong's works will receive ever more attention abroad; therefore, the emergence of a global 'Jiang Zilong fever' is not impossible."[102] The assumption here is that with just a little effort and efficiency, works portraying the new collective, national imaginary of Deng's China and its reforms would attain global acclaim.

This faith in a straightforward 'march towards the world' was largely an extension of enthusiasm left over from Maoism. "One reason for this," Dai Jinhua believes, "was that 'the world' wasn't something very precise, it was something imagined. . . . This started to change between 1985 and 1987, when 'the world' started to become more and more real. . . . Previously, it had always been imagined that what was accepted as good writing in China would be accepted as good writing everywhere; the two were seen as two identical processes."[103] With the emergence mid-decade of the writer Can Xue (1953–) and the director Zhang Yimou, it began to dawn on writers that success in China did not mean success in "the world." Can Xue, renowned for her Kafkaesque fiction during the mid-1980s, was one of the first writers to launch a career in post-Mao China *after* getting translated into foreign languages.[104] Starting with *Red Sorghum* in 1987, Zhang Yimou has made an international (and secondarily domestic) reputation for himself with films viewed as portraying "the true China" in the West but often severely criticized at home. By the late 1980s, the contrast between Zhang and his onetime fellow student, colleague, and later rival, Chen Kaige (1952–), provided a revealing and instructive lesson to Chinese intellectuals and artists concerned about winning global audiences. Zhang Yimou's films — in particular those that made his name as an international director — *Red Sorghum, Raise the Red Lantern*, and *Judou* — are unapologetically ethnographic, verging on Orientalist, a fact that has generated suspicion that he is making films to suit the tastes of foreigners. Chen Kaige's more esoteric films of the same period, such as *King of the Children*, adopted a critical, questioning stance toward Chinese tradition that echoed that of many roots-seeking works of literature and proved far more palatable to Chinese critics. Yet while Chen's films were winning him the dubious plaudit of "the philosophical director" at home, they were failing to win him any international awards.[105] The contrast between the levels of success these two directors achieved with overseas audiences punctured the universalistic aspirations of many post-Mao writers, seriously undermining their hopes of joining an idealized and liberating creative realm where art was ruled by autonomous aesthetic values harmoniously fused with national characteristics. It was at this time, remembered Dai Jinhua,

> that writers and artists began to become aware of the close connection between China and their own identity, that it was like a part of their bodies when they stood before the world. They realized that they weren't independent artists. Before, they felt, "I'm an artist and I write in China. If I write well, the world will recognize me." Moreover, at that time, they wanted to break away from China and politics, to feel "I'm *not* writing for China." Then they discovered they couldn't break away from it. . . . Zhang Yimou showed that you could be a successful artist in the West, but that it was related to your status as a Chinese — it felt very contradictory. Zhang Yimou was successful because he was Chinese, but it was almost as if he wasn't a Chinese director. His films didn't appear in China and he didn't care what Chinese viewers thought of them. So "China" became something artificial, something to be performed.[106]

It was discussion of the Nobel Prize that even earlier had indicated a discrepancy between domestic and international recognition. Göran Malmqvist's speech at the Jinshan Conference in 1986 made two things clear. Firstly, as a representative of the Nobel Committee, he was far more interested in Shen Congwen and the Misty Poets than in China's official candidates. Secondly, translation was of paramount importance to any author who aspired to win the Nobel Prize. If the first point cooled the enthusiasm of Chinese officialdom, the second undermined the idealistic equation of a world readership and a Chinese audience in the minds of Chinese writers, making the issue of "national identity" in world literature far more problematic. If, as Malmqvist has frequently repeated since 1986, the main obstacle China faces in competing for a Nobel is the problem of translation, then the very use of the Chinese language must be factored into China's inability to produce "great" or "world" writers (as defined by Nobel recognition).[107] Writing in Chinese is the mainstay of Chinese literary identity; equally, however, it is one of the obstacles between Chinese writers and world recognition.

"Other writers are always asking me how authors like Rushdie can be successful in the West," said Li Dawei (1963–), a writer and graduate of an English department. Rather than drawing the conclusion that his use of English helps and that they could learn more from Chinese writers like Ha Jin who also write in English, "they don't consider them Chinese writers: Jung Chang [the author of *Wild Swans*, who writes in English] doesn't count for anything."[108]

Ha Jin's PEN/Faulkner Prize in 2000 for his novel *Waiting* was instant news in Beijing; equally, however, few Chinese literary intellectuals would admit he was a Chinese writer. Ha Jin's choosing to write in English about uncomfortably "orientalized" subject matter such as bound feet made him the plaything of foreigners. "After the Roots Seekers and experimentalist writers," says Dai Jinhua, "it was clear that the quality of literature derived from its language. On the other hand, the better the language, the harder it is to reproduce in translation and introduce to the world."[109] Dai Jinhua's comments imply it is not just the use of Chinese that hinders translation; it is the way in which Chinese is used, the range of aesthetic techniques (including imagery, *bense*, *quwei*) and the effects evoked that hinder the straightforward transferral of meanings. This further validates the importance of the Roots Seekers as engineers of the collapse of equivalences between intellectual-official and national-international literary identities during the 1980s.

It was precisely the tension between Chinese literature and Chinese literature-in-the-world that Stephen Owen addressed in his criticisms of Bei Dao's "translation poetry." In 1990 Owen claimed that Bei Dao (for years the most prominent Chinese candidate for the Nobel) courted international constituencies with his easily translatable "political virtue" and "local color"; these, he argued, were based in a superficial reading of Western romanticism and modernism and only worked to the detriment of Chinese aesthetics.[110] But amidst his sweeping pronouncements about Chinese poetic modernity, Owen raised important questions about the consequences of a world (i.e., Western) cultural market that is supported by the translation industry, and whose arbiters are the judges of the Nobel Prize for Literature. Owen acknowledged Bei Dao's talent but regretted that interest in the world literary economy was turning poetry into an international traveler, with the luggage of poetic values and traditions lost in transit. This was, moreover, a literary economy marked by inequalities of cultural capital, Owen noted:

> By writing a supremely translatable poetry, by the good fortune of a gifted translator and publicist, he may well attain in the West the absolute preeminence that he cannot quite attain in China itself. And the very fact of wide foreign (Western) recognition could, in turn, grant him preeminence in China. Thus we would have the strange phenomenon of a poet who became the leading poet in his own country because he translated well.[111]

Owen's criticisms highlight the difficulties experienced by Chinese writers as they struggle to reach global audiences and impress the Nobel judges, raising the all-important questions of literary technique and craft. Following a century in which Chinese writers have endlessly imported and studied foreign techniques, what can now be considered sufficiently "Chinese" to maintain its distinctiveness in a world literary economy made up of translations? Ethnographic detail is insufficient to satisfy all constituencies. For example, China's nativist roots-seeking authors have not attained the quick international success of their cinematic counterparts, the Fifth Generation. Moreover, ethnographic color is viewed as deeply problematic in the Chinese postcolonial mindset, exemplified by the resentment Zhang Yimou's work has generated in China, where it is proclaimed to be *zuo gei waiguo ren kan* (made for the gaze of foreigners).[112] Interestingly, Rey Chow views the complexity of Zhang Yimou's cinematic ethnography as going far beyond straightforward Orientalism. Translation between the languages and cultures of East and West, Talal Asad has noted, is shot through with inequalities, due to the "unequal power encounter between the West and Third World, which goes back to the emergence of bourgeois Europe."[113] But by invoking the idea of a multidirectional "gaze" integral to the cinematic experience — the gaze of the creative director, of the viewer (Chinese or Western), of the figures on screen that both command the audience's gaze and return it — Chow finds in Zhang's films a fruitful new way of envisioning the implied passive/active balance of power between the object/viewer. The immediacy of the medium, underlined by the primitive nature of many of the themes used by the Fifth Generation, is a powerful and empowering way of communicating ideas about nation and people — not just to foreigners but also to the Chinese audience. Through his exaggerated use of exotica and fictionalized ethnography, Zhang Yimou's films undermine the basic tenet of Orientalism (to gaze upon, encroach upon, and know a passive East) by making the object of our gaze *knowing*: for example, when Judou consciously decides to allow Tianqing to peep at her nakedness. Zhang's knowing self-exhibitionism undermines any pretence to incontrovertible realism or ethnographic accuracy.[114]

Literature, needless to say, relies on a range of techniques very different from that of cinema, and international success depends predominantly on the mediation of translation. To create appeal in a work of literature that rivals the directness of film for an international audience means in most cases emulating "international" (i.e., Western) cinematographic techniques in literary terms — through skillful combination of "local color" with easily translatable techniques such as liberal use of imagery, through reliance on expert cultural brokers such as Western translators, agents, and publicists, or simply by writing directly into Western languages. All such devices tend to affirm the "superiority" of Western languages and expectations of cultural production.

Nevertheless, to the end of the 1980s, it seemed possible that the divergence between international and national tastes could be resolved thanks to the re-

CHAPTER FOUR

spect accorded to Western acclaim. There was, for example, a resurgence of interest in Shen Congwen (rumored to be the leading Nobel candidate in the mid-1980s, up until his death in 1988) in both literary (for example, among the roots-seeking writers) and official circles: *Wenyi bao* even publicized the upgrading of his living conditions (such as his moving to a better apartment) in 1986.[115] But 1989 represented a watershed in the constitution of the Chinese literary field which, with the emergence of a group of prominent dissident exiles, became more nationally and internationally fragmented than ever before, creating new tensions in relation to Chinese literature's presence on a global stage. True enough, expectations for a Chinese Nobel Prize until 2000 continued to hover uncertainly around Bei Dao who, though in exile, possessed broadly national, symbolic value as leader of the first artistically liberating literary movement to rise to prominence after Mao's death. But the outcome of the Nobel Prize in 2000 exacerbated rather than resolved these ongoing divisions in the Chinese literary world. Beneath the euphoria that a Chinese person had won the Nobel lay a reservoir of baffled resentment that someone so totally cut off from China and its literary scene had been chosen as a global representative of Chinese literature.

The 1990s: Back to the Margins

If assumptions concerning the centrality of intellectual culture to national modernization underpinned the Nobel discourse of the 1980s, their fate in the 1990s had an equal bearing on attitudes towards the Nobel Prize. Intellectuals, and writers in particular, were dislodged from their role as forgers of a new national consciousness following the demise of the intellectual liberalism at the center fostered by Hu Yaobang (1913–1989) in the 1980s. In theoretical terms, the opposition between China and the West (China as the civilizational other of the West, awaiting its moment to rise up and be recognized as such) was undermined by the introduction of postmodernism and postcolonialism into Chinese intellectual life, and by the increasing influence of globalization within China through the socialist market economy. According to critics such as Zhang Yiwu, the "Post-New Era," starting in 1990, marked the beginning of new possibilities for a third-world nation with a developing market economy, which included reevaluating the "idea of modernity" through opposition to Western reason, history, and subjectivity.[116] Did this mean the end of the Nobel Complex and the Chinese obsession with winning recognition from the West?

The radical critic Wang Hui is doubtful of how much far-reaching intellectual change took place in the 1990s, asserting the absence of fundamentally fresh critical considerations of the idea of modernization, which in China was still envisioned as an equal encounter between China and the West. Of the late 1990s, he writes, "Chinese intellectuals are now engaged in discussions of the question of globalization. Most of them, however, understand globalization within the context of the Confucian ideal of universal harmony . . . this type of universalism is nothing more than another version of the century-long modernist dream of 'meeting the world' (really, 'meeting the West')."[117]

Furthermore, there is little sign that nation building, China's most significant import from Western modernity, took any kind of a backseat in 1990s China. If anything, nationalism was on the rise, as indicated by the enormous popularity of TV series such as *Beijing ren zai Niuyue* (A Beijinger in New York).[118] Politicians, intellectuals, and ordinary people believed that although China had produced an economic miracle in a short time, it had still failed to achieve the global recognition it deserved. Meanwhile, the West was demonized as the prejudiced cause of all China's troubles. Yet these feelings intensified the desire for recognition from external sources, rather than nullifying it. The strong sense that the world/the West owed China something "came to the fore during China's Olympic bid in 1993 when mainland media called on the rest of the world to 'give China a chance.'"[119] Intellectual developments mirrored popular opinion: postmodern and postcolonial theorists emphasized a unique notion of "Chineseness" while blaming China's ills in the modern era on the influence of alien Western culture — a simple formula for antiforeign nationalism. Thus, old binaries — official vs. unofficial identities, high vs. low — blurred, as feelings of nationalism ran high alongside worship of American-style global capitalism, and intellectuals embraced a mass culture entangled with state ideology.

This amalgam of ideological and cultural forces in the 1990s can be seen in developments in the Nobel Complex. Although pursuit of a Nobel Prize ceased to be official policy after 1989, continuing discussion indicated that the desire for international recognition had by no means dissipated. As popular culture marginalized and encroached upon elite literature, the Nobel Complex entered the realm of mass culture and became a subject for media spin, taken up by journalists or critics attempting to make literature a newsworthy subject once more. Despite this hubbub, neither officialdom nor writers continued to fixate on the Nobel Prize as before. Recognizing that it could probably do little to determine any Nobel outcome, the state instead shifted its highest-profile efforts to achieve international recognition to the sporting, scientific, and economic spheres: the Olympic Games for Beijing and the Nobel science and economics prizes, for example. For writers, meanwhile, the advent of a Chinese mass culture made certain questions of brute economics more pressing than thoughts of Nobel glory. Even if the wealth and prestige of Western markets could still attract writers, the effects of globalization and commercialization within China brought with them the means to achieve these desirable goals other than through aspiring for the Nobel. Yet the desire for a position in world literature and for the ideal of a universal literary standard (symbolized by the Nobel Prize) was intensified in some writers by a siege mentality resulting from the pressures of commercialism. The 1990s thus undermined the status of Chinese literature, leaving writers and critics bemused and resentful at their turn in fortune: some writers became more pragmatic, others pinned their hopes even more on the ideal of a universal aesthetic, on representing the nation through winning a Nobel Prize. Whatever strategy was adopted, suspicions continued to run rife that everyone had the complex: writers suspected the critics who kept the complex spinning in public discourse; critics suspected China's writers of angling for the prize and for international recognition.

Critics Debate the Nobel Prize

Critical debates around the Nobel Prize in 1990s academic journals covered a broad spectrum: postcolonial readings of its Eurocentrism; discussions of the Nobel Prize as a literary United Nations or as a great literary family recording "the cultural consciousness of modern humanity";[120] and, above all, rationalizations of China's failure to win Nobel laurels and repeated calls for a Nobel Prize winner to represent Chinese civilization in the world.

As knowledge of the prize grew, so did awareness of the extraliterary networking necessary, for example efforts made by the Japanese government to ensure that the Western literary world came to appreciate Japanese literature. "So that Kawabata should win the prize," wrote Zhao Li, "the Japanese government specially arranged that the 1968 PEN meeting should take place in Tokyo; at the same time it invited a member of the Swedish Academy to visit Japan and diligently engaged in a whole series of publicizing activities."[121] Such knowledge led not so much to skepticism, as to pleas for renewed efforts on the part of the Chinese government towards winning the prize. Under normal circumstances, the idea of directly imitating the Japanese example would have appeared to Chinese commentators uncomfortably craven, but the general absence of such objections in Chinese discussions of the need to learn from Japanese success suggests that the strength of the Chinese yearning for a Nobel overrode even the usual nationalistic edginess of modern Chinese attitudes toward Japan.[122] Although some commentators remarked rather sourly on the extraliterary factors that had helped Japan win a Nobel — namely, its global influence due to economic growth — the dominant response of critics was one of admiration for the literary achievements of Kawabata and Oe, and of an earnest desire to learn from the Japanese Nobel success.[123]

But rather than reflecting the centrality of literature to the national modernizing project, these campaign manifestos instead betrayed an almost desperate consciousness of literature's new marginality. The stress laid on the centrality of the Nobel Literature Prize to twentieth-century civilization and national liberation was far more revealing of the psychology of Chinese commentators than of the actual importance of the prize itself within and without China. While some critics railed throughout the 1990s that China should produce a Nobel winner to enlighten both nation and world, the rest of Chinese society was busy "looking forward/towards money" (*wang qian kan*), and many Chinese writers were joining in the capitalist free-for-all. Literary production was no longer concerned with the idealism or national enlightenment preached in articles about the Nobel Prize; writers instead pursued commercial profit. Articles calling for renewed government efforts to promote Chinese literature worldwide indicated a desire for literary questions (and thus literary critics) to be reinstated as central to national affairs. As the novelist Li Feng recalls, though few writers were interested in the Nobel Prize in the 1990s,

> every critic worried about it. Criticism and fiction have a complementary relationship: if fiction has no influence, criticism will have even less influence. So critics were all very anxious: they felt that novelists were hopeless and tried to draw ordinary people's attention to literature by talking about the Nobel Prize, because ordinary people all knew about the Nobel Prize.[124]

In tune with growing nationalism, Nobel discussions often reverberated with a new patriotic pride. China's lack of a Nobel Prize, Cai Yi wrote in 1995, "has puzzled and astonished the peoples of many countries; it has also made countless Chinese writers fume with anger or become tongue-tied with shame."[125] In addition to the old-style China-meets-the-West self-approbatory visions of China's deserved position in world literature came postcolonial readings of relations between China and the Nobel Prize. In 1992 Wang Hongtu asserted that China's lack of a laureate was not due simply to problems of translation or exchange, but to Western hegemony. "The cold-shouldering of China by the Nobel Prize [Committee] is the inevitable result of Western-centrism in the global cultural structure."[126] In the development of modern Chinese literature, "because the power of foreign literature has been too great, the native literary tradition has had no way of producing its own rich, vital literary discourse, thus for the time being it can only use foreign forms to express the national life and emotions of the New Era."[127] Tagore's winning of the Nobel Prize, Wang considered, was a sobering reminder of the hazards of Western cultural imperialism. Acclaimed by the Nobel Committee as "a part of the literature of the West," Tagore was absorbed into the oppressive literary discourse of the West.[128]

The significance of this critical development should not be overlooked: Wang had seen through the idealized vision of a universal world literature, exposing the predicament of writers from the non-West. Recognition from the West, he realized, would not alter the fact of cultural hegemony; indeed, it results to a greater or lesser degree in that writer being expropriated by and strengthening the Western value system dominant in world literature. Yet while Wang's insights provided a postcolonial reading of East-West cultural dynamics, his remarks were still locked into that familiar conundrum of Chinese modernity: they ultimately addressed (and so accepted) the Western gaze as arbiter of value in the world of letters. His appeal for Chinese literary intellectuals to create their own literary discourse seemed in the end aimed at winning the respect of foreigners. "If ancient Chinese literature can still inspire Westerners through its intrinsically creative qualities, then contemporary Chinese literature, as an echo of the West . . . will have great difficulty stimulating deep interest."[129] Such was the quandary faced even by skeptical analysts of the world literary economy.

Writers Turn Elsewhere

This activity on the part of critics appears to have had relatively little influence on writers themselves. After a decade of unrequited love for the Nobel and the realization that literature was no longer an issue central to the national modernizing project, pragmatic writers began to turn their attention to domestic economic matters. As the market economy took off in the 1990s, the government began to phase out the iron rice bowl (the communist promise of a salary for life to its state-sponsored writers). In the new economic climate, the novelist Wang Shuo (1958–) led the way in showing writers how to profit from their pens, repackaging his words as songs, screenplays, and television shows.[130] With the literary market flooded by commercial entertainment products (love stories from Taiwan, kung-fu novels from Hong Kong), some novelists abandoned literature almost completely. One of the most prominent examples is Zhang Xianliang (1936–): acclaimed in the 1980s as China's Milan Kundera for his novels on sex and the Chinese gulag, he started his own film studio in north China in the 1990s.

The growth of mass consumer culture not only marginalized but also encroached upon high culture. Jia Pingwa's 1993 novel, *Feidu* (The ruined capital), was one of the first and most notorious cases of a serious writer surrendering to sensationalism.[131] A Roots Seeker in the 1980s, Jia Pingwa's themes in *Feidu* are a revealing portrait of provincial literati and of intellectual reactions to the times. Jia combined depiction of the greed and hypocrisy in a decaying contemporary Chinese city with graphic emphasis on the sexual exploits of his hero, Zhuang Zhidie, a famous middle-aged writer. Jia's portrayal of a male writer's spermatic journey through the spiritual corruption of contemporary China gave voice to intellectuals' feelings of malaise and their struggle to reassert themselves during the early 1990s, making the novel an heir to the lingering marginality complex of the 1980s. *Feidu* formulated one strategy for coping with the 1990s version of the complex: making money. The novel was rumored to have sold up to several million copies by the end of 1993.[132] Despite its explicit sexual content, the Chinese authorities failed to ban it until 1994, when the sensation it caused was in any case dying down; Jia Pingwa himself was not persecuted. The political message was clear: sex and sensation meant high sales figures and high sales figures promoted state ideology, "to get rich is glorious."

Just as 1993 saw the emergence of a new recipe for domestic success with *Feidu*, it marked also an adjustment in views of Chinese literature's route to the world. Zhang Yimou hired five well-known authors to write novels on the Empress Wu to serve as the basis of a screenplay; a sixth author, offended to be left out, wrote one anyway. A television drama on the Empress that year also produced a book. Thus, seven books on the subject were produced, all hoping to cash in on the gold mine represented by Zhang's path to world recognition. What this phenomenon reveals is not a resolution of the divergence between national and international recognition first highlighted by Zhang's career in the 1980s, but a new cynical pragmatism that pervaded Chinese society, and the literary world in particular, resulting in part from the confusion and disillusionment generated by the Tian'anmen repression. In the eyes of some critics in China, the previously anti-Orientalist Chen Kaige apparently embraced Zhang's exoticist approach to wooing international audiences, directed *Farewell My Concubine*, a sumptuous historical saga about life and death at the Peking opera (starring Zhang's leading lady Gong Li) through the twentieth century, and picked up the Palme d'Or at Cannes. "After *Farewell My Concubine* won the Cannes prize, I no longer had any faith in film prizes, because this film was made for the film world, for their prize," said Dai Jinhua. "After I'd seen the film, I laughed . . . because it had all the elements needed to win the prize, and then it actually won. I thought, you can't give the prize to someone for sucking up to you like that."[133] Finally, 1993 was the year in which many novelists turned to writing television and film scripts. "There were two reasons for this," analyzed Dai Jinhua. "Some wanted to follow Zhang Yimou's path to international renown. But even more people did it for the money."

> I think that Yu Hua's *Huozhe* (To live) had elements of this; as soon as Yu Hua had written it, before it had even been officially published, he gave it to Zhang Yimou . . . After the news that Zhang Yimou wanted to film it came out, European publishers immediately asked Yu Hua for the rights. Writers adapted by Zhang Yimou became the most famous writers in China, famous among nonliterary people. They had the world's attention; Europe and America took notice. That's what the relations between China and the world turned into.[134]

Not everyone rejoiced at this development, and postcolonialists were more than ready to criticize Zhang Yimou's techniques. In 1995 Zhang Rongyi blamed Zhang Yimou for perpetuating inequalities within world literature. "So-called 'world literature' today is based on Western standards; in this system, after third-world literature has been 'encoded' as 'other' by the West, it is often twisted or understood in a distorted way. This 'encoding' forces the literatures of all third-world countries to detach themselves from tradition and lose their capacity to reflect national characteristics, thus increasing their tendency towards otherness."[135] Zhang Yimou's simulacra of real local customs "in fact . . . are fake customs," complained Zhang Rongyi, "Westerners now expect China to be a rural society, while descriptions of city life are considered to be too 'Westernized.'"[136] Like Wang Hongtu in 1992, Zhang Rongyi broke through the idealistic vision of China as one nation among many equals, resulting in a more clear-sighted understanding of China's predicament in global culture: "If Chinese literature wants to 'march towards the world,' this isn't moving towards a homogenized world in which each country has a neutral, equal position; it is a world largely encoded by Western others. Zhang Yimou's success lies in his finding the secret of success in this code."[137]

Zhang Rongyi's comments point to the understandable wish to attain some degree of overlap between the contemporary Chinese experience and views of China on the global stage, at that moment dominated by Zhang Yimou's images of a backward, exotic past. Such a demand, however, risked placing writers and artists in thrall to a new, contemporary essentialization of "China." Rey Chow's analysis of Zhang Yimou's "self-orientalizing" views his fictionalization of Chinese tradition as a technique for subverting the binaries of East/West national identity, rendering all such essentializations inauthentic. Zhang Rongyi, however, allowed for no such nuance in his belief that ultimately there was a "genuine" China to be portrayed, in opposition to Zhang Yimou's simulacra. His analysis carried revealing echoes of the male marginality complex—insisting on a strong, "true" Chinese identity and likening Zhang Yimou's inauthentic images of China to the "feminization" of male prostitution. Moreover, while protesting the unequal distribution of cultural capital in the world, Zhang Rongyi only wished to reorder the world hierarchy to the extent that it granted China equality with the West, *not* with other marginal cultures. He remarked with distaste of China's "encoding" as the Other, that "China has been placed in a position near that of African blacks and Indian aboriginal culture."[138] The postmodern maelstrom of commercialization and postcolonialism notwithstanding, the belief in China as the civilizational Other of the West and the quest for the *echt* China lived on.

Exile Writing and the Poetics of Disorientation: Performing China, Act II

One development that kept the Nobel Complex evolving in the 1990s was the emergence of a group of exiled writers in the West and the subsequent exacerbation of difference between national and international aesthetic identities that resulted. Hostility quickly developed between writers still working in China and those in exile—both of whom had become marginal within the national political unit post-1989 — concerning who could best represent China on a world stage. A writer who "is forever floating internationally with the express aim of becoming a writer of world stature," commented Wang Lijiu pointedly in 1992, "is at best a rootless freak," and his works are "like airplane food, a totally flavorless international mixed platter."[139] "China" had long been written outside the geographical center of the Mainland by, for example, writers based in Taiwan or foreigners such as Pearl Buck. The exiles, however, threatened a new rivalry to the claims and capacity of Mainland writers to represent the Chinese nation, thanks to their Mainland background, their residence in the West, and the international media spotlight that focused on them after the events of 1989. They were given an automatic head start in the international arena by the networking, publishing and translation opportunities available to them overseas (opportunities they had to develop to survive in a foreign environment) and by Western audiences' comfortable latent sense that the exiles, by the fact of their leaving Communist China, had acknowledged the inexorable logic of Western victory in the Cold War.

In the post-Tiananmen world, it was exiled writers—three of the best known being Bei Dao, Gao Xingjian, and Yang Lian—who always stood the best chance of winning a Nobel Prize. Göran Malmqvist had begun translating Misty Poets such as Bei Dao in the early 1980s, and many exiles spent time in Stockholm shortly after leaving China. Having been refounded in Oslo in 1990 as a forum for writers in exile, the underground magazine *Jintian* (Today) moved to the Swedish capital in 1991. Praising Bei Dao and Yang Lian highly in a 1990 interview, Nobel Committee member Göran Malmqvist, who is also Gao Xingjian's translator, commented, "It is quite obvious that there is growing now in China and perhaps even more so among the exiled Chinese writers a very first class literature, and sooner or later that literature will have to be rewarded . . . it really is high time that a Chinese got the Literary Nobel Prize."[140] Writers in China have been well aware of this phenomenon and have registered objections to the way exiled writers came to be regarded as representatives of China, even though some have been out of China for well over a decade and have not contributed to the evolving literary scene of the Mainland. "Exiled writers become internationalized," considered the poet Ouyang Jianghe (1956–). "They're filling a quota, they're willing to say that they're a Chinese voice. Every year, a British or American newspaper will publish an article and they'll always call on them. They become representatives of China, but I put a big question mark by this."[141]

This role as representatives (or performers) of China for the West has proved problematic also to exiled writers themselves, who have struggled against the limited political definitions of Chineseness that are an inescapable part of how they make their living abroad. During the 1990s, it became increasingly difficult for dissident poets to achieve any kind of artistic voice independent of their political significance, that of representing an oppressed China. Maghiel van Crevel has revealed the politicized workings of the Western marketing machine behind the poet Duo Duo (1951–) and others. Ignoring the title chosen by Duo Duo's translators, the publishers dubbed his 1989 poetry collection *Looking Out From Death: From the Cultural Revolution to Tian'anmen Square*, imposing narrow political limits on Duo Duo's significance as a poet.[142] The exiles' predicament was expressed in 1998 by the poet Yang Lian, who relative to other Chinese authors commands a strong media presence in Great Britain. He was rumored to have been a likely candidate for the 1998 Nobel Prize.

> Of all the Chinese brand names which sell well in the West, the most conspicuous and best-selling is Chinese politics. For Westerners, if a Chinese writer writes in China, he must be "underground"; if he lives abroad, he must be an "exile." If a Chinese poet is introduced to a Western audience, as soon as the word "dissident" is mentioned, the audience immediately relaxes—the poet's opponents have guaranteed that the poem must be good.[143]

In the late 1990s, Yang Lian spoke out against this mode of reception with criticisms of many of his fellow writers and contemporary Chinese poetry generally, in which he outlined the "exotic localism" plus "political virtue" trap. He saw only two terms for literature in the new period: "5000 years" (namely, superficial, exotic Chineseness) and "Communist Party" (namely, a force against which writers appear in sensationally heroic relief when telling their stories of political repression).[144] For Yang, the superficiality of Western reception was further tainted by the influence of the market. "It is even rumored that Western literary agents have defined 'Chinese pain' as a product," he wrote, "because a profit can be made from it."[145] Although Yang spared no one in his criticism — neither writers in exile nor those in the Mainland — these questions were of particular relevance to exiled authors who, despite enjoying a status of momentarily heady interest to the Western media, soon had to make independent sense of their position as Chinese writers in the West. Cut off from their linguistic homeland, how should they maintain a rapport with their own culture? What should they write about, and for whom? "Is exile literature defined by its author's being in exile?" ponders Maghiel van Crevel, considering contemporary Chinese poets. "Do all authors in exile write exile literature? Can they write anything else?...Is exile literature political by nature, directly or by implication?"[146] Yang Lian felt strongly that literature directly about exile, just like literature directly about the Cultural Revolution, was of limited value. The Cultural Revolution, he asserted, should not offer writers simply the thematic opportunity to describe politics, but rather a platform to explore the horizons of mental possibilities, not to construct tales of heroic resistance but to portray enduring psychological reality.[147] The impasse that Yang felt Chinese writing had reached poses familiar questions: how can Chinese literature be valorized in the world while preserving its artistic integrity, originality, and particularity? This is once more the struggle of the autonomous aesthetic ideal versus the demands of a national imaginary that have continued to loom large not only for modern Chinese literature but also in the very conceptualization of world literature.

Yang Lian reacted against the current sociopolitical specificity of Chinese literature by developing a theory of the uniqueness of the Chinese language related not to boxed-in categories of political virtue or cute Chinoiserie, but rather to its capacity to "delete time" (*quxiao shijian*). Although language that records concrete happenings risks giving up its open-ended qualities and becoming overly concrete, Yang considered that the nonspecificity of Chinese (which can omit verbal tense and subject markers) inherently retains a degree of abstraction. For Yang, the Chinese language served as a perfectly efficient linguistic bridge between reality and imagination, capturing all time and space without being tied down to specifics.[148] Yang hoped that this vastness of vision would enable his poetry to take off from the commodified, predictable corner to which post-Mao Chinese poetics had been confined. A poet fascinated by the long reach of tradition, Yang believed language and poetry should constitute a totality of time and space, using all possible means at their disposal (visual, aural, musical, structural). Yang aimed at a global, universal literary perspective.

His theories have been embodied in a series of long poems or poem cycles, culminating at the end of the 1990s with two collections, *Da hai tingzhi zhi chu* (Where the sea stands still) and *Tongxinyuan* (Concentric circles).[149] Yang set out his central aims thus:

> Tradition and modernity: how can we accomplish a modern transformation of China's cultural (including poetic) tradition?
> - China and the West: where does Chinese literature stand in today's world?
> - The "depth" and "originality" of creative work: what in the end is the perceived value and standing of modern Chinese poetry?[150]

These are complex and ambitious goals which, as the roots-seeking manifesto did earlier, address the question of Chinese aesthetic identity in world literature. What kind of literature, however, results from Yang's reaction against political and aesthetic pressures? Yang has produced a poetry preoccupied with enormous themes: the position of the "I" in the universe, the inescapable approach of death, the mystery of the past, the interplay of dream and material reality. The idea of synchronic form plays a central role in achieving these expansive goals in his poetry, not only through the grammatical and ideogrammatic nature of the Chinese language but also in the structures he employs, in the way that images and lines are chosen and combined; it is thus reproduced in translation.[151] His poetry gives the reader few clues, flinging objects and images together. The significance of his images and symbols remains constantly fluid, dependent on context and juxtapositions. The reader is confronted with an authorial perspective that leaps nonsequentially between disjointed images and mutating forms. Although his is clearly a highly personal poetry, the path by which personal experience becomes poetic material is often abstruse and quasi-metaphysical.

Yang is therefore asserting a poetics of disorientation, of "pure" literary intent, which attempts to obliterate all recognizable signifiers of a limited historical or artistic shelf life that Yang thinks a reader might expect to find in modern Chinese poetry. His confusing lines contain neither Chinoiserie nor easily deciphered political associations. Yang wishes to avoid producing a poetry that will pander to clichéd expectations and to devote himself to the boundless terrain of pure, universal poetics. But in his struggle to do this, he goes so far as to lose the reader. The purity of message often results from the reader's simple inability to follow the sense of his meaning and therefore from the impossibility of projecting any kind of meaning onto it, "impure" or otherwise.

Almost all the poems in his 1998 collection *Where the Sea Stands Still* bear the hallmarks of Yang's obscure poetics, with their lack of historical and geographical specifics, leaps of temporal and spatial perspective, unremittingly surreal descriptions, bizarre material transformations, and indecipherable images: "sharks with sinister intent climb trees behind your back"; "flowers book operations to come."[152] One example from within the collection suffices to illustrate how Yang's quest for a disoriented purity results in pure disorientation. The four-poem cycle of the title, "Where the Sea Stands Still," takes a panoramic view of the sea, which serves as symbol for the world, even the universe. It juxtaposes the limited view taken by humans, hemmed in by cliffs, with the boundless reality of the ocean. Through it, Yang aims to take in the vastness of time and space. A unifying theme emerges over the course of the cycle, concerning the halting of time, the fleeing of time, the repetition of time, its denial, irreversibility, and finality, until he reaches a climax of realization relevant to all humans: that we are all alone in death.

> Who accompanies you to the brink of every one of your deaths
> who says   the only harvested stone
> makes the sea sink down to the level of your own water
> as you look   birdsong sounds only like a funeral dirge
> you listen   but dream of the ocean's deep red book jacket
> lodged on the windowsill
> nightmares subject you to a yet more critical reading
> corpses are stuffed with chalk re-remembered
> who enjoys with you this mournful distance
>
> is now furthest away[153]

In this extract the first and last two lines convey a simple and direct truth: the fact that each of us must face our own death in isolation. What comes in between is disorienting and surreal, and makes jumps that could cause the reader to give up before the crucial part of the poetic message is reached.

The questions that Yang Lian has raised about literature and poetry are important, yet he has perhaps set the objectives too high, in view of the difficult path that modern Chinese poetry treads. 1990s poets found themselves at a crossroads regarding their aims, audience, and aesthetic standards. On one side they faced demands for a kind of political virtue and exotica that fit the expectations of Western audiences, on the other, were the demands of doing justice to lived experience and their language art. Yang writes within a context in which thoughtful Chinese writers are ever more apprehensive of the confines of a new "obsession with China" now thrust upon them not just by internal political circumstances but by the view of Chinese literature dominant in the world literary economy. But while Yang's poetics of disorientation have escaped the traps of political virtue and poetic Chinoiserie and assert the translatable vitality and individuality of the Chinese language within world literature, the incomprehension that it may produce is an equally imprisoning state.

Yang Lian's advocacy of a "pure," hard, but strongly Chinese poetry to gain entrance to the modern realm of universal artistic validity is only one of the most recent demonstrations of the faith modern Chinese literary intellectuals continue to have in the power of the autonomous aesthetic to smooth over the contradictions between national and international aspirations. But poets who remained in China in the 1990s were deeply distrustful of the political implications of the exiles' aesthetic solutions: on one hand they had broken free of the nation, but on the other, they are forever tied to China since to some extent they must rely on their Chinese identity to make a living in the West. Bei Dao and Yang Lian, Ouyang Jianghe considered, have each come to represent a different but equally "inauthentic" approach to the question of representing Chinese poetry in the world. Bei Dao, for instance, "uses a language that's easily translated." Ouyang continues:

> [There is also] another sort of language, one that is particularly Chinese, full of classical Chinese elements, of strongly eastern characteristics. But this is a China that comes from the Western understanding of China, the China that the West is willing to understand, a classical, imperial, exotic China. Take Yang Lian: although he's tried so hard to bring so many Chinese things into his poetry, it's not written for Chinese readers . . . this isn't the China of Chinese people, it's the China of Westerners.[154]

Yet despite their criticism of exiles — which could be challenged on various counts[155] — Mainland poets have come no closer to resolving the tensions between the autonomous aesthetic and national identity, indeed many have adopted strategies similar to those of Yang Lian. Whether written in the Mainland or in exile, Chinese poetry became almost universally more obscure during the 1990s, glorifying the autonomous, independent voice of the poet. This exacerbated a growing estrangement from the reading public: since the 1990s, it has been often observed that there are more writers than readers of poetry in China. While "pure" literature in all shapes and forms was increasingly sidelined during the 1990s, no genre suffered a more dramatic demotion than poetry. Yet avant-garde poets were not straightforwardly accepting of this marginal status: they cultivated an identity and consciousness in which "poetry is not just a private and personal endeavor of a creative and spiritual nature; rather, it is elevated to being the supreme ideal in life and a religious faith."[156]

This stance taken by contemporary poets highlights again the workings of the marginality complex in the construction of national and literary identities. Poets have displayed a consciousness of marginality through their verse, whose obscurity has completed the divorce between poetry and a narrow, nation-state-defined realism first envisioned by the Misty Poets; yet this is a marginality that views itself as a powerful alternative to the political, social, and economic status quo, and that now looks abroad for validation. Although avant-garde poets (in particular, the so-called "intellectual," *zhishifenzi*, poets, such as Ouyang Jianghe and Wang Jiaxin (1957–) clearly feel a strong spiritual kinship with foreign poets and with the idea of an autonomous poetry, theirs is also very much a Romantic vision of the poet as both solitary hero floating above the gritty sociopolitical realm of contemporary reality *and* representative of the nation. Hence the conflict with exile writers. Just as Mainland poets feel that contemporary China is an integral part of their poetic and personal profiles and as they admire leading Western poets (once more, juxtaposing national and international identities), they also feel *their* China is not the one the West is determined to see:

> If the West has one representative for China, Bei Dao, then that's enough. . . . A lot of people are only interested in Chinese politics, in China as a great dictatorship. If they don't see politics in poetry they're not interested. A journalist interviewed me in Venice and asked me "Why are your poems so different from Chinese films? Films are really Chinese." They thought I was too internationalized. I replied with a quotation from Borges: "Mohammed doesn't need a camel to be an Arab." From my poems, you can see I'm a Chinese person, but I'm not a traditional person, I'm a now person. I don't need to write about the Great Wall or Tian'anmen to be Chinese.[157]

This remark by Wang Jiaxin illustrates how the self-image of contemporary Chinese poets has been caught between two impulses: to be recognized in the world as an international poet *and* to have the world acknowledge his/her Chineseness. Certain contemporary Mainland poets venerate Western poets (often Nobel laureates) such as Eliot and Heaney as leading representatives of world literature who occupy a central position of literary authority for which they yearn. The marginalization of poetry in 1990s China, Michelle Yeh believes, led to an ever greater need to identify with a world poetic community symbolized by institutions such as the Nobel Prize. The "intense attention that Chinese avant-garde poets have focused on the Nobel Prize is itself significant. . . . For the avant-garde poet, the indifference of society and the hostility from the establishment probably make him particularly eager to be recognized by, and become part of, the international literary community."[158] This ideal of a universal literary community is real enough, kept alive by afficionados of "difficult" poetry everywhere. Yet the universal aesthetic recognition for which Chinese poets long is, to a degree, a phantasm. The role played by exiles in representing Chinese literature internationally has made them aware that Western publishing and reading markets have their own nonuniversalistic axe to grind when they appraise Chinese literature. Ouyang Jianghe frankly acknowledged the balance of power in the world literary economy.

> In the West, people don't read Chinese poems for the poems themselves, they use them to understand Chinese social or political phenomena. . . . If you don't satisfy this need, but pay more attention to the poetry itself, they're not interested. . . . Poets writing in the 1990s represent contemporary China; the China that Misty Poets were representing doesn't exist any more. But that China perhaps is the China that the West wants to see. It's too simple: it shows Chinese people not living well . . . this is where exchange between East and West is unequal. We don't need Westerners' suffering, we need their literary value, their artistic qualities and style. The West is the other way round: it needs the bitterness we express through literature. This is the current state of Western-Chinese cultural exchange. . . . It looks like a literary and poetic phenomenon, but there's a great deal of historical, economic background to it. The Nobel Prize doesn't only reflect literature, but also the relationship between literature and politics.[159]

1990s Chinese poetry suffered from a deep confusion about its audience and aims both in China and abroad. Since the 1980s, Misty and post-Misty generations of poets (wherever they now write) have largely shunned the heroic socially engaged voice associated with Bei Dao's early work, aspiring to a "purer," more independent poetry. However, it has proved hard to walk out from under this shadow, as the poet Wang Jiaxin discovered when, following a lecture at Beijing University in 2000, he was asked by a student, "Why don't you write with your blood and your life?" (as, by implication, the early Bei Dao did).[160] Put another way, why does he not write to protest about politics, society, the nation? While poets still writing in China acknowledge the achievement of the Misty Poets such as Bei Dao and Yang Lian who went into exile after 1989, they feel these poets can say nothing about 1990s China. As Ouyang Jianghe commented, "There's absolutely no reflection of post-1980s literary development in their works. This isn't to say that Nobel literature *has* to represent the present day, but I think their literary achievement is extremely limited."[161] However, it is the Misty model (one that speaks for the nation) that lives on in popular memory as true poetry. Poets still writing in China today find themselves considered inauthentic in comparison to those who left in 1989, even though the former see themselves as the more authentic voice of contemporary China.

At the close of the millennium, this confusion in contemporary Chinese poetry became rather more heated, as controversy broke out between two poetry factions: "intellectual writing" (*zhishifenzi xiezuo*) and "people's writing" (*minjian xiezuo*). "Intellectual writers," represented by Wang Jiaxin, Ouyang Jianghe, and others, were labeled pro-Western, elitist and, in their own view, artistically autonomous. "People's writers," represented by Yu Jian (1954–) and others, placed themselves in conscious opposition to the "intellectuals," emphasizing their poetry's honesty and closeness to the common people. In practice, however, the distinctions between the two groups seemed more rhetorical than actual. Adherents of both groups declared their independence from official and commercial pressures, claiming that everyday life provided the basis of their poetic inspiration. Both groups, thus, asserted a romantic function for the poet, that of the *Volkstimme* towering about the *Volk*, practicing the autonomous, self-sufficient religion of poetry.[162] Yet the polemic's heated arguments over poetry's links to the "common people" in fact had little relevance outside middle-class poetic circles. "Of all writers, poets have the least influence on society," remarked Dai Jinhua in 2001. "Even people who research literature—let alone society at large—don't look at poetry."[163] The whole exchange highlighted the disputed nature of the contemporary Chinese poetic space and the degree to which the various possible sociopolitical roles of poetry remained confused in the minds of poets: poetry as an autonomous value system, as the voice of nation and people, as a cosmopolitan, universal aesthetic currency, and as marginalia.

The Nobel Complex and Chinese Literature at the Fin de Siècle

By the close of the 1990s, the fading of overt politicization in Chinese literature and the growth of literature for entertainment suggested that the literary field in China was more autonomous than ever before, that it had "its own logic and its own power structure," increasingly independent of value systems both domestic and foreign.[164] Membership in the official Writers' Association was no longer a prerequisite for professional status as a writer, and China's "New Generation" (*xin shengdai*) of writers, born in the 1960s–1970s, existed increasingly outside the old-style socialist literary system, living by the market economy and holding down day jobs with newspapers, publishers, or businesses. In 1998 Zhu Wen (1967–), a New Generation leader, published a survey entitled "Rupture" (*Duanlie*) that polled his peer group about the Chinese literary scene. Questions such as "What assistance does the Writers' Association offer you?" garnered the response "public washroom." "Dressed-up piles of shit," someone else commented on state literary prizes.[165] But it would be naïve to assume that political restrictions had disappeared. According to many critics and writers, Chinese authors could now write about anything they wanted without fear of severe reprisal, and even with the prospect of financial gain — only as long as they did not write about politics. The flip side of this new literary freedom is that since 1989, serious political discussion has largely been sidelined by a popular literature that responds to the market demand for entertainment and thus fits nicely with the CCP's emphasis on market development over political reform.

The choices intellectuals faced, however, were not so simply polarized between remaining on the elitist margins or becoming slaves to market forces; instead, the old high-low, official-unofficial binaries that looked increasingly uncertain at the start of the 1990s had been largely displaced by the second half of the decade. After 1996, Jing Wang has noted, culture became a source of capital both economic and political as the state embarked on a new legitimizing, modernizing, civilizing project based around the consumption of culture. The state actively sponsored the culture industry in the late 1990s, planning to invest five billion RMB over the coming ten years to build large-scale cultural institutions such as museums, libraries, and bookstores. In short, "culture gives impetus to, and serves as an index of, economic boom."[166] Intellectuals (through print, among other, media) began to abandon foreign theoretical imports such as the "post-isms" and, in conjunction with state "leisure culture campaigns," sought to democratize culture for the new-style collective of consuming masses. Cultural consumption and production became the two interlinking halves of a state economic policy that drew in intellectuals. The jury is out concerning the degree to which this new state legitimation policy has reinforced official hegemony or fostered (consumerist) democracy; this, Jing Wang muses, is perhaps even a question of limited value "in a world where parties of conflicting interests negotiate in the boardroom rather than duel on the battlefield. Domination is not total; resistance is never complete."[167]

Yet despite the growing resistance to foreign theoretical agendas, China and its literary worlds had not shaken free of the desire for international recognition. A glance at the publishing situation of 1996 highlights the survival of old-style oppositions between nationalism and universality, working in tandem in the Chinese modernizing project. The best-selling anti-American nationalist tract *Zhongguo keyi shuo bu* (China can say no) and a host of like-minded titles stood on the best-seller racks next to foreign novels and self-help books preaching the values of the American dream. Western goods continued to maintain a high profile in the Chinese market, despite the promotion of domestic competitors. This juxtaposition of market forces reexpressed the enduring conflict between national identity and global/Western conscious-ness in Chinese modernity: "the American dream is a comprehensive model and the object of emulation. At the same time, it is that which is desired to be replaced and, at the very least, contested with."[168]

Chinese culture and literature, in short, remained a muddled concept aptly expressed by the developments in the Nobel Complex. The doubts and suspi-cions that clouded the complex in the late 1990s — turning critics on writers, writers on critics and on each other, as the bureaucrats sat back and watched the fur fly — highlights the confusion experienced by literary intellectuals as they tried to locate a meaning or aim for their work, whether in a search for international recognition such as the Nobel, for domestic popularity, official acclaim, literary autonomy, or financial rewards.

Although by 2000 the Nobel Complex was a fully acknowledged feature of the Chinese literary scene, it was harder to pin down than ever before. "The Nobel Complex is in the minds of writers," the novelist Xu Xiaobin (1951–) was sure.[169] Of herself, however, she wrote: "I win very few prizes and I'm un-connected with mainstream literature. . . . I've never hoped for any prize that would bring great honor."[170] "The Nobel Complex still exists, but I don't have it," the New Generation writer Mian Mian (1970–) asserted.[171] Li Feng was unequivocal: "All my effort goes into writing novels. I have no time to think about the Nobel Prize."[172] Critics gave little credence to these denials. "In the 1990s," considered Li Tuo in 2000, "a lot of Chinese writers wanted to get the Nobel Prize. They still think about it, but nobody says anything."[173] "All writ-ers in China would like to get the Nobel Prize. They're interested in anything of benefit to them," said the critic Chen Xiaoming.[174] "Of course people are going to want to win the Nobel. It's a big prize, they want the money," Jin Jian-fan, secretary of the Writers' Association, laughed.[175]

In the 1980s the push for a Nobel Prize testified to a certain faith in the lit-erature prize (and therefore in literature itself) as a universal panacea capable of resolving the tensions between modern Chinese literature and national, global and individual identities. Yet the continued dislocation between writers and a centralized national identity through the 1990s heightened these ten-sions, and by the close of the decade, serious writers started to express doubts. "Even if we win the prize," remarked Mo Yan in 2000, "it doesn't mean we've 'marched towards the world.' The issue of the Nobel Prize should be separated from Chinese literature. The burden is too big."[176] If in the 1980s the Nobel Prize represented a unified world standard to Chinese writers, by the late 1990s the idea of a single authoritative value system ceased to exist for Chinese literati. "When Dario Fo won, people were very confused about the Nobel. What kind of thing was this post-Cold War? How could [the prize] go to this leftist revolutionary? Was it symbolic of something? I didn't understand," puzzled Dai Jinhua.[177] Writers became increasingly selective about what they took from the West, and translations from the West lost the absolute preeminence they enjoyed in the 1980s. Established authors such as Mo Yan instead turned increasingly to traditional popular literary forms.

Eighty years after the concept of realist fiction was first introduced to China, and following twenty years of literary experiments, Chinese writers at the fin de siècle returned to pondering the question of how to reflect "real life" and produce a literature relevant to Chinese society. This suggests an intriguing overlap between official rhetoric and writers' aims, whereby the Nobel Prize and the politics of international recognition were designated subsidiary issues. Compare the following four statements, all made in 2000:

1. In the 1980s, we had a valuable role to play for the people. Now we have no influence, except on writers. We should try to influence ordinary people, we should write the life of ordinary Chinese. . . . Right now, not one writer is doing this. . . . In the 1990s, the real worry is how to get readers. The Nobel Prize is no yardstick, or an unimportant yardstick.[178]

2. The crucial question is not, can we win the Nobel Prize, but can we produce a literature of a critical nature, which can attract support and attention from a broad spectrum of readers and ordinary people?[179]

3. I'm very unsatisfied with contemporary Chinese writers . . . I feel that most Chinese writers today avoid reality . . . really great writers should directly face their lives, society. If you haven't faced up to your own life or society, you can't be great.[180]

4. We should be writing for the people, not for the Nobel Prize.[181]

The first three statements were by the New Generation writer Li Feng, and the internationally noted critics Li Tuo and Wang Xiaoming, respectively; all three are nonofficial literary figures. The fourth was by Jin Jianfan, secretary of the Writers' Association. This convergence of views echoes Jing Wang's analysis of the blurring between the state and intellectuals in the project to democratize culture in the late 1990s, with its turn away from "traveling . . . agendas," including preoccupation with the Nobel Prize.

But even if the old exponents of global value systems such as the Nobel Prize began to be doubted, the desire for international recognition that originally generated the Nobel Complex still existed, despite official denials. "We wouldn't help a Chinese writer try to win the Nobel Prize, because writing has to be for the Chinese people" declared Jin Jianfan in 2000.[182] However, in 1998 the Writers' Association, working with the All-America Chinese Writers' Friendship Association, began to promote selected works of Chinese literature in America, donating copies to universities and libraries "in order to 'march towards the world.'" Describing these efforts, the director of the American Friendship Association, Bing Ling, criticized blind worship of the Nobel Prize as the sole signifier of global status in literature: "Classical and modern China has produced so many great writers and immortal works . . . this can't be summed up in a couple of Nobel Prizes; the problem is that people sometimes turn prizes into the standard for defining global status." Yet these critical comments were followed by a diligent analysis of why China had failed to win a Nobel Prize: "The biggest problem is that of . . . how to promote [literature]. . . . Our Chinese writers living abroad ought to take action and take advantage of their position . . . we will be unstinting in our efforts to promote Chinese literature to the world!"[183]

Although the 1980s solutions to narratives of national liberation and universal modernity were discredited in the 1990s, the narratives themselves and the faith in progress, in Chinese literature's capacity to succeed in the international arena and win glory for the nation, still remained. As a representative of the New Left, an intellectual opposition group doubtful about China's embrace of global capitalism, Dai Jinhua's was one of the few voices skeptical of the optimism that literature would be able to mediate the national inequalities inherent in universalism and globalization. "To me," she reflected, "world literature is a lie, a very beautiful lie."

> The Nobel Complex can't be resolved by literature or culture. The Nobel Prize is part of the whole process of globalization, it's linked with all its political and economic problems, all China's problems. China's experiences in globalization should be seen as the post-cold war Cold War: China is practicing capitalism, but we still have to talk socialism. . . . I feel that this element exists for each Chinese writer, after his works enter world literature. When people read them, they know they're Chinese works, and bring to them all their attitudes towards socialism. . . . Only when people understand this can we discuss world literature.[184]

Yet the paucity of such opinions testified to the tenacious hold ideals of modern universality had over the Chinese intellectual imagination, to the ongoing hope for validation from external (Western) sources of authority, and to the persisting belief in the ambassadorial powers of literature, even on the eve of Gao Xingjian's Nobel Prize.

OVER THE TWO DECADES since 1979, the Nobel Complex developed from an official policy issue, to an intellectual publicity stunt, to a phantasmal disorder, rising and falling with the public profile of literature. Despite the changing face of the complex, the amalgam of cultural forces it signified — the mix of desire, sense of inferiority, and faith in the power of literature to mediate between national and international spheres — showed no signs of disappearing at the turn of the century. In conjunction with the hundredth anniversary of the Nobel Prize in 2000, China's Nobel Complex erupted in full force, and the very week Gao Xingjian's award was announced a popular Beijing newspaper ran articles on the "Nobel Blues."[185] Even after news of Gao's prize broke, one newspaper ran a prescheduled article bemoaning the continued lack of a Chinese laureate.[186] Official professions of detachment, as expressed above by Jin Jianfan, offered no solid proof that any of the sensitivities surrounding the complex and questions it raised had abated for the state. It was, perhaps, simply that officialdom had braced itself against the realities of the world literary economy, namely that a writer in exile was far more likely to find favor with world and Nobel audiences than one based on the Mainland. The idea of this clash of imagined literary communities, however, was still no more palatable within official circles. Jin declared in 2000 that if Stockholm were to award the Nobel Prize to Bei Dao, "Most Chinese people would think this was a highly unfriendly expression of feeling by the Nobel Prize Committee towards the Chinese people, whose patriotism is very deeply rooted."[187]

A sideways glance at post-Mao Chinese attitudes to winning international recognition in areas other than literature — in sports, science, and economics — provides a revealing contrast with the degree of nationalistic sensitivity and ideological ambivalence exhibited toward the Nobel Literature Prize. Post-Mao China's reentry into the international sporting realm has, admittedly, spurred some of its most public outbursts of both jubilant and angry nationalism: the passionate rejoicing at the victory of the Chinese women's volleyball team in the 1981 World Cup; the riot that followed the defeat of the Chinese football team by Hong Kong on 19 May 1988; the strenuous efforts made by the Chinese government to win the right to host the Olympics in 2000 and 2008; the thousands of Chinese weeping with joy in Tian'anmen Square in 2001 after the announcement of Beijing's successful 2008 Olympic bid. But although China's international sporting aspirations have indisputably provided a sometimes explosive focus for nationalist feeling, for several reasons they have not caused the levels of controversy generated by the literary nationalism and internationalism tied up with efforts to win a Nobel Literature Prize.

Firstly, sports are judged by criteria far less subjective and politically contentious than those used for literature. Athletes, moreover, do not need a translator to win international success. Secondly, unlike literature — by its nature elitist and individualistic — sports provide a direct, populist symbolic framework for representing the nation: athletes train their bodies to win international glory for the larger national body.[188] Thirdly, sports have not been as closely linked with political dissidence as have literature and the arts. This is not to claim that sports stand entirely outside politics. Susan Brownell, for example, has shown that the public space occupied by sports in post-Mao China has been used by a variety of political interest groups, ranging from officialdom to democratic protestors.[189] Both of China's bids for the Olympic Games were politicized by international protests about its poor human rights record. Nonetheless, as a nonverbal discipline, sport in China has not generated political dissidence the same way literature has.

Fourthly, and perhaps most importantly, in sports, China has had little grounds for feeling insecure about its international achievements. Despite a few publicly perceived failures (such as a poor performance at the 1988 Seoul Olympics), Chinese men and women in the post-Mao era have put in strong international performances in a wide range of sports, including track and field, gymnastics, racquet sports, and volleyball. Chinese competitors achieved their best medal-winning performance yet at the 2004 Athens Olympics, winning thirty-two gold, seventeen silver, and fourteen bronze medals. Although Chinese soccer fans have complained bitterly about the poor standard of the men's game, many Chinese are becoming relatively philosophical about the time and investment required for their teams to catch up with the world leaders in the sport. General reactions to the Chinese team's performance in its first World Cup Finals in 2002 reflected this attitude: although some web commentators raged that the Chinese team had "lost face" for the nation, others seemed resigned to China's early exit and expressed satisfaction that the Chinese team had at least made sufficient progress to participate in the finals for the first time. China's rapidly won success in modern international sports — a discipline the Chinese began developing little more than a century ago — has contrasted jarringly with the lack of global plaudits won by Chinese literature, which has a history of about three thousand years.

Post-Mao China's greatest source of insecurity in the international sporting realm has probably derived from its bids to host the Olympics, which failed for 2000 but succeeded for 2008. Both bids combined the sense of insecurity and entitlement that has characterized modern Chinese nationalism and the Nobel Literature Prize Complex. In 1993, during the run-up to the announcement of the 2000 Olympics, Chinese articles made predictably nationalistic arguments about China's right to host the Olympic Games, as an ancient civilization now home to one fifth of the world's population.[190] Taking a more petulantly supplicatory tone, the Sino-American Committee for the Promotion of Beijing's 2000 Olympic Bid (Zhong-Mei Beijing 2000 nian aoyunhui shenban cujin hui) begged the Olympic Committee to "give China a chance and China will give the world a miracle."[191] In its sometimes abject desire to impress the Olympic Committee with a tidy Beijing, Chinese officialdom was willing to commit acts both absurd and brutal in Beijing, such as spray painting yellowed patches of grass green and purging the streets of handicapped people.[192] The bids were frequently overshadowed by political controversy: by international criticisms of China's human rights situation, and by voices within China protesting that a Beijing Olympics would divert crucial funds from other, needier parts of the country.

But the quest for the Olympics, despite its anxiously nationalistic elements, did not suffer from quite the same ideological unease and suspicion of dissidence that dogged the quest for the Nobel Literature Prize: the worry that aspiring to an international literary award such as the Nobel Prize was tantamount to capitulating to Western cultural and economic domination. Chinese officials involved in the Olympic bids accepted virtually wholesale the Movement's claims to universalism, such as its professed ambition to foster world peace.[193] Even after the disappointment of the failure of the Chinese bid in 1993, there was little suspicion voiced by China of national bias within the Olympic Movement. Indeed, the resignation with which the announcement was received led one senior sports official to conclude that "China has matured."[194] A 1996 article in the official press continued to draw attention primarily to the Movement's universalistic aspirations for world peace, adding only as a final afterthought the fact that "the Olympics originate in capitalist countries...and therefore inevitably have their own historical limitations."[195] Desire for international glory in the form of the Olympics, therefore, never provoked the uneasy soul-searching about national identity and Western hegemony that the Nobel Literature Prize Complex did.

Anxiety about the Nobel Science and Economics Prizes seems to bear a closer resemblance to attitudes to the literature prize. As with the literature prize, the print media could express admiring interest in the science and economics prizes with the advent of Deng Xiaoping's rule.[196] This interest persisted all the way into the twenty-first century with, for example, an exhibition held at the Beijing Military Affairs Museum (Junshi bowuguan) entitled "The

Gateway to Science: A Look at the Development of Twentieth-Century Science as Reflected through the Nobel Prize," sponsored by the Chinese Academy of Science.[197]

Particularly after the mid-1990s, press articles concerning the Nobel science prizes started to become not just informative, but also speculative and introspective, revealing a desire for Nobel prizes and anxiety about why China had failed to garner one. In 1996 Xu Jiayue lamented that "the annual Nobel Prize announcement was a source of mental turmoil for China's scientists, as this most influential, most global of science prizes still seems very far from the Chinese people."[198] From the late 1990s onwards, three or four articles were published annually with titles such as "Why Has China Never Managed to Win a Nobel Science Prize?" and "Creative Education: Thoughts on China's Failure to Win a Nobel Prize."[199] Rather more patchy interest was also expressed in the idea of a Chinese economist winning the Nobel: in 2001 Fan Yuejin and Yi Yuji published one such discussion in "How Chinese Economists Can Contend for the Nobel Prize."[200] Explanations put forward by these and other articles concerning China's lack of Nobel prizes cited the relative youth of modern science and economics as academic disciplines in China, the highly disruptive intrusion of ideology and politics (principally during the Cultural Revolution) into both spheres, the lack of institutional funding (relative to the West), and failings in traditional Chinese philosophy that hindered the development of a creative knowledge culture.[201]

On the surface, this discussion appears to contain many of the anxious, nationalistic elements present in the complex around China's lack of a Nobel Literature Prize: the belief that such recognition for individuals amounts to recognition of the nation; the desire for and strong sense of entitlement to international recognition; the sense of shame at China's failure to win a prize that other, equally "backward" developing countries have; the self-flagellating search for historical reasons for this failure.[202] But two facets of this public discussion indicate that the quest for the science and economics prizes never reached the levels of controversy generated by Chinese interest in the literature prize.

Firstly, although the Nobel Science and Economics Prizes have historically been even more Western-dominated than the literature prize, Chinese discussions of the former seemed largely content to accept at face value assertions of these prizes' universalistic image. In contrast to debates about the literature prize, there was little sense that pursuit of a Nobel Science or Economics Prize equaled capitulation to Western values. No commentator attempted to draw a distinction, for example, between "Chinese" and "American" quantum mechanics, in a way comparable to the post-Mao debates about "Chinese" versus

"Western" modernism. Chinese journalists and academics could, of course, speak enviously of the local conditions, such as access to generous funding and institutional support, that favored American scientists in the Nobel competition, but the prizes' basic claims to internationalism were seldom challenged. Vying for recognition in sciences, therefore, has constituted a far less ideologically ambivalent project than competing for a literature prize, probably because of the general assumption that science as a modern global discipline is free from nationalistic bias and is judged by criteria more objective than those used in appraising literature.[203] One commentator observed that "the Nobel science prizes are the greatest, fairest, most authoritative evaluation of scientific achievement. Winning a Nobel Prize is a symbol of a country's scientific and technological development, and of a country's ability to create knowledge. If China wants to make a greater contribution to humanity, it needs the Nobel Prize and the spirit of Nobel science."[204] A similar faith in the universalism of modern economics led the author of one article to remark that "in methodology, our nation's study of economics needs to learn from Western economics."[205] Desire for science and economics prizes, thus, was simplified by a sense that the two disciplines, despite originating in and being dominated by the West, were universalistic fields of enquiry, and that it was ideologically unproblematic to learn from the West in the cause of competing for Nobel glory. Indeed, far from being seen as slavish worship of the West, aspiring to the level of scientific and economic achievement represented by Nobel prizes was viewed as a patriotic contribution to China's material knowledge.

A second crucial difference is that science, like sports, has not been as closely associated with dissidence and political nonconformism in the post-Mao era as have literature and the arts in general.[206] This is not to say that science stands entirely above politics. Both the former Soviet Union and the People's Republic of China have produced prominent dissident scientists, notably, Andrei Sakharov and Fang Lizhi.[207] But it remains true that science has not attracted dissident controversy as consistently as have the arts.

This is illustrated by contrasting official attitudes towards Chinese-born winners of the literature and science prizes. Six ethnic Chinese have won Nobel Science Prizes: Chen Ning Yang and Tsung-Dao Lee (Physics, 1957); Samuel Ding (Physics, 1976); Yuan Tseh Lee (Chemistry, 1986); Steven Chu (Physics, 1997); Daniel Tsui (Physics, 1998). Of these, three (Yang, Tsung-Dao Lee, and Tsui) were born on the Mainland, but almost all the prize-winning work was carried out in the United States. And by the time they were awarded the prize all six either already were, or would later become U.S. citizens. While in Sweden to collect their awards in 1957, Yang and Tsung-Dao Lee required Swedish government protection from Chinese Embassy overtures to persuade them to return to the motherland, even though both were in the process of securing U.S. citizenship.[208] Yet despite the laureates' distance from Mainland China at the time of their awards, the post-Mao government has been far readier to bask in reflected glory from ethnic Chinese science prize winners who worked in the United States than it was with Gao Xingjian. It is the awkwardly dissident tendencies of certain Chinese writers that have made the state so hostile to international recognition for them. The Chinese writers most familiar to international audiences have either been exiles (such as the former Misty Poets), or authors working beyond the reach of the official Chinese literary establishment (such as Mo Yan). Some Chinese-born Nobel Science Prize winners, by contrast, have been more patriotic and eager to establish links with the state. In the Central China Television program of 29 April 2000, which asked "How far are we from a Nobel [Science] Prize?," Yang, Lee, and Tsui were all invited to comment on the patriotic significance of their prizes and on how China should strive to foster Nobel-winning research. In the same year, a journal pictured the six ethnic Chinese Nobel laureates below an exhortation by Jiang Zemin that the Chinese people build a strong, rich, democratic, civilized, and modern socialist country, and canvassed their opinions on the outlook for China in the twenty-first century.[209]

As would soon become apparent, similar officially sponsored overtures to Gao Xingjian were unthinkable. Reactions to his 2000 Nobel Prize confirmed that despite disillusionment, professed nonchalance, and growing pragmatism about the Nobel Literature competition, modern Chinese literature remained a uniquely sensitive touchstone for national identity within and outside China.

CHAPTER FIVE

The Nobel Prize, 2000

Unsurprisingly, given its history, the Swedish Academy's response to the Chinese Nobel Complex on 12 October 2000 left few parties satisfied. While Mainland writers kept their own counsel for the first thirty-six hours, the Taiwanese expressed delight; Chinese Internet users throughout the world veered between surprised pleasure at a Chinese Nobel winner, and bemused resentment at the unfamiliarity of Gao's name. In a truly universal world literature, Gao Xingjian's prize would have been feted as an award to an individual writer, who happened to be born in China, for his achievements in both Chinese and French. However, the much dreamed of liberating potential of the idealized autonomous aesthetic has rarely, if ever, been realized. In this instance, the context of recent Chinese intellectual history, the Nobel Complex, and the marginal position of modern Chinese work in the world literary economy determined that Gao's prize would become a contentious political issue.

The discussion below of Chinese reactions to Gao's prize will focus principally on the Mainland. This is not a dismissal of responses from Taiwan or Hong Kong, but the Mainland figures more importantly here because of themes developed above, and also because there has been little public forum for discussion of these issues within Mainland intellectual circles, beyond anonymous discussion on the Internet. Reactions from Taiwan, Hong Kong, and diasporic Chinese communities, meanwhile, have been more easily accessible. Due to the politicized nature of Gao Xingjian's Nobel Prize in China, I have for the most part omitted the names of my respondents.[1] Quotations attributed to Critic A, Poet A, etc. are taken from interviews with well-known critics, writers, and editors in Beijing in spring of 2001. Although this anonymity in some ways may compromise readers' interest in the opinions of my interviewees, I still considered inclusion of these viewpoints important, in order to provide a public forum for views of influential Mainland literary intellectuals that might not otherwise reach a wider audience.

Gao Xingjian and the Swedish Academy's Appraisal

The awarding of the Nobel Prize to Gao Xingjian looks like the perfect counter to the Chinese Nobel Complex and the intellectual marginality complex, or the "obsession with China" that lies behind them. Gao is a figure who has denounced the "China complex" and who revels in his marginality without, it seems, any desire to recover the center by seeking recognition or declaring a particular identity. Apart from one public outburst about the Tian'anmen crackdown, Gao has led a life of hardworking exile, far away, he claims, from the hustle and bustle of exile activity.[2] Both in his writing and public persona, Gao has worked to cultivate a studied detachment and artistic neutrality, declaring he writes neither for politics nor for money. Gao lays claim to a truly universalistic range of options, in which he can make free use of his Chinese cultural heritage, retain his freedom of sociopolitical commentary, and speak out on whatever he chooses. In exile, he has built up (particularly in Europe) a dedicated following for his drama and fiction, generating a small but enthusiastic body of critical work.[3]

The theoretical basis behind Gao's stance was expounded in his 1996 collection of essays, *Meiyou zhuyi* ("No-ism"), in which he defines what he is and, most importantly, what he is not: no-ism is an individual stance of positively engaged doubt. "No-ism approves of individual choice, but it doesn't view the individual as a supreme being . . . it's best to stand on the sidelines and not harbor wild dreams of dominating the world."[4] The primary function of the writer and intellectual is to engage in detached, independent, and individual reflection. Gao advocates a "cold literature" (*leng de wenxue*), in which the writer is not a hero, a revolutionary, or a sacrificial object, and has no moral responsibility to his readers and no duty owed to society. Cold literature "won't attract mass attention, of course."[5] Neither, however, does Gao advocate an abstract purity in literature. No-ism "is nonpolitical, it doesn't follow politics, but it doesn't oppose other people following politics. . . . No-ism is the most basic condition of freedom for the contemporary individual."[6] Gao sets himself apart from other modern Chinese intellectuals, blaming the stranglehold of "isms" for impoverishing modern Chinese literature and obscuring the works themselves with banners and slogans. Fleeing from the motherland and leading a marginal existence are the only means by which he can achieve his authorial ideal of cold detachment.[7] Instead, Gao's principal source of identity derives from his art and his subjectivity: "I express, I exist."[8] Literature, Gao observed in his Nobel lecture, "can only be the voice of the individual."

> Once literature is contrived as the hymn of the nation, the flag of the race, the mouthpiece of a political party or the voice of a class or a group, it . . . loses what

is inherent in literature . . . and becomes a substitute for power and profit . . . for a writer of the present to strive to emphasize a national culture is problematical. Because of where I was born and the language I use, the cultural traditions of China naturally reside within me. . . . Literature transcends ideology, national boundaries, and racial consciousness . . . .[9]

These declarations of aesthetic neutrality, asserting disinterest in, though not indifference to, political matters and disavowal of commercial temptations, epitomize the stance of "neutral engagement" that the Nobel Committee has sought in recent decades.

The principal coordinates of Gao's avant-garde position — independence from nation, people, and commercial pressures; antidogmatism; individual artistic and political integrity; and skepticism — emerge in his biographical details and drama. Born nine years before the founding of the People's Republic, Gao grew up in a creative home environment, encouraged by his mother (an amateur actress) from a young age to write and draw. (As an adult, Gao has continued to paint as actively as he writes, and has had his work exhibited in Europe, the United States, Taiwan, and Hong Kong.) During the Cultural Revolution, he demonstrated his commitment to independent artistic creation, writing for personal expression despite personal danger. After Mao's death, Gao was at the forefront of those disseminating Western modernism within China. *Chezhan* (Bus stop, 1981), influenced by Beckett and the Theater of the Absurd, caused an immediate sensation among theater audiences.[10] Victim to the 1983 Anti-Spiritual Pollution campaign, Gao asserted his independence from political threats by taking off on a five-month tour of China. The trip eventually yielded *Lingshan* (1990), an exploration of the self in eighty-one chapters, written, Gao claims, "for myself and without the hope that it would be published."[11]

In tune with his independent stance built on artistic neutrality, Gao's reasons for exile emphasized the artistic over the political: on leaving China for Germany in 1987, he remarked, "An artist who wishes to express freely would not want to stay in this country unless he goes against his conscience."[12] The events of 1989 led to *Taowang* (Fugitives, 1990), a play about the massacre that criticizes both Party brutality and the protesters' radicalism. Gao's plays of the 1990s — including *Sheng si zhi jie* (Between life and death, 1991), *Duihua yu fanjie* (Dialogue and rebuttal, 1992), *Yeyou shen* (The nocturnal wanderer, 1993) — have been resolutely experimental, addressing the fragmentation and insufficiency of the human self.[13] Settings are unspecified and his protagonists are not given names, leaving them open to interpretation as universal types ("Man," "Woman," "Girl," "Prostitute"). He makes frequent use of symbolic devices and stylized dream sequences that break down the barriers between internal and external realities. Buddhist influences are unobtrusively and enigmatically present, for example, the appearance of a nun in *Sheng si zhi jie* and the silent antics of the Zen monk in *Duihua yu fanjie*.

These puzzling devices are part of Gao Xingjian's project of alienating the audience from their normal assumptions and thoughts in order to stimulate deeper reflection on the state of consciousness. In *Sheng si zhi jie* and *Yeyou shen*, his protagonists refer to themselves as "she" and "you," giving their speech and thoughts a detached, disembodied quality. Committed to an avant-garde stance, he has been "under the enormous pressure he has brought upon himself, as he vows not to repeat anyone, least of all himself, and every new work has to be a step forward."[14] Doubt could be cast both on the fundamental feasibility of such an aspiration, and on Gao's success in fulfilling it. Whether intentional or not, the influence of Beckett, for example, is apparent in both his earlier and later works. But in life, rhetoric, and dramatic art, Gao has striven to live up to the demanding manifesto of *Meiyou zhuyi*, and Henry Zhao makes an impassioned case for the originality of Gao's "modern Zen theater" within world drama. Gao's work, he argues, has broken with the anxiety of influence in world literature that holds Chinese (along with much of non-Western literature) to be either derivative of Western models or exotic marginalia, and has injected a fresh aesthetic into jaded Postmodern Theater.[15]

Zhao's emphatic treatment of this question — he devotes the entire final chapter of his book on Gao's drama to discussing it — highlights a familiar problem in the reception of Chinese literature in the West: the denigration of Chinese literature for being derivative of Western models and for lacking artistic value independent of its sociopolitical exotica. Awarding the prize to Gao, the exile who has broken with the "obsession with China," for his "universal validity" appears to break from this pattern, acclaiming his artistic originality as separate from his marginalia value as a "Chinese dissident." Yet it seems a little odd that mention of his achievements in existentialist, nonreferential avant-garde drama occupied only one quarter of the Swedish Academy's press release announcing Gao Xingjian's laureateship on 12 October 2000. The rest was devoted to his two largely autobiographical novels set predominantly in China, *Lingshan* and *Yige ren de shengjing* (One man's bible, 1999), and to his play with the most specific political setting, *Taowang*. Is it perhaps the case that despite the Swedish Academy's welcoming of the Chinese-born Gao into the fold of universal literary modernity, the Academy has disguised the longstanding Western view of Chinese literature as "obsession with China," with praise for his "universal validity"? Do Gao's novels depict an acceptably dissident Chinese "imagined community" that the judges of world literature find lacking in his drama, and thus fulfill the long-established requirement that marginal literatures should be nationally representative to win a Nobel Prize?

These reservations recall earlier observations about the role of the Nobel Prize in arbitrating world literature and its inclusion of "marginal" non-Western literatures. Since the Second World War, the Nobel Committee has sought to satisfy Alfred Nobel's stipulation that Nobel winners should demonstrate "an idealistic tendency" of benefit to all mankind by selecting oeuvres of "universal validity," honoring the difficult writing of figures such as Eliot and Beckett, and seeking a universal, autonomous artistic neutralism, unrestricted by the concrete, social reference points of realism. But Nobel winners from outside the Western tradition have rarely been commended for their universal artistic qualities. It is instead their links to national cultural roots that have been praised, implying that non-Western literatures are insufficiently advanced to be prized for their intrinsic artistic qualities and are valuable mainly as sociopolitical documents, as national obsessions. The two-tier treatment of Western and non-Western writers reemerges in the Swedish Academy's appraisal of Gao Xingjian. Chinese intellectuals' marginality complex and their obsession with China, it turns out, is a discourse not only projected by the Chinese onto their relationship with the West, but also by the West back onto Chinese literature. Nobel developments in 2000 may be seen to express discomfort on an international scale regarding "China" the nation-state and its literature.

In theoretical terms, Gao's two novels continue the aesthetic concerns and modernist schema of his drama and essays. Both pick up on devices and themes from Gao's plays: most notably the disorienting and alienating use of personal pronouns; the concern with consciousness and definition of the self; and confusion and skepticism about what constitutes reality, history, and memory. Towards the end of *Lingshan*, Gao inserts a self-mocking dialogue between the author and an imagined critic: "'This isn't a novel! . . . This is modernist, it's imitating the West but falling short. . . . You've slapped together travel notes, moralistic ramblings, feelings, notes, jottings, untheoretical discussions, unfablelike fables, copied out some folk songs, added some legend-like nonsense of your own invention, and are calling it fiction!'"[16] Thus described, the narrative sounds like a reassuringly open-ended mix of myth and fact, past and present, supernatural and natural. In its quest for an alternative fictional form reminiscent of the traditional Chinese *biji* style, *Lingshan* is an experiment in narrative. The narrator's voice moves between pronouns ("I," "you," "she," "he"), which function as extensions of a fractured self and conflicted subjectivity used to alleviate the narrator's loneliness and restore the completeness of his being, while the author ponders the perils of modernity, environmental degradation, the horrors of political repression and collectivism, and the alienated individual.

Despite these innovations, however, *Lingshan* contains certain obstacles to achieving the open-ended skepticism characteristic of Gao's plays. The principal difficulty lies in the tone and presence of the narrator(s). In Gao's drama, the portentousness of the questions raised in dialogue is undermined by their stylized, performed quality. This element of artificiality undermines the audience's faith in the realist meaning of the lines, opening up a broader space for reflection. Moreover, Gao achieves greater detachment since he is not writing lines for himself. In his fiction, the strongly autobiographical elements combined with the ponderous quality of the linking prose give his message a fixedness that is a long way from the skepticism that he advocates elsewhere. The Nobel Committee called Gao a "perspicacious skeptic," but Romanticism conquers skepticism in *Lingshan*, and Gao's voice can sound baldly naïve. "I am perpetually searching for meaning, but what in fact *is* meaning?" (p. 308). He seems torn between marginality and heroism, as both "a refugee from birth" (p. 381) and a speaker of truths who suffers for his sincerity. "It's because of this damn portraying the truth that misfortune has befallen me and I have fled here" (p. 384). It emerges that the self being sought in *Lingshan* has regressed to a Romantic core hiding behind a modernist façade, a marginal individual both detached from and capable of speaking truth for the people, a *Volkstimme* towering above the *Volk*.

This Romanticism undermines the claims to skepticism and neutrality Gao put forward in *Meiyou zhuyi*, setting up a self-supporting opposition between the political center and the dissident, marginal hero. As such, *Lingshan* firmly reinstates the "obsession with China" at the heart of the marginality complex from which Gao has proclaimed his detachment. *Lingshan* falls neatly into the category of roots-seeking fiction, a movement that Xueping Zhong views as fundamentally implicated in the intellectual search for a strong Chinese identity. Zhong's observations about the Roots Seekers' preoccupation with and celebration of the marginal male (intellectual) through fantasies of sexual potency and about the return of the repressed intellectual to power by expressing truth through his own alternative language, echo themes present in *Lingshan*. Through his "truth telling" and largely autobiographical narrator, Gao is also celebrating and attempting to recenter the marginal male, an impression strengthened by the wandering narrator's assertion of potency through frequent sexual conquests. Gao the dramatist and theorist emphatically proclaims skeptical detachment from the nation, and from the desire for national and international recognition. Gao the (Nobel Prize–winning) novelist valorizes the heroic individual living in (oppositional) symbiosis with the nation-state. *Lingshan* thus begins to edge towards Gao's dissident version of the old obsession with China. It is a strongly political novel, as Gao meditates on his escape from politically and environmentally contaminated Beijing. The narrator travels on the margins of society to evade persecution, and the horrors of collectivism in China's past are often evoked. "Are you the people, or am I the people, or is it the so-called we who are the people? I speak only for myself" (p. 498). Hell is crowds of other people, menacing nature and the individual, and Communist officials are villains who ruin a good Daoist ritual (p. 298). Thus, the message of the novel polarizes the beleaguered, but all-important marginal Self and the repressive regime, rather than attempting the disinterested criticism of belief systems present in Gao's other politicized work, *Taowang*.

These points can be reiterated for Gao's 1999 novel *Yige ren de shengjing*, a semi-autobiographical account of the author's experiences under the Communist regime, interleaved with episodes (generally sexual) from exile. The novel nods to preoccupations similar to those of *Lingshan*, *Meiyou zhuyi*, and Gao's drama — namely the persecuted self, the difficulties of human communication (particularly under the distorting influence of ideological repression), and the need for individual exile. Like the wandering narrator(s) in *Lingshan*, the protagonist denoted by "you" (Gao in exile) and "he" (Gao in China) lacks a place, and certainly a motherland, in which to settle. The narration moves in and out of the protagonist's experiences as political activist, victim, and external observer; the lack of a first-person pronoun intensifies the alienated tone of the narrator. Once more, however, inconsistencies emerge in Gao's rhetoric. That he should in 1999 produce a novel so preoccupied with China and its politics is surprising, given that he claimed the "China Complex" had ceased to influence his writing after the completion of *Lingshan*, *Mingcheng* (The Netherworld, 1989), and *Shan hai jing* (The Classic of Mountains and Seas, 1993) by the early 1990s.[17] His exhortation to Chinese intellectuals to abandon such concerns forms an important theme in the *Meiyou zhuyi* collection. *Yige ren de shengjing*, however, appears to be little more than a reversion to the "obsession with China" dressed up in Gao's modernist, individualist claims.

Writing in 1998, Yang Lian bemoaned the status of Chinese literature in the West, trapped in a ghetto of dissident virtue:

> Though the writing may be mediocre, the style drab, as long as a book fits into the West's conception of Chinese politics — along the lines of *Hollywood-Style Resistance Hero Challenges Commie Devils* — it qualifies as "serious literature" and boards the China Express.[18]

Yang went on to chastise Zhang Xianliang's formulaic pandering to Western tastes: "this 'Chinese Milan Kundera' . . . uses the best-selling formula of hero plus beauty plus sex to describe the monstrous and abnormal atmosphere of Chinese prisons, allowing the reader to enjoy the twin pleasures of . . . 'freedom' and voyeurism." There is a case to be made for applying Yang's comments (who, by contrast, has highly praised his friend Gao Xingjian's writing) to Gao's novels. The novelistic technique of *Yige ren de shengjing* is strikingly close to that of Zhang's strategy, particularly in his novel *Xiguan siwang* (Getting used to dying, 1989) — a work analyzed at some length by Xueping Zhong in her account of the intellectual marginality complex — in its use of multiple personal pronouns and heavy dual emphasis on the sexual exploits of its main male protagonist and his political ordeals.[19] Gao's book is also, by and large, a spermatic journey through modern Chinese political history and exile. Born within four years of each other, Gao and Zhang (and their autobiographical narrators) share important historical and literary influences and experiences, such as the Soviet-style idealism of the 1950s and the sense of loss resulting from the Maoist years of internal exile. After Mao's death, these marginal male narrators try (without necessarily succeeding) to reassert their freedom, strength, and masculinity, expressing a deep sense of anguish at their recollections of impotence while suffering political repression.

As in *Lingshan*, Gao's narrator in *Yige ren de shengjing* seems torn between marginality and a heroic individual stance. Gao's narrator is portrayed as an exile, without "-ism," who decides to attend only to his own salvation. However, pronouncements on his own position and its significance undermine his advocacy of an existence spent floating on the sidelines, portraying him as an embattled, self-determining Romantic individualist. "You're not a dragon, not a worm, not a this, not a that, that 'not' is just you, that 'not' isn't a denial. . . . You're writing yourself in this book, this book of fleeing, your one man's bible; you are your own God and disciple" (pp. 203–204). Endlessly repeated proclamations on the nature of freedom, writing, and most of all his own character and position leave the reader battered by the narrator's posturing. "[H]e has no leader, he doesn't come under the jurisdiction of a party or any organization; neither has he a motherland. . . . The reason why he still writes is because it is a need for him: only thus can he write in freedom and without using his writing to make money. Neither does he turn his pen into a weapon that struggles for some cause or other: he has no sense of mission" (p. 419).

Yet Gao still reserves the right to affect an attitude of wry skepticism totally at odds with these pronouncements. He thumbs his nose at the nation, empty glory, revolution, readers, himself: "You laugh at this world, you also laugh at yourself" (p. 423). He reverts to the device used in *Lingshan*, that of stepping outside the narrative to write an ironic dialogue between the narrators, he and you (pp. 439–440). This playful tone is immediately contradicted in the following chapter. When presented with a reader's copy of his novel to sign, he starts to write: "Language is a miracle that enables people to communicate; however, very often people are unable to communicate with each other. But the second half of the sentence you didn't write, you can't write so carelessly, so thoughtlessly, trampling on other people's feelings . . . you can't play carelessly with language" (p. 444). Behind the linguistically playful modernist front, fervent belief in a holistic language-using subject shows through. Since, in terms of subject matter, the book falls squarely into the category of "obsession with China," Gao's Romantic individualism reduces the central thrust of the novel to that of the marginal self battling political oppressors, or, in Yang Lian's words, "Hollywood-style Resistance Hero Challenges Commie Devils."

Praise for the "universal validity" of Gao Xingjian's metaphysical dramatic experiments seems reasonable. But by specifically commending his two novels, rather than mentioning by name any of Gao's corpus of drama other than the sociopolitically specific *Taowang*, the Swedish Academy preserved the age-old link between Chinese literature and (some version of) obsession with China, and the two-tier treatment of Western and non-Western literatures. The Academy's praise conveys a backhanded compliment, pegging "universal validity" in Chinese literature to "obsession with China," as exemplified by the Romantic tendencies in Gao's fiction. Beyond the simplistic ideology-driven response of the Chinese government, this rhetorical inconsistency between the universal and the national has generated far-reaching disillusionment among Mainland Chinese writers.

The Chinese Debate Gao Xingjian

When the news of Gao Xingjian's prize broke in China, most critics, scholars, and journalists waited for instructions from above. After a thirty-six-hour suspension of comment, the *Renmin ribao* pronounced:

> It seems the Nobel Committee has used a political criterion for giving the prize for literature, instead of doing so from the perspective of literary value. . . . This shows that the Nobel Prize for Literature has essentially been used for political purposes and thus has lost its authority.[20]

An immediate ban on publishing or discussing Gao followed; intellectuals abroad who had responded enthusiastically to the news were reproved and asked to explain themselves. In Taiwan, meanwhile, audiences embraced Gao as their own, though Gao's works had barely sold there in previous years. Both political and cultural leaders (President Chen Shuibian and Long Yingtai, director of Taipei Cultural Bureau, respectively) cheered Gao's prize.

The news quickly moved through the global Chinese community on the Internet and was followed by fierce debate. Internet users expressed joy at a Chinese writer winning the Nobel Prize, puzzlement at the unfamiliarity of Gao Xingjian's name and resentment that here was a Chinese writer, acclaimed for his global stature, that only Westerners could enjoy. Prominent exiles such as Yang Lian enthusiastically endorsed Gao's prize, while in Internet chat rooms commentators pondered whether Gao's Nobel meant that good Chinese literature could only be produced abroad. Yang proclaimed the award "the victory of exile" and reported how in 1993 he and Gao had both agreed that "the experience of exile was extremely necessary to writers who had grown up in the Mainland."[21] But not all exiles were delighted at the news. Internet articles published by a Chinese democracy activist accused the Nobel Committee of disobeying Alfred Nobel's stipulation of idealism by giving the prize to an author who espouses "coldness" in writing. Members of the democracy movement had clearly hoped to stake a claim for their cause in a Chinese Nobel Prize. "It seems the Chinese Nobel Prize winner doesn't think it his responsibility to struggle for freedom for others."[22]

But in the rush to draw broader significance from Gao's prize, it was on the Mainland that reactions revealed most clearly the uncertain nature of Chinese literary identities at the start of the new millennium. The spontaneous reaction of a substantial number of writers and intellectuals was delight, accompanied by discontent at the public reaction of the Writers' Association. Chen Pingyuan, a professor at Beijing University, expressed jubilation that a Nobel Prize had gone to writing in Chinese; his place of origin and current residence were less important.[23] All these were largely instinctive statements of approval for global recognition of Chinese culture; very few people in Mainland China had read the works for which Gao was awarded the prize when the Nobel announcement was made.

Yet jubilation at this first Chinese Nobel Prize faltered over the details of Gao's personification of Chinese identity and over his right to represent this identity on a global stage. Despite having spent the first forty-seven years of his life in Mainland China, Gao was defined variously as a "Chinese writer in inverted commas," "foreign literature worker," "exiled writer," "French writer" in discussions of his prize. Even the reactions of those who welcomed Gao's prize revealed a sense of insecurity with respect to Chinese national literary identity. Having praised the progress Gao had made since the 1980s, Editor A commented: "We'd always thought only a writer like Faulkner could win a

Nobel Prize; now we know that someone like Gao Xingjian can. I think he's strong among Chinese writers but weak compared to Nobel Prize winners." Intellectuals have long harbored illusions of a longed-for center (implied by Western recognition) which, once reached, is compromised instantly either through a Chinese writer (inevitably presumed to be below the world standard) attaining it or through the ambivalence resulting from its location in the West. Having spent years idealizing an aesthetically universal world literature and struggling to reconcile it with their own Chinese imagined community, intellectuals were shocked when the outcome differed so radically from their own imaginings.

There was no question of support for the Party-state nationalism in the reaction of the Writers' Association. "They criticize the Swedish Academy for being political? What organization," Critic D wished to know, "is more political than the Writers' Association?" However, Professor A, who supported a protest petition addressed to the Association, later felt rebuffed by the resolute individualism Gao asserted in his Nobel lecture. "He was too proud, not like Brodsky, who acknowledged the greatness of Russian literature that came before him." Critic C expressed his disappointment with Gao's later behavior. "Originally, Gao stood for artistic creativity, but now he's changed, he's expressing opinions about the Mainland." Gao is clearly in a no-win situation: standing as an individual, he is deemed arrogant; taking a position on China, he is accused of abandoning his independent artistic conscience.

Conscious of the marginality of literature in 1990s China, one group of contemporary poets responded by identifying increasingly with an idealized pinnacle of world literature represented by Western Nobel winners such as Yeats, Heaney, and Eliot. But it was these pro-Western members of China's literary field who appeared most resentful of Gao Xingjian's Nobel Prize, believing it smacked of tokenism and mired "pure" literary values in politics. To Poet A, Gao Xingjian represents a merely transitional generation of writers active in the 1980s, a period when literature was breaking out of the Maoist political mold but had not yet attained the greater artistic autonomy of the 1990s. Yet despite this poet's feeling of marginality from national politics, the desire to represent the nation runs parallel to a yearning for Chinese literature to attain the imagined universality of world literature. If the Nobel Committee was determined to give a prize to China, Poet A believed, they should have given it to Bei Dao, whom he regards as the most influential representative of a literary breakthrough in post-Mao Chinese writing. "It seems the Nobel Committee had begun to feel obliged to give the prize to someone Chinese," mused Poet A. "So it wasn't a breakthrough for pure literature: there were cultural, social, political factors at work. . . . And this whole question of whether to give it to someone Chinese and whom to give it to mutated into something even stranger, because in the end they gave it to a French person: it became a prize to works in Chinese." To this poet, Gao Xingjian is neither sufficiently literary, nor sufficiently Chinese and representative. This sense of disappointment was echoed by Critic A. "I don't believe he represents China; the problem is that the world thinks he represents China. If he was a good writer, we wouldn't need to raise the issue of whether he represents China or not. But because he's not good enough, and he's taken to represent China, I find it all very strange — I don't see why he should represent China."

A serious issue lies behind these unhappy complaints: the literary representation of contemporary China. The works of Gao Xingjian seized upon by such critics were those mentioned by name in the Swedish Academy's press release: *Lingshan*, *Yige ren de shengjing*, and *Taowang*, all of which, as shown above, take a very particular political stance on life in China, one that ties China to images of the Cultural Revolution, struggle sessions, and Tian'anmen. Contemporary China and its literature, meanwhile, remain a blank in average Western perceptions. There is a feeling among contemporary Chinese writers that China has changed greatly since 1989 and that the exiles, seized upon by the West as representatives, are not necessarily qualified spokesmen. Poet A spoke of his current disillusionment with Western views of China, which he sees as gripped by a superiority complex called the "China fantasy" (*Zhongguo huanxiang*).

> One manifestation of this is Westerners showing sympathy towards the weak, the unfortunate: people who live in China, under a dictatorship. . . . If Gao Xingjian was just one of them, they wouldn't have given him a prize. . . . Another manifestation of this is Chinese literati who go to the West. They know what China is like, even if Westerners don't. But living in the West, they discover their only capital is China. It's advantageous to them to turn China into a fantasy, something to be pitied. They put lots of nonliterary things into their works: they know it's not right, but it enables them to make a living. . . . This means that China can never be examined from a serious literary point of view by Western thinkers, critics and writers. . . . I think that giving Gao this prize is like giving a ping pong player a golf prize. Tell me, is this really a prize for Chinese literature? Or is it a prize for the political things that Westerners like to read about China?

But reception of Chinese literature in the West is not necessarily as simple as Poet A describes it, particularly in non-Anglophone areas: the success of Zhang Jie's nondissident *Chenzhong de chibang* (Heavy wings) in Germany is a contradictory case in point. Yet perhaps Poet A's assumptions are not too far from the truth in the economically and culturally powerful Anglophone reading market, in which émigré memoirs continued to occupy a far larger sector than Chinese literature in translation in 2001. Poet A's comments indicate how vehemently contemporary writers object to the imputation of national weakness and exotic marginality to China; at the same time his complaint highlights the painful disappointment of the long-cherished nationalist-universalist dream of Chinese writers and intellectuals: to be central at once in both national and international culture.

But where do the rumblings of Chinese intellectual nationalism end and questions of legitimate aesthetic concern (the literary representation of contemporary China) begin? China today is no longer the China of Mao Zedong or of the 1980s, despite all its manifest problems and lack of civil liberties. Since Zhang Yimou became an international and national cultural phenomenon, Chinese commentators have been highly suspicious of the international success of compatriots who have supplied a vision of a backward, benighted, politically oppressed China to the West. Yet does this mean that cataclysmic events in modern Chinese history such as the Cultural Revolution and 4 June 1989 are no more than junk-food literary topics designed to tempt Western appetites (as is implied by Poet A's dismissal of the "China fantasy")? Moreover, neither is writing about China's consumerist present-day a guarantee of literary quality. The fact that the first Chinese Nobel Prize has gone to a writer practically unconnected with contemporary China has brought out in Mainland authors (writing in the wake of a firmly entrenched realist tradition) a commitment to a literature that portrays the here-and-now of life around them — their very own imagined community. Yet critics lambaste contemporary Chinese literature for its superficiality, and for its failure to plumb the depths of experience in China.[24] The whole issue is tangled with feelings of cultural anxiety and marginality that have produced an acutely sensitive sense of copyright over the representation of China in modern global culture. While no one would dispute James Joyce's moral right or accomplishment in portraying the Dublin of *Ulysses* from Paris, modern Chinese history and the marginal position occupied by modern Chinese works in the world literary economy complicate questions of right to representation.

True enough, the commitment of Mainland writers to contemporaneity is not necessarily a rigidly nationalist project or a fixation with their exclusive right to represent a precisely defined China. One web commentator complained that giving a Nobel Prize to a writer as unknown in China as Gao was a "humiliation" (*chiru*) to the 1.3 billion Chinese, a turn of phrase deeply rooted in the Chinese marginality complex, registering both protest at foreign bullying and the desire to avenge such insults. Virtually no one involved in literary work in China, however, would be deluded enough to claim that any one writer could represent the nation or the people. Most writers in contemporary China are accepting of the marginal position of literature in society and hardly aspire to reach *all* the Chinese people. Instead they struggle with two redoubtable challenges: making sense of the amalgam that is China today (free market economy fronted by a tightly controlled media machine), and fulfilling the desire to create some small point of intersection between the life and language experienced by China's contemporary writers, and global literary perceptions.

This task is seen not simply as a question of subject matter and style (for example realism), but also of language and technique. "It's not that the things Gao Xingjian writes about can't be written," remarked Poet B, "but it's a question of how you write about them, what mode of thinking you use." Gao's works from the 1990s have been circulating among readers in China since he won the prize, eliciting more disappointment than approval. Gao himself emphasizes the importance of a free poetic and musical quality to his language, yet Chinese readers have criticized his language for lacking these very qualities. But such criticisms inevitably return to the question of portraying contemporary national reality in Chinese literature. "Your language should reflect the changes going on in Chinese reality," asserted Poet A.

> But when we read the works of poets who left the country ten years ago, it's as if they're still writing ten years ago. It's out-of-date, it's China of the 1980s. Gao Xingjian reflects that age very strongly in his grammar and vocabulary. The basic feelings of an era are embodied in its language and it's very important for novelists, particularly those who write about reality in their own country, to live in that country.

Mainland critics of his works generally prefer *Lingshan* to *Yige ren de shengjing*, primarily because the former was written in China, the latter abroad. Gao's modernist language and philosophy, it is felt, have too much of a studied quality, lacking a basis in the experience of contemporary Chinese life. "The level of Gao Xingjian's language in *Yige ren de shengjing* is that of a high school student," complained Critic B. "It's been washed and simplified by French." Although such comments raise generally valid aesthetic concerns, a suggestion of Chinese cultural exceptionalism remains apparent in the belief that the Chinese language is uniquely subtle and expressive in comparison with the efficient transparency of Western languages. The emotive force attached to representing contemporary Chinese reality, moreover, hints at the nationalistic sensitivity that has lain at the heart of modern Chinese literature and intellectual nation building since the May Fourth movement embraced literary realism.

Furthermore, while the need to use new types of language and thought from the 1990s to replace those of the 1980s is perceived, the search for new forms of literary and linguistic representation begun anew in the 1990s is by no means complete. Gao's Mainland critics themselves have few satisfactory solutions to the problematic relationship between intellectuals and literature, on the one hand, and Chinese history, politics, and society, on the other. China's pro-Western poets maintain faith in the universal power of art to transcend national political boundaries and place themselves in resolute opposition to the "nonliterary" elements and aims of Gao Xingjian's oeuvre. Poet A, however, refers to himself as "a pure, serious literary creator," while claiming he does not write "pure literature, because my writing contains a lot of nonliterary elements — political elements, factual elements, and historical elements, as well as my feelings about contemporary life and my experiences — all these are my materials. . . . I use nonliterary things to do literary things." He later attempted to be more specific in mapping out the complex interrelations between China and its literature.

> It's very hard to define China, but you can define literature through your own writing. I think the power of literature lies in fictionality (*xugou*). But now it seems that to be successful, Chinese writers have to discard fictionality. They have to write about reality, or about a Chinese reality defined by the West: the China fantasy, sympathy for China, criticism of dictatorship, only rotten, corrupt things. Chinese reality isn't like that any more, that's the China of the past.

This poet's reverence for "fictionality" as the basis of autonomous literary production is not as freewheeling as it appears. The Chinese reality described in works such as *Yige ren de shengjing* can lay an equally strong claim to being fictional. As Professor B pointed out, "Gao Xingjian could be imagining all this stuff about the past — who knows any more what's truth, what's illusion? He could have made it all up!" Gao Xingjian's fictional technique, however, is considered unacceptable because of its detachment from Chinese reality of the here-and-now. The desire expressed by contemporary poets for a universal literature rendered independent of the national political unit by the artistic power of its fictionality must be considered in tandem with their objections to the currency in the West of an "incorrect" Chinese reality. While the attachment of these writers to a universal, autonomous literary ideal is doubtless genuine, it is complicated by an undercurrent of "obsession with China." The concept of a "pure" art-for-art's-sake literature still mixes uneasily with China's entrenched realist tradition and cultural nationalism. Writers are anxious both for international recognition as creative agents and as acute chroniclers of contemporary Chinese society.

There are those, however, who have seen past the mirage of literary universalism and through the inequalities of the global system in which Chinese intellectuals have longed to participate. Critic A felt recent Nobel developments "highlight the position of contemporary Chinese culture since the end of the Cold War."

> For the Nobel Committee, the question of Chinese writers has been a difficult one, due to the Committee's contradictory feelings towards the CCP and towards socialism. I think if they'd given the prize to a French writer, they'd look at that writer's literary achievement, but when they gave it to a Chinese writer, in the end what they saw as important was China.

Gao Xingjian's prize, this critic believes, is symbolic in two ways. "It reveals the Nobel Committee's unchanging Eurocentric position. They very probably believe that only a writer who's lived for such a long time in France could blaze a new path for Chinese literature." Secondly, largely thanks to the reaction of the Chinese government, the latent ideological aspects of the prize "were turned into something public and exaggerated: Gao Xingjian has become this symbol of ideological resistance. Actually, I think he's independent of this, he isn't like this." This suggests that everyone is participating in a strange dance around the concept of China and its literature: the Chinese government has transformed an artistic exile into a Cold Warrior; Gao Xingjian, who claims to have broken with China, has become a literary freedom fighter; the Nobel Committee, which claims to be honoring a Chinese writer for his "universal validity," only mentions by name his works related to China, which happens to be one of the last great political stumbling blocks to the global victory of liberal democratic capitalism.

The only way out of this quagmire, Critic A believes, is to remain clear-sighted about the contradictions raised by Gao Xingjian's Nobel Prize.

> I feel that most good Chinese writers and scholars, on the one hand, strongly reject nationalism. But on the other hand, if they're reflective, they'll discover that they can't escape this national status so easily and that when they face the Euro-American world, it's no use denying this national status and saying "I don't represent China, I'm not speaking out as a Chinese person." ... In the end it's still, "Hey, that Chinese person's talking." Denying it is not only no use, it's also problematic, because there are still unequal power relations in place.

While acknowledging this quandary for Chinese writers, this critic did not find any virtue in the poets' assertions about "pure literature."

> Contemporary poets hallucinate that they can write as independent artists, with no relation to contemporary Chinese society and reality. First, I feel they lack a clear understanding of the globalization process and of the position of third-world countries in this process. Second, their attitude results in a loss, not a gain, in resources. I feel that the process of change to China's substructure, this brutal reality, is a resource for artists, not the other way round. . . . You have to face up to the nation. Ignoring it is a kind of self-deception.

This viewpoint demands a necessary skepticism towards the sources of authority and recognition in both China and the West for which Chinese intellectuals have yearned. It requires a reevaluation of the hopes invested by literary intellectuals in the dream of Chinese culture recovering lost power and glory through international acknowledgement, in the neutrality of modern international organizations and the autonomous aesthetic, and in their role as ambassadors for individual, national, and international identities. The final section will consider evidence for the emergence of this newly skeptical mode of thinking.

Post-Nobelism

"This Nobel Prize is mostly harmful," pronounced Poet A, "because Chinese people will think that Westerners don't take them seriously." China certainly takes itself extremely seriously as a political and cultural unity, a seriousness compounded by its terrible experiences in the twentieth century. Western observers have not failed to acknowledge and even appreciate this, as, for example, in the rumor that by 1998 Western literary agents had defined "Chinese pain" as a product because a profit could be made from it.[25] China's Nobel Complex was the (somewhat undignified) product of this almost melodramatic sense of historical seriousness.

Are Chinese intellectuals developing a sense of humor or irony over the Nobel Prize, however, and with it a calmer conception of the links between writing, nation, and the world? "The Nobel Committee has played a big joke on China!" proclaimed Shu Yi, head of the Institute of Modern Chinese Literature in Beijing. Shu Yi's remark, however, was tinged with a deep seriousness. The Nobel Prize remains a legitimate source for Chinese concern, he believed. "China is a great literary nation and has a very strong modern literature that isn't in the slightest inferior to international literature — it ought to have fair treatment in the world. . . . Why don't they give the prize to China?"[26] Doubt-less with this grievance in mind, Shu Yi has publicly endorsed and promoted a virtually unsubstantiated story concerning the planned award of the Nobel Prize to his father Lao She in 1968, claiming that in the chaos of the Cultural Revolution the Swedish Academy only found out about Lao She's death two years after it occurred. Still determined to give the prize to an East Asian writer, the committee made the award instead to the Japanese writer Yasunari Kawabata. Shu Yi's affectation of scorn about Gao's prize overlies a sense of cultural grievance directed at the recognition denied his nation and (alleg-edly) his father.[27]

This feeling of grievance, however, is far from universal: to other Chinese critics, the Nobel Prize has laid open the machinations of the international cultural scene. "Writers said themselves," Critic A reported, "this was the first time they understood that the Nobel Literature Prize was a lottery . . . Gao Xingjian is like the buyer of a winning lottery ticket. . . . They take this political game, cultural game, racial game, put them all together and Gao Xingjian wins the prize." The affirmation that acquaintance with (and trans-lation by) Göran Malmqvist amounted to a prerequisite for Chinese candi-dacy finally destroyed many people's hopes. Writer B expressed surprise at Göran Malmqvist accompanying Gao Xingjian on his post-Nobel visits to Hong Kong and Taiwan, both as translator of Gao's work and as Nobel judge. "Göran Malmqvist hasn't just awarded the prize, he's also won the prize, be-cause he's the translator. Therefore he should talk about translation questions, but no, he talks about Nobel problems, he talks about the problems of Chinese literature. It doesn't feel like a relationship between author and translator, it looks much more like a relationship between teacher and student — and he's the teacher. Or it's a favor relationship," he laughed. "He's Gao's mentor."[28] However, he has little patience with those disgruntled at the decision. "It's ridiculous to criticize the Swedish Academy for lacking fairness or authority, because that would be tantamount to acknowledging the Swedish Academy has the power and the ability to make judgments over the literature of the whole world — surely that's impossible?"

There is a substantial number of writers of all ages for whom the deflation of China's Nobel Complex was the most welcome cultural event of 2000. For the younger generation of free writers, the Nobel issue represents little more than a source of amusement, a curious cultural phenomenon well detached from their lives. "We don't particularly identify with it, but neither do we oppose it," commented Writer C, a young author. "Maybe older writers will despair, because they'll have no chance now. But there's no general reaction in Chinese writers, no envy because of the money, no jealousy because we think we write better. . . . Gao Xingjian's prize has more individual significance than anything else." He doubts Gao's winning the prize will have any influence on the development of Chinese literature, at least in the short term. "The society of such a big country as China has its own natural direction and Chinese literature will inevitably be influenced by this direction . . . if China is a river, Gao Xingjian is a different river, maybe a very pretty one, but we can only pass it by." Writer C considers Gao Xingjian's writing for foreigners, but this is not a cause for censure, merely a question of market logic. "If you're in exile, you don't have any choice other than to consider the tastes of Westerners, because you're floating. It's no good imagining what Chinese people want to read, because they can't get to read you now."

Yet despite such nonchalance, a sense of China's national uniqueness that overlaps with official nationalist rhetoric remains in those writing in the Mainland. "As a writer," asserts Li Feng, "I worry about how to be in China. The value in China of [Chinese] writers abroad has to be very low, because although they seem powerful abroad, they don't understand much of what's going on inside China." As Jiang Zemin has commented elsewhere: "Foreigners do not sufficiently understand China's goals."[29] Li continues: "As a writer, the greatest honor is acknowledgment from your own people. . . . Your works have to exercise influence and provoke discussion among this people."[30] He is concerned less about the Nobel Prize than about reestablishing links between Chinese society and a marginalized Chinese literature. In 2001 Li had spent the last two years devising the screenplay for *Hero* a martial arts film to be shot by Zhang Yimou, whose films of the late 1990s represented a more effective channel for simultaneously achieving international recognition, national popularity, and for raising social issues. "After *Not One Less* [which addressed the lack of funding for rural schools]," Li observed, "everyone was discussing the problem of rural education, everyone was crying and worrying about poverty, about children. Chinese literature doesn't have this reach."[31] Is this more "obsession with China"? A neosocialist reformulation of "serve the people" (*wei renmin fuwu*) for the new millennium?

Above all, Li Feng's remarks reinforce earlier observations about the self-positioning of intellectuals within the socialist market economy since the late 1990s. In conjunction with the marginalization of literature in the 1990s, writers during the second half of the decade sought to consolidate their position with respect to the domestic readership, turning away from foreign institutions such as the Nobel Prize. Reactions to the Nobel Prize 2000 thus reflect the dynamics of intellectual marginality during the 1990s. Perhaps even the political treatment of Gao Xingjian's prize within China was indicative of literature's peripheral status. The discomfort of the authorities was manifest in their pronouncements and in their acts of censorship: all of Gao's works, including those written before he left China and his translations from French into Chinese, were officially banned. Yet the authorities' handling of the incident through brief public statements recalled little of the virulent 1980s campaigns against writers such as Liu Binyan and Wang Ruowang. The CCP's relatively laissez-faire attitude implies that literature is seen as a marginal business, and that the party expects most intellectuals and writers to view Gao Xingjian's values as largely detached from and irrelevant to the everyday, pragmatic concerns faced by Chinese people and represented in Mainland culture. "This Nobel Prize won't influence ordinary people," said Writer C. "Winning a million dollars isn't that much money in China now—people are far more interested in Zhang Zhaoyang [an Internet millionaire]." Even if the Nobel Prize is now irrelevant, however, writers such as Li Feng continue to struggle to provide a voice for nation and people through alternative routes.

But by 2001 the heyday of serious literature seemed long past in China, and reading habits had changed with the younger generation: "My graduate students roared with laughter when they read *Yige ren de shengjing*," reported Professor B. "What's this, they said, sex then politics, sex then politics? What are the two doing together? They didn't understand at all, they're from a different age." His more traditional intellectual "worrying consciousness" (*youhuan yishi*), however, was still very much in evidence. He outlined the endemic problems within Chinese society resulting from uneven development, from collapse of the iron rice bowl, and from taxation burdens, all of which he feels have been obscured by the Western focus on Gao Xingjian's account of China's political predicament:

> The West has been fooled by Gao Xingjian! All these issues are beyond the worldview of Chinese writers abroad, of most writers in China. Nowadays, "human rights" have become a topic for discussion exclusively between overseas exiles, Gao Xingjian, the West, and the Chinese government, completely detached from the lives of ordinary Chinese people.

This statement, quite apart from the doubt that could be cast on its accuracy, begs the question of whether Chinese literature is the proper vehicle for raising such questions. Following a century during which Chinese literature has shouldered enormous burdens of responsibility with respect to social and political transformation, it is still trying to find its level under the rule of mass consumer culture at the start of the new millennium. It would probably be rash to assume that long-cherished hopes for a Nobel literature laureate resident on the Mainland permanently disappeared after the events of October 2000. In 2001, for example, Wenhua yishu chubanshe (Art and Culture Press) launched a series of anthologies of works by leading post-Mao Mainland authors, such as Yu Hua and Mo Yan, under the series title "Marching towards a Nobel" (*Zou xiang Nuobeier*). But for a few months after 12 October 2000, at least, Chinese literary intellectuals seemed willing to leave international diplomacy to the fliers of spy planes and the Nobel Prize to its own business.

AFTERWORD

The roots of China's Nobel Complex lie in the key intellectual question of Chinese modernity: how to respond to a historical situation that at once requires national and transnational consciousness. Modern intellectuals, and writers in particular, took on a heavy ideological and artistic burden at the start of the twentieth century as they worried about the fate of the nation and strove to produce a culture that would enable China to vie with the West. In the broad and ill-defined arena of national identity, and under pressure from international stimuli, aesthetics and politics in twentieth-century China have thus both supported and struggled with each other, but only rarely operated in clear-cut, self-sufficient states of detachment. The development of the Nobel Complex highlights the ongoing confusion over aims and audience among modern Chinese writers caught between national, international, and individual aspirations.

Chinese preoccupation with the Nobel Literature Prize has provided insights into the development of these century-old concerns during the past twenty-five years, and into the self-image of Chinese intellectuals under the rule of Dengist internationalism. While the events of October 2000 quieted the Complex, other issues such as hosting the 2008 Olympics and engineering China's entry to the WTO have taken its place as symbolic foci for Chinese anxieties about their nation's status as a modern global civilization. Yet although both these events will doubtless continue to generate international controversy, they are securely rooted in the sporting and economic spheres, which are judged by criteria generally less contentious than those used for literature. Neither sport nor economics embodies as clearly as the Nobel Complex the links between intellectuals, the practices of literature and nation building, and the tensions that run along those links. Intellectual nation building and the desire for a Nobel Prize have held literary intellectuals ransom to a collective identification with "the people," and turned literature into an international ambassador for China. But as long as the nation-state remains the principal unit of accounting in global transactions, and as long as intellectuals remain opinion makers in nations around the world, national

185

identity and literature continue to exercise a powerful hold over global con-sciousness — even in once-neutral Sweden. In twentieth-century China, it is simply the case that for historical and cultural reasons, these connections have been closer and more exposed than in other parts of the world.

With all this in mind, it is hardly surprising that virtually no party emerged with any particular clarity of standpoint from the controversies surround-ing China's Nobel Complex: neither the Swedish Academy, which conflated criticism of Chinese politics with praise for "universal validity," nor Gao's critics inside China, who struggle on the margins to find their own literary manifesto and constituency of readers. The only real winner is, of course, Gao Xingjian, who has demonstrated impressive commitment to literary creativ-ity in the solitude of exile and who has received recognition of this fact in the form of the world's most famous literary prize. Literary prizes, as Kingsley Amis sensibly said, are "obviously all right if you win them."[1]

NOTES

Prologue

1. Although in the complete index of laureates, Gao Xingjian's Nobel Prize is now listed as going to France, the original press release states that "The Nobel Prize for Literature 2000 goes to the Chinese writer Gao Xingjian." See Swedish Academy, http://www.nobel.se/literature/laureates/2000/index.html and http://www.nobel.se/literature/laureates/2000/press.html, respectively.

2. Swedish Academy, "Press Release: The Nobel Prize for Literature," 12 October 2000, at http://www.nobel.se/literature/laureates/2000/press.html.

3. After being effectively muted, like many writers of his generation, by the political campaigns of the Cultural Revolution, Gao rose to fame in the 1980s as a pioneer of avant-garde, modernist techniques in drama and literary theory, before leaving China in 1987 for Europe and, ultimately, France. Since taking up residence abroad, he has developed an increasingly surrealist, avant-garde dramatic style with echoes of Beckett, at the same time as completing two novels set in China. In 1998, he was granted French citizenship (for further biographical details and references, see pp. 164–166). Although by October 2000, Gao was still remembered by intellectuals and writers who resumed or began their careers in the early 1980s and in avant-garde drama circles, the rapid changes in the Chinese literary scene in the 1990s ensured that he was not well known to younger readers. Outside literary circles and in the general literate community, moreover, his audience was very small.

4. See ibid and http://www.nobel.se/literature/laureates/2000/presentation-speech.html.

Chapter 1: Introduction — Diagnosing the Complex

1. See, for example, Zhou Changcai, "Ba Jin he Nuobeier wenxue jiang" (Ba Jin and the Nobel Literature Prize), *Waiguo wenxue* no. 5 (2000): 43–51; Zhao Zhizhong, "Shen Congwen yu Nuobeier wenxue jiang" (Shen Congwen and the Nobel Literature Prize), *Waiguo wenxue* no. 4 (2000): 87–90.

2. Lydia Liu, *Translingual Practice: Literature, National Culture, and Translated Modernity; China, 1900–1937* (Stanford: Stanford University Press, 1995), 50.

3. Lu Xun, "Zi xu," (Preface) to *Nahan* (Call to arms), in *Lu Xun quanji* (Collected works by Lu Xun) (Beijing: Renmin wenxue chubanshe, 1982), vol. 1, 417.

4. See Vera Schwarcz, *The Chinese Enlightenment: Intellectuals and the Legacy of*

the May Fourth Movement of 1919 (Berkeley: University of California Press, 1986), for example, 170.

5. Ibid., 7.

6. Perry Link, *Evening Chats in Beijing* (New York: Norton, 1992).

7. See reference and further discussion on p. 6.

8. See, for example, Sun Wanning, *Leaving China: Media, Migration, and Transnational Imagination* (Maryland: Rowman and Littlefield, 2002).

9. C. T. Hsia, "Appendix 1: Obsession with China: The Moral Burden of Modern Chinese Literature," in idem, *A History of Modern Chinese Fiction*, 2nd ed. (New Haven: Yale University Press, 1971), 533–534. It should be pointed out, however, that "obsession with China" is not a disorder suffered uniformly throughout the broad community of Chinese intellectuals, literary or otherwise. Critics such as Bonnie McDougall and Xueping Zhong have specifically identified it as an overwhelmingly male disorder, a view that many of my findings on the Nobel Complex (as an offspring of "obsession with China") corroborate. See, for example, Bonnie S. McDougall, "Disappearing Women and Disappearing Men in May Fourth Narrative: a Post-feminist Survey of Short Stories by Mao Dun, Bing Xin, Ling Shuhua and Shen Congwen," in *Fictional Authors, Imaginary Audiences: Modern Chinese Literature in the Twentieth Century* (Hong Kong: The Chinese University Press, 2003), 133–167; "Writing Self: Author/Audience Complicity in Modern Chinese Fiction," in *Fictional Authors*, 45–74; Xueping Zhong, *Masculinity Besieged? Issues of Modernity and Male Subjectivity in Chinese Literature of the Late Twentieth Century* (Durham: Duke University Press, 2000). Elsewhere, McDougall redefines the intellectual "obsession with China" as an obsession with the fate of Chinese intellectuals themselves (see "Modern Chinese Literature and Its Critics," in *Fictional Authors*, 36). In the context of China's complex about the Nobel Literature Prize, this redefinition further accentuates the ironies and paradoxes of the way in which the development of the elite individualistic cultural form of literature and the preoccupations of Chinese intellectuals have over the past hundred years become so closely identified with the collective state of the Chinese nation.

10. For discussions of this phenomenon, see Suisheng Zhao, "Chinese Intellectuals' Quest for National Greatness and Nationalistic Writing in the 1990s," *China Quarterly* 152 (December 1997): 725–745; Peter Hays Gries, *China's New Nationalism: Pride, Politics and Diplomacy* (Berkeley: University of California Press, 2004). The post-Mao fixation on face-giving prizes was mercilessly satirized in fictional form by the contemporary novelist Wang Shuo in *Please Don't Call Me Human*, trans. Howard Goldblatt (Harpenden, London: No Exit Press, 2000).

11. Geremie Barmé, *In the Red: On Contemporary Chinese Culture* (New York: Columbia University Press, 1999), 265–272.

12. Writers and the estate of literature have, of course, enjoyed varying fortunes in China's turbulent twentieth century, the Maoist years (in particular 1966–1976) representing the high point of political repression suffered by many writers. As will become apparent from my later discussion, however, I believe that the efforts and ideas of intellectuals have overall played a central role in modernization and reform movements in twentieth-century China. Starting from Yan Fu and Liang Qichao,

moreover, literary intellectuals (and hence literature itself) have assumed a central role in Chinese modernizing schemas. Even at the peaks of literary and intellectual repression in the twentieth century, ideological struggles and political campaigns were often fought out *between* factions of literary intellectuals and not necessarily *against* literary intellectuals en masse, for example, the 1957 Anti-Rightist campaign that banished the novelist Ding Ling (see Merle Goldman, *Literary Dissent in Communist China*, Cambridge, Mass.: Harvard University Press, 1967: 203–242). Years later, Ding Ling and the poet Ai Qing themselves turned on their fellow writers, by supporting the 1983 Anti-Spiritual Pollution campaign directed at the Misty Poets (*Menglong shiren*), among others.

13. China is not alone in its Nobel Complex. The Japanese government made strenuous efforts in translation and promotion to bring Kawabata and other Japanese authors to international and Nobel attention in the 1960s, in the lead-up to the awarding of the 1967 Nobel Prize to Kawabata. More recently, the Japanese government has expressed anxiety about Japan's paucity of Nobel Science Prizes, declaring that Japan should strive to win thirty Nobel Prizes in fifty years (see "Round Table Talk: Are Japan's research hopes really so 'Nobel'?" *The Asahi Shimbun*, http://www.asahi.com/english/op-ed/K2001121200562.html. In China, meanwhile, from the late 1990s, media interest in Nobel prizes focused increasingly on the science prizes. National anxiety about global sources of recognition and prestige are, furthermore, not restricted to the Nobel Prize. Both Japan and China have exhibited marked determination to "catch up" with the West in, for example, the sporting sphere. See Sebastian Moffett, *Japanese Rules* (London: Yellow Jersey Press, 2002) for Japan's campaign to reinvent itself as an international footballing presence, culminating in the hosting of the 2002 World Cup finals; see Susan Brownell, *Training the Body for China: Sports in the Moral Order of the People's Republic* (Chicago: University of Chicago Press, 1995) for the links between modern Chinese nationalism and sport, and for commentary on China's 1993 campaign for the 2000 Olympics; see also the discussion in Barmé, *In the Red*, 258.

14. China's international sporting achievements in the post-Mao era have included the women's volleyball World Cup in 1981, the hosting of the Asian Games in 1990, the women's football World Cup in 1999, 28 gold medals in the 2000 Sydney Olympics, qualification by the men's team for the 2002 football World Cup finals, and Beijing's successful bid to host the 2008 Olympics. China has also established itself as a world economic power, trumpeting miracle growth rates and, in December 2001, engineering accession to the World Trade Organization (WTO). See, for example, Peter Nolan, *China and the Global Economy: National Champions, Industrial Policy and the Big Business Revolution* (New York: Palgrave Macmillan, 2001) and Nicholas R. Lardy, *Integrating China into the Global Economy* (Washington, D.C.: The Brookings Institution, 2002).

15. The situation is different in the reading markets of other European languages. In August 2001, for example, the Spanish translation of Gao Xingjian's Nobel Prize–winning novel, *Lingshan*, was the sixth best-selling work of fiction in Spain. See "Bestsellers in Spain: What the World Is Reading," *The Economist*, 25–31 August 2001, 77. Consider also the success of the novelist Ah Cheng in continental Europe relative to

Britain (McDougall, *Modern Chinese Literature*, 37). See also discussion on p. 31 and 196n.99 below.

16. Benedict Anderson, *Imagined Communities: Reflections on the Origin and Spread of Nationalism* (London: Verso, 1991).

17. Liah Greenfeld, *Nationalism: Five Roads to Modernity* (Cambridge, Mass.: Harvard University Press, 1992). John Fitzgerald, *Awakening China: Politics, Culture and Class in the Nationalist Revolution* (Stanford: Stanford University Press, 1996).

18. Ernest Gellner, *Nations and Nationalism* (Oxford: Blackwell, 1983).

19. Susan Daruvala, *Zhou Zuoren and an Alternative Chinese Response to Modernity* (Cambridge, Mass.: Harvard University Press, 2000), 14–35.

20. The philosophical contradictions within nationalist thought between particularism and universalism emerged with the crisis of liberal nationalism towards the end of the nineteenth century, when organicist, race-based conceptions of the nation rose up to challenge Enlightenment notions of universal human liberty. These tensions contributed to the emergence of totalitarian nation-states in the twentieth century such as Nazi Germany and formed the backdrop to the nation-building experiences of many non-Western states. See the discussion in Pericles Lewis, *Nationalism, Modernism, and the Novel* (Cambridge, Eng.: Cambridge University Press, 2000).

21. Anderson, *Imagined Communities*, 5.

22. Prasenjit Duara, *Rescuing History from the Nation* (Chicago: University of Chicago Press, 1995), 20.

23. My reading of Hegel is influenced by Prasenjit Duara's account of the Hegelian Enlightenment mode of thinking about "History," which he designates "with a capital H to distinguish it from other modes of figuring the past" (Duara, *Rescuing History*, 4). While I have chosen to focus on particular aspects of the intellectual legacy of the Enlightenment (namely its contribution to modern nation building); it is, of course, important not to overlook the complexities of the philosophy and thought associated with the Enlightenment: for example, its manifestly liberal advocacy of the natural rights of man and of religious tolerance. Hegel's date of birth, moreover, would seem to mark him out as a Romantic rather than an Enlightenment thinker. However, through his twin preoccupations with rationality and (the national) spirit, Hegel demonstrated how the Enlightenment belief in universal reason and progress could be harnessed to a (post-) Herderian Romantic preoccupation with national particularity. The development of the late eighteenth- and nineteenth-century view of individual national cultures as unique entities bound together by their own language, folklore, and institutions, combined with historical circumstances (the rise of the nation-state in Europe following the French Revolution) cemented this link and oversaw the emergence of an increasingly aggressive and competitive nationalism as the dominant mode of political organization and consciousness in the nineteenth-century European world and beyond.

24. David Held et al., *Global Transformations: Politics, Economics and Culture* (Cambridge: Polity Press, 1999), 37–38.

25. Although tributary practices can be traced as far back as the Shang period (second half of the second millennium BC), they were first fully institutionalized under the Han, reaching a peak of maturity and complexity during the Qing dynasty. For more

details, see John K. Fairbank ed., *The Chinese World Order* (Cambridge, Mass: Harvard University Press, 1968); John K. Fairbank and S. Y. Teng, "On the Ch'ing Tributary System," *Harvard Journal of Asiatic Studies* 6.2 (1942) 135–246; Yü Ying-Shih, "Han Foreign Relations," in *The Cambridge History of China, Volume 1: the Ch'in and Han Empires, 221 B.C. —A.D. 220*, eds. Dennis Twitchett and Michael Loewe (Cambridge: Cambridge University Press, 1986), 377–383.

26. Takeshi Hamashita has recently argued that the introduction of the treaty port system in the mid-nineteenth century did not bring about the instant cessation of old-style tribute relations in China, but rather a half century of negotiations that combined elements from both the Western notion of trade between sovereign nations and the Chinese notion of tributary relations involving vassal states. See Hamashita, "Tribute and Treaties: Maritime Asia and Treaty Port Networks in the Era of Negotiation, 1800–1900," in Giovanni Arrighi, Takeshi Hamashita, and Mark Selden, eds., *The Resurgence of East Asia: 500, 150 and 50 year perspectives* (London: Routledge, 2003), 17–50.

27. On the relative equalities in economic development between Europe and Asia as late as the eighteenth century, see, for example, Kenneth Pomeranz, *The Great Divergence: China, Europe, and the Making of the Modern World Economy* (Princeton: Princeton University Press, 2000). Arrighi et al. eds., *The Resurgence of East Asia* offers wide-ranging temporal perspectives on the internal dynamism of the East Asia region from the early modern period onwards, together with detailed insights into the complexities of interregional transactions during these centuries.

28. Joseph Levenson, "The Genesis of *Confucian China and Its Modern Fate*," in *The Historian's Workshop: Original Essays by Sixteen Historians*, ed. L. P. Curtis, Jr., (New York: Knopf, 1970), 288.

29. Xiaobing Tang, *Global Space and the Nationalist Discourse of Modernity: The Historical Thinking of Liang Qichao* (Stanford: Stanford University Press, 1996), 8.

30. Rey Chow, *Woman and Chinese Modernity* (Minneapolis: University of Minnesota Press, 1991); David Der-wei Wang, *Fin-de-siècle Splendor: Repressed Modernities in Late Qing Fiction* (Stanford: Stanford University Press, 1997). Chow, in particular, has persuasively argued that a strong current of traditional Confucian didacticism runs through the May Fourth theorization of a new, modern, and artistically autonomous literature.

31. Leo Ou-fan Lee, *Shanghai Modern: The Flowering of a New Urban Culture in China 1930–1945* (Cambridge, Mass.: Harvard University Press, 1999), 62.

32. Perry Link, *The Uses of Literature: Life in the Socialist Literary System* (Princeton: Princeton University Press, 2000), 104–105.

33. Philip C. C. Huang, "Liang Ch'i-ch'ao: The Idea of the New Citizen and the Influence of Meiji Japan," in *Transition and Permanence: Chinese History and Culture. A Festschrift in Honor of Dr Hsiao Kung-ch'uan*, ed. David C. Buxbaum and Frederick T. Mote (Hong Kong: privately printed, 1972), 85–86.

34. See, for example, Liang Qichao, "On the Relationship Between Fiction and the Government of the People," in *Modern Chinese Literary Thought: Writings on Literature, 1893–1945*, ed. Kirk Denton (Stanford: Stanford University Press, 1996), 74–81.

35. Fitzgerald, *Awakening China*, 35.

36. Rey Chow, *Writing Diaspora* (Bloomington: University of Indiana, 1993), 102.

37. Liu Kang, "Is There an Alternative to (Capitalist) Globalization? The Debate about Modernity in China," in *The Cultures of Globalization*, ed. Fredric Jameson and Masao Miyoshi (Durham: Duke University Press, 1998), 170.

38. Tang, *Global Space*, 75.

39. It could be countered that global modernity should be defined as a general complex of socioeconomic processes and practices arising globally during the early modern period, and far from exclusive to the West, such as growing commercialization, the rise of an urban leisure culture and double-entry bookkeeping. In attributing primacy here to a Western-dominated model of global modernity, however, I attach particular importance to political processes and forms of Western dominance that have arisen during the past two to three centuries, in direct connection with the rise of imperialism and nation building. My reading of the links between modernity, globalization, and nation building is influenced by Daruvala's division of "modernity" as a category for analysis into an earlier "first-order modernity," ("a general, somewhat Braudelian, set of processes of socioeconomic change in different parts of the world that led to higher levels of global economic integration" during the early modern period) and a later "second-order modernity" (springing from "the simultaneous emergence of the modern nation-state and the establishment of colonial empires, from the late eighteenth century through the nineteenth century and into the twentieth.") See Daruvala, *Zhou Zuoren*, 14–16.

40. Bin Zhao, "Consumerism, Confucianism, Communism: Making Sense of China Today," *New Left Review* 222 (1997): 44.

41. See, for example, Matei Calinescu's comments on the "two modernities" in *Five Faces of Modernity: Modernism, Avant-Garde, Decadence, Kitsch, Postmodernism* (Durham: Duke University Press, 1987), 41–58.

42. That said, the unsettling effects of modernity's endless pursuit of novelty and development have manifested themselves as much in the West as in the non-West, as is illustrated in Marshall Berman's study of aesthetic experiences of modernity in the West, *All That Is Solid Melts Into Air: The Experience of Modernity* (London: Verso, 1983). At present, there are also signs that the Western-dominated paradigm of modernity in historical studies is beginning to be challenged by non-Western-centric and comparative perspectives, as exemplified by R. Bin Wong's approach in *China Transformed: Historical Change and the Limits of European Experience* (Ithaca: Cornell University Press, 1997). More recently, in *The Birth of the Modern World, 1780–1914: Global Connections and Comparisons* (Oxford: Blackwell, 2004), C. A. Bayly adopts a similar historical viewpoint. Essays in the *Journal of Asian Studies* (61.2 [May 2002]) and the *American Historical Review* (Gale Stokes, "The Fates of Human Societies," in 102.2 [April 2001], 508–525) have provided a forum for discussing these mooted paradigm shifts. In the view of the author, although these new currents of debate signpost a significant change in ways models of modernity are conceptualized, it will take time for them to impact fully on general public consciousness beyond academia.

43. Duara, *Rescuing History*, 17–19.

44. Edward Said, *Orientalism* (New York: Random House, 1978).

45. Partha Chatterjee, *Nationalist Thought and the Colonial World: A Derivative*

Discourse? (London: Zed Books, 1986). This is not to deny Chatterjee's observations about the space nationalism also provides for developing alternatives.

46. Partha Chatterjee, *The Nation and Its Fragments: Colonial and Postcolonial Histories* (Princeton: Princeton University Press, 1993), 5. See also the discussion in Daruvala, *Zhou Zuoren*, 24–29.

47. Gregory Jusdanis, *Belated Modernity and Aesthetic Culture: Inventing National Literature* (Minneapolis: University of Minnesota Press, 1991). His focus on Greece demonstrates that the anxieties linked to modern nation building are not a uniquely non-Western phenomenon.

48. The label Enlightenment–Romantic is used to signal the way in which the life and work of Herder, one of the most influential theorizers of the uniqueness of national peoples, straddled and connected two broad phases of modern Western thought, the Enlightenment and Romanticism.

49. See Pierre Bourdieu, *The Cultural Field of Production*, ed. Randall Johnson (Cambridge: Polity Press, 1993).

50. Fitzgerald, *Awakening China*, 123–126 and 131–132.

51. See discussion in Liu, *Translingual Practice*, 183–195.

52. Zhong, *Masculinity Besieged?*, 11.

53. Martin Jacques, "The Interregnum," *London Review of Books*, 5 February 2004, p. 8.

54. David Held and Anthony McGrew, "The Great Globalization Debate: An Introduction," in *The Global Transformations Reader: An Introduction to the Globalization Debate*, ed. David Held and Anthony McGrew (Cambridge: Polity Press, 2000), 1–45. The selection of books on global politics and society reviewed in Jacques, "The Interregnum"—ranging from Ellen Meiksins Wood's opinion that "the world today is more than ever a world of nation-states," via Michael Ignatieff's view of American international interventionism as, overall, a benevolently globalized policeman, to Mary Kaldor's conceptualization of an openly global civil society—testify to the continuing existence, post-September 11, of hugely divergent views on the balance of power between national and global forces in the current world order. See Wood, *Empire of Capital* (London: Verso, 2003); Ignatieff, *Empire Lite: Nation-Building in Bosnia, Kosovo, Afghanistan* (London: Vintage, 2003); Kaldor, *Global Civil Society: An Answer to War* (London: Polity, 2003).

55. Held and McGrew, "The Great Globalization Debate: An Introduction."

56. Arjun Appadurai, "Disjuncture and Difference in the Global Cultural Economy," in *Global Culture*, ed. Mike Featherstone (London: Sage Publications, 1990), 295–310.

57. Chatterjee, *The Nation and Its Fragments*, 3.

58. Gyan Prakash, "Writing Post-Orientalist Histories of the Third World: Perspectives from Indian Historiography," *Comparative Studies in Society and History* 32.2 (April 1990): 384. See also Henk Wesseling, "Overseas History," in Peter Burke ed. *New Perspectives on Historical Writing* (Cambridge: Polity Press, 2001), 71–96, for a useful overview of trends in colonial and postcolonial historiography from the late nineteenth century onwards.

59. Ziauddin Sardar, *Postmodernism and the Other* (London: Pluto Press, 1998),

6–7. See Calinescu, *Five Faces of Modernity*, 263–312, on the epistemological diffusion of postmodernism; see Linda Hutcheon, *A Poetics of Postmodernism: History, Theory, Fiction* (New York: Routledge, 1988) on the literary aesthetics of postmodernism; see Jean-Francois Lyotard, *The Postmodern Condition: A Report on Knowledge* (Manchester: Manchester University Press, 1984) on postmodern consciousness.

60. Fredric Jameson, "Preface," in Jameson and Miyoshi, *The Cultures of Globalization*, xvii.

61. Frederick Buell, *National Culture and the New Global System* (Baltimore: Johns Hopkins University Press, 1994), 137.

62. Ibid., 337–338.

63. Homi K. Bhabha, "DissemiNation: time, narrative and the margins of the modern nation," in *Nation and Narration*, ed. Bhabha (London: Routledge, 1990), 291–320.

64. Daruvala, *Zhou Zuoren*, 27.

65. Buell, *National Culture*, 341–342.

66. Dirlik does not address the challenge to Western economic dominance presented by the rise of East Asia since the 1960s and of China since the 1990s. His omission is perhaps still justified in the case of China which, despite enjoying phenomenal growth figures over the past ten to fifteen years — 14 percent was the highest annual increase achieved in the 1990s — is building itself up from a tiny base of national wealth. In 1990, the Gross National Product was barely $330 per capita (Joe Studwell, *The China Dream: The Elusive Quest for the Greatest Untapped Market on Earth* [London: Profile, 2002], 99). In short, China's economic miracle, although impressive, is still in its early days.

67. See also Wesseling, "Overseas History" for comments on the paradoxical dependence of non-Western postcolonial historians on the West, and on the survival after decolonization of the Western "empire of capital."

68. Buell, *National Culture*, 342. See also Jacques, "The Interregnum," 9, for the failure of Western conceptualizations of a "global civil society" to make significant reference to models of civil society from the non-West.

69. Arif Dirlik, *The Postcolonial Aura: Third World Criticism in the Age of Global Capitalism* (Boulder, Co.: Westview Press, 1997), 60.

70. Sardar, *Postmodernism*, 13.

71. Ibid., 13.

72. Ibid., 168.

73. In Fredric Jameson, *Postmodernism, or the Cultural Logic of Late Capitalism* (Durham: Duke University Press, 1991), for example, Jameson fully identifies global capitalism as the driving force behind the making of postmodern culture and argues that, in its inability to maintain critical distance from consumer society, postmodern culture becomes little more than an embellishment of that society.

74. See, for instance, Hutcheon, *A Poetics of Postmodernism*.

75. See, for example, Gandhi, *Postcolonial Theory: A Critical Introduction* (Edinburgh: Edinburgh University Press, 1998) and Chow, *Ethics After Idealism* (Bloomington: Indiana University Press, 1998) 1–13. Gandhi's book is an excellent introduction to the context and debates of postcolonial theory.

76. Ien Ang, *On Not Speaking Chinese* (London: Routledge, 2001).

77. Arif Dirlik and Xudong Zhang, "Introduction: Postmodernism and China," *boundary 2* 24.3 (1997): 3.

78. Jing Wang, *High Culture Fever: Politics, Aesthetics, and Ideology in Deng's China* (Berkeley: University of California Press, 1996), 233–259.

79. Dirlik and Zhang, "Introduction," 4.

80. Ben Xu, "From Modernity to Chineseness": The Rise of Nativist Cultural Theory in Post-1989 China," *Positions* 6, no. 1 (1998): 203–237. Zhao Yiheng, " 'Houxue' yu Zhongguo xin baoshou zhuyi," *Ershiyi shiji* 27 (February 1995): 4–15.

81. Xu, "From Modernity to Chineseness," 224.

82. Ibid., 220.

83. The ripostes to Xu and Zhao from the scholars they are criticizing are discussed in Michelle Yeh, "International Theory and the Transnational Critic: China in the Age of Multiculturalism," *boundary 2* 25.3 (1998): 193–222. In sum, the debate highlights the tensions between different camps of the now diasporic Chinese scholarly community as well as the development during the 1990s of a hostile nationalist essentialism among Mainland critics directed at Chinese scholars and writers abroad.

84. Jing Wang's later work observes a greater degree of indeterminacy within late 1990s Chinese culture. While the florescence of consumerist popular culture coexists with one-party state nationalism, however, it is difficult to affirm the pluralizing results of economic liberalization. See Jing Wang, "Culture as Leisure and Culture as Capital," *Positions* 9, no. 1 (2001): 69–104.

85. See Fritz Strich, *Goethe and World Literature*, trans. C. A. M. Sym (New York: Kennikat Press, 1972).

86. Karl Marx, *The Communist Manifesto* (London: Harmondsworth, 1967), 84.

87. Richard Kraus and Wendy Larson, "China's Writers, the Nobel Prize, and the International Politics of Literature," *The Australian Journal of Chinese Affairs* 21 (January 1989): 155.

88. See Kjell Espmark, *The Nobel Prize in Literature: A Study of the Criteria Behind the Choices* (Boston: G. K. Hall, 1991).

89. See also Andrew Jones' lucid remarks on the position of Chinese writing within world literature in "Chinese Literature in the 'World' Literary Economy," *Modern Chinese Literature* 8.1–2 (Spring/Fall 1994): 171–190.

90. I am indebted for many of the statistics given on Chinese-English translation in this section to Red Chan's doctoral thesis, "Politics of Translation: Mainland Chinese Novels in the Anglophone World in the Post-Mao Era" (Oxford: University of Oxford, 2003). Although references are made where possible to non-Anglophone translations of Mainland Chinese literature and to Taiwanese literature, this section focuses predominantly on Mainland Chinese literature in English translation. This decision to narrow the scope of discussion was governed partly by considerations of space, but mainly because of the global linguistic dominance of English and to maintain the thematic focus on Mainland Chinese literature elsewhere in the book.

91. Only one translator of contemporary Chinese literature — Howard Goldblatt — has any track record in placing Chinese literature with prominent commercial presses, and even his achievements have produced few best-sellers or critical *succes d'estime*.

92. See, for example, the series of modern Chinese fictional works published by University of Hawai'i Press and Columbia University Press.

93. One example is Michael Berry's translation of *Nanjing 1937* (*1937 nian de ai-qing*) by Ye Zhaoyan. Originally published by Columbia University Press, it was published in Great Britain in 2003 by the renowned poetry and fiction publisher, Faber and Faber. The latter, however, did not bother to anglicize the translation's original Americanized usages, much less iron out some of the translation's stylistic infelicities. A notable exception to this carelessness towards Chinese literature in translation is the skillful editing by Rebecca Carter at the equally famous London publishing house Chatto & Windus of books such as *Red Dust* and *The Noodlemaker* (Ma Jian, 2001, 2004). Much of the credit for the high production quality of both these books is also due to the efforts of the London literary agent Toby Eady, who has championed the mainstream publishing of writing on China since the start of the 1990s (his first and most notable success was Jung Chang's *Wild Swans* (London: HarperCollins, 1991). Eady originally commissioned *Red Dust* and ensured sympathetic and meticulous editing for both books.

94. Bonnie McDougall, *Fictional Authors, Imaginary Audiences*, 6.

95. See, for example, the remarks made by Bonnie McDougall in "Modern Chinese Literature and Its Critics" in her *Fictional Authors*; Howard Goldblatt in "Words Don't Come Easy," *South China Morning Post*, 12 June 1999; and Michael S. Duke in "The Problematic Nature of Modern and Contemporary Chinese Fiction in English Translation," in Howard Goldblatt ed., *Worlds Apart: Recent Chinese Writing and Its Audiences* (New York: M. E. Sharpe, 1990), 198–227.

96. One instance is W. J. F. Jenner's essay, "Insuperable Barriers? Some thoughts on the Reception of Chinese Writing in English Translation," in Goldblatt ed., *Worlds Apart*, 177–197.

97. McDougall, "Modern Chinese Literature and Its Critics," in *Fictional Authors*, 17–18.

98. Any list of "the best" modern Chinese authors is inevitably personal, but pre-1949 authors such as Lu Xun, Shen Congwen, Zhang Ailing and Qian Zhongshu can be rated highly without inciting too much controversy; canonization of significant contemporary authors is more open to debate, but most critics would probably select one or more names from a group of authors born in the 1940s, 1950s, and 1960s that includes Bei Dao, Mo Yan, Han Shaogong, Wang Anyi, Liu Heng, Yu Hua, Jia Pingwa, and Ma Jian. Some of the best Anglophone translators of the post-Mao period are Bonnie McDougall, Howard Goldblatt, and Flora Drew.

99. Reading markets in countries such as Spain (see note 15 above), the Netherlands, and France are far more open to translations, even from Chinese. In the months following the awarding of the Nobel Prize to the relatively unknown Gao Xingjian in October 2000, a series of translations of both his best- and lesser-known works into Dutch was promptly organized. British readers, however, had to wait until February 2001 for a translation of Gao's novel *Soul Mountain* (*Lingshan*) to be brought out. In France, meanwhile, translations of contemporary Chinese literature win review space in national broadsheets such as *Le Monde* more often than in Britain. Nevertheless, the position occupied by Chinese literature in the rest of Europe is still far from main-

stream: the success of Zhang Jie's 1981 novel *Heavy Wings* (*Chenzhong de chibang*) in Germany is often cited to disprove European aversion to reading Chinese literature in translation, but German sinologists themselves view its popularity as an exception rather than the rule. And although some European publishers maintain impressive China lists, it remains the case that breaking into Anglophone markets is frequently key to international success. Despite some notable exceptions — such as Ah Cheng's *Qiwang*, the English translation of which was commissioned on the strength of its success in French — the sale of translation rights to other European countries often follows translation into English: for example, Han Shaogong's 1995 novel, *Maqiao cidian*, was translated into German as a consequence of the publication of the English translation (*A Dictionary of Maqiao*, New York: Columbia University Press, 2003). Often, moreover, where there is an existing English translation, publishers in other European languages will save time and money by commissioning a translation from the English, rather than from the original Chinese version.

100. Stephen Kinzer, "America Yawns at Foreign Fiction," *New York Times*, 26 July 2003, http://www.nytimes.com/2003/07/26/books/26BOOK.html.

101. See note 120 below for further reading on the modern Chinese enthusiasm for Western fiction. One of the recent translations from the West to become a best-seller in the Mainland is the Harry Potter series, which by May 2001 had sold 1.3 million copies in China.

102. Notable examples are Nien Cheng's *Life and Death in Shanghai* (London: Grafton, 1986), Jung Chang's best-selling *Wild Swans*, and Ha Jin's *Waiting* (New York: Random House, 1999). The latter won the U.S. National Book Award in 2000.

103. Several works by the first three have been published by commercial presses in Britain (Penguin, Harvill, and Faber and Faber, respectively). Books by Murakami and Yoshimoto are consistently reviewed in serious literary review journals such as *The Times Literary Supplement*. Murakami's *Sputnik Sweetheart* was discussed on publication in translation on the BBC arts program, *Late Night Review* — a very rare honor for a translation. For a discussion of the recent history of publishing translated Japanese fiction in the West, see Edward Fowler, "Rendering Words, Translating Cultures: On the Art and Politics of Translating Modern Japanese Fiction," *Journal of Japanese Studies*, 18.1 (Winter 1992), 1–44.

104. On the link between Japan's economic development and Western appreciation of its literature, see comments by the Nobel judge Artur Lundkvist in Peter Lennon, "Why Graham Greene hasn't won a Nobel Prize and Solzhenitsyn has," *Washington Post* (Book World), 28 December 1980, p. 6. A telling illustration of the differing reception of Chinese and Japanese writing among literary Anglophone audiences is provided by the juxtaposition of three reviews (two on Japanese fiction, one on fiction by a Chinese author) on one page of *The Times Literary Supplement* in 2001. The review of the China fiction (Ha Jin's *The Bridegroom*) dismisses all Mainland Chinese fiction as "Socialist Realism." By contrast, the reviews of the two Japanese novels (Haruki Murakami's *Sputnik Sweetheart* and Akira Yoshimura's *Shipwrecks*) respectfully focus on the books' literary and universally human qualities, thereby adopting the analytical tone predominantly used in the paper to review Western fiction. Murakami's themes are identified as the "politics of affection, rites of passage, the relationship

between self and society . . . the difficulty of communication"; *Shipwrecks* is praised as "a hymn to the resilience of the human spirit." It is further indicative of the low esteem in which the Anglophone literary world holds Chinese, relative to Japanese, fiction in translation that the two Japanese novels reviewed are translated from the Japanese; the reviewer cites short stories by Ha Jin—who lives in the United States and writes directly in English—to justify denigrating all Chinese-language fiction. See *The Times Literary Supplement*, 11 May 2001, p. 23.

105. Michael Specter, "The Nobel Syndrome," *The New Yorker*, 5 October 1998, 53.

106. McDougall, "Modern Chinese Literature and Its Critics," 23–24. By "inferior literary texts," McDougall is thinking particularly of works by modern Chinese writers who accepted positions in the Communist literary bureaucracy after 1949, for example Mao Dun, Guo Moruo, and Ba Jin. Private communication, 26 November 2004.

107. Ibid., 29.

108. Jenner, "Insuperable Barriers?" 186. See also Chan, "Politics of Translation," 111–121, which includes a discussion of the Foreign Language Press's most conspicuous instance of wasting talent and effort: the careers of Gladys and Xianyi Yang. See also Li Hui, *Going Through Together: Yang Xianyi and Gladys Yang* (Hong Kong: The Chinese University Press, 2001).

109. Jeffrey Kinkley, "A Bibliographic Survey of Publications on Chinese Literature in Translation from 1949 to 1999," in Pang-yuan Chi and David Der-wei Wang eds., *Chinese Literature in the Second Half of a Modern Century: A Critical Survey* (Bloomington: Indiana University Press, 2000), 243. Further examples of the politicized bent of much post-Mao translation include *Roses and Thorns: The Second Blooming of the Hundred Flowers in Chinese Fiction 1979–1980* (Perry Link ed., Berkeley: University of California Press, 1984); Helen Siu and Zelda Stern eds., *Mao's Harvest: Voices from China's New Generation* (New York and Oxford: Oxford University Press, 1983); Geremie Barmé and John Minford eds., *Seeds of Fire: Chinese Voices of Conscience* (Newcastle, Eng.: Bloodaxe, 1989). For more references, see Chan, "Politics of Translation," 43–102.

110. Many have sought to follow the successful example of *Wild Swans*, a memoir of the twentieth century told through three generations of women, in narrating Chinese Communist history through autobiographical family experiences: a few instances are Gao Anhua, *To the Edge of the Sky* (London: Viking, 2000), Aiping Mu, *The Vermilion Gate* (London: Little Brown, 2000), and Anchee Min, *Red Azalea: Life and Love in China* (London: Victor Gollancz, 1993). As a genre, the Chinese memoir admittedly has recently shown signs of moving onto events and experiences other than political persecution under Mao, for example in Annping Chin's *Four Sisters of Hofei* (London: Bloomsbury, 2003) and Da Chen's *Sounds of the River* (London: William Heinemann, 2003); see Julia Lovell, "Making History," *The Guardian*, 15 February 2003, for more details. Nevertheless, the phenomenal sales figures for *Wild Swans* still attract hopeful imitators: Toby Eady Associates, the London literary agency originally responsible for *Wild Swans*, continues to be approached with proposals for "family under Communism"-style memoirs (private conversation with Toby Eady, May 2002).

111. Dian Li, "Ideology and Conflicts in Bei Dao's Poetry," *Modern Chinese Literature* 9.2 (Fall 1996): 369–384.

112. The back and inside covers of Wei Hui's *Shanghai Baby*, trans. Bruce Humes (London: Robinson, 2001) provide apposite examples of both these phenomena.

113. Henry Y. H. Zhao ed., *The Lost Boat: Avant-garde Fiction from China* (London: The Wellsweep Press, 1993); Jing Wang ed., *China's Avant-garde Fiction: An Anthology* (Durham: Duke University Press, 1998); David Der-wei Wang and Jeanne Tai eds., *Running Wild: New Chinese Writers* (New York: Columbia University Press, 1994). Henry Zhao, in particular, has made a passionate case for Chinese literature to be read in the West as literature. The blurbs on the back cover of *The Lost Boat* inform the reader: "You will learn something new about life and literature, not just life and literature *in China*. . . . The world of these writers . . . is one aspect of a sophisticated, maturing artistic vision which distinguishes a new generation of young Chinese writers who will demand recognition in the West."

114. Authors translated by Goldblatt include Mo Yan (for example, *Red Sorghum: A Novel of China* [New York: Viking, 1993]); Li Rui (*Silver City* [New York: Holt, 1997]); Wang Shuo (*Playing for Thrills: A Mystery* [London: No Exit Press, 1997]); Hong Ying (*Daughter of the River* [London: Bloomsbury, 1998]). Probably the most successful of these among a general readership was *Red Sorghum*, which benefited from the renown in the West of Zhang Yimou's 1987 film of the book. The title of Goldblatt's own anthology of avant-garde Chinese writing, *Chairman Mao Would Not Be Amused: Fiction from Today's China* (New York: Grove Press, 1995), attempts to attract audiences, once more, by trading on reference to Chinese politics.

115. Justin Hill, "Democratic Devices," *The Times Literary Supplement*, 11 May 2001, p. 23.

116. Jones, "Chinese Literature in the 'World' Literary Economy," 184.

117. Gregory Lee, *Troubadours, Trumpeters, Troubled Makers* (London: Hurst and Company, 1996), 79.

118. Stephen Owen, "What is World Poetry? The Anxiety of Global Influence," *The New Republic*, 19 November 1990, 28–30.

119. Ibid., 29–30.

120. The critical literature concerning Western influence on modern Chinese literature is extensive. For the May Fourth period, see Leo Ou-fan Lee, *The Romantic Generation of Modern Chinese Writers* (Cambridge, Mass.: Harvard University Press, 1973); Mau-sang Ng, *The Russian Hero in Modern Chinese Fiction* (Hong Kong: Chinese University Press, 1988); Bonnie S. McDougall, *The Introduction of Western Literary Theories into Modern China 1919–25* (Tokyo: Centre for East Asian Cultural Studies, 1971). For the 1980s and 1990s, see, for example, Chen Xiaomei, *Occidentalism: A Theory of Counter-Discourse in Post-Mao China* (Oxford: Oxford University Press, 1995), Xudong Zhang, *Chinese Modernism in the Era of Reforms: Cultural Fever, Avant-garde Fiction and the New Chinese Cinema* (Durham: Duke University Press, 1997); Maghiel van Crevel, *Language Shattered: Contemporary Chinese Poetry and Duoduo* (Leiden: Research School CNWS, 1996).

121. See Liu, *Translingual Practice* and Wang, *Fictional Realism in Twentieth-*

Century China: Mao Dun, Lao She, Shen Congwen (New York: Columbia University Press, 1992).

122. Jenner, "Insuperable Barriers?" 181.

123. Stephen Owen, "What is World Poetry?"

124. Swedish Academy, "Press Release."

125. Fredric Jameson, "Third-World Literature in the Era of Multinational Capitalism," *Social Text* 15 (Fall 1986): 65–88. Aijaz Ahmad, "Jameson's Rhetoric of Otherness and the 'National Allegory,'" in *In Theory: Classes, Nations, Literatures* (London: Verso, 1992), 92–122.

126. Jameson, "Third-World Literature," 65.

127. Ahmad, "Jameson's Rhetoric," 102.

128. Fredric Jameson, "A Brief Response," *Social Text* 17 (Fall 1987): 26.

129. The 2001 essay collection *Unacknowledged Legislation* (London: Verso) by the influential critic Christopher Hitchens probed this very issue in the modern Western encounter between politics and literature. The title derives from Shelley's acclamation of poets as the "unacknowledged legislators of the world."

Chapter 2: The Nobel Prize for Literature: Philosophy and Practice

* *Statutes of the Nobel Foundation* (Stockholm: The Nobel Foundation, 1994), 1.

1. Lars-Åke Skagegård, *The Remarkable Story of Alfred Nobel and the Nobel Prize* (Uppsala, Sweden: Konsultförlaged AB, 1994), 11.

2. Herta Pauli, *Alfred Nobel* (London: Nicholson & Watson, 1947), 263.

3. For a recent, impassioned discussion of the manipulation of the United Nations by the world's most powerful countries, see Linda Polman, *We Did Nothing: Why the Truth Doesn't Always Come Out when the UN Goes In*, trans. Rob Bland (London: Penguin, 2003).

4. Charles Taylor, *Sources of the Self* (Cambridge, Mass.: Harvard University Press, 1989), 6–7.

5. Burton Feldman, *The Nobel Prize: A History of Genius, Controversy, and Prestige* (New York: Arcade, 2000), ix.

6. The first winners to capture the media's imagination thus were Marie and Pierre Curie (1867–1934 and 1859–1906, respectively). See ibid., 5–8.

7. Ibid., 16.

8. *Nobel Museum Newsletter* no. 4 (Autumn 1999).

9. W. Odelberg, ed., *Nobel the Man and His Prizes* (New York: American Elsevier Press, 1972), 635.

10. Specter, "The Nobel Syndrome," 52.

11. Due to the number of writers mentioned in this chapter, to give all their dates would disrupt the text. This practice is thus suspended until the following chapter.

12. One of the first genuinely analytical histories of the Nobel Prize as an institution was produced in (as late as) 2000 by Burton Feldman.

13. See Espmark, *The Nobel Prize* (1991).

14. Feldman, *The Nobel Prize*, iv.

15. Anders Österling, "The Literary Prize," in Odelberg, *Nobel the Man*, 76.

16. Linda Dowling, *Language and Decadence in the Victorian Fin de Siècle* (Princeton: Princeton University Press, 1986), 37.

17. H. de Balzac, *Traité de la vie élégante* (Paris: Delmas, 1952), 16, quoted in Pierre Bourdieu, *The Rules of Art*, trans. Susan Emanuel (Cambridge: Polity Press, 1996), 56.

18. Bourdieu, *The Rules of Art*, 129–130.

19. Chen Sihe, interview by author, Shanghai, 8 April 2000. For remarks on the modern Chinese understanding of "pure literature," see Torbjörn Lodén, "Why Pure Literature? Random Thoughts on Aestheticism in Contemporary Chinese Literature," in Wendy Larson and Anne Wedell-Wedellsborg eds., *Inside Out: Modernism and Postmodernism in Chinese Literary Culture* (Aarhus, Denmark: Aarhus University Press, 1993), 156–160.

20. Here, I am thinking particularly of the premodern moralistic exhortation that "literature should convey the Way" (*wen yi zai dao*). I do not wish to claim this is the single dominant influence on Chinese literary practice across the millennia; the individualistic belief that "poetry should speak intent" (*shi yan zhi*) is an equally important plank of premodern Chinese thinking about literature. Nevertheless, the idea that "literature should convey the Way" is an undeniably influential strand of Confucian humanism.

21. R. Nisbet Bain, *Gustavus III and His Contemporaries, 1746–1792* (London: K. Paul, Trench, Trubner & Co., 1894), vol. 2, 261–263.

22. Liu, *Translingual Practice*, 183.

23. Taylor, *Sources of the Self*, 143–167, 338–367.

24. Strich, *Goethe and World Literature*, 5.

25. Ibid., 13.

26. Ibid., 9.

27. Ibid., 13–14.

28. These statistics imply a certain indifference on the part of the judges of the Nobel Science Prizes towards possible accusations of national bias in judging scientific achievement, and hence a state of relaxed universalism within the scientific world, as compared to the literary world. We should not, however, overlook key eruptions of nationalism in modern science and in the Nobel Science Prizes, particularly around the time of the First World War. For more details, see Elisabeth Crawford, *Nationalism and Internationalism in Science, 1880–1939: Four Studies of the Nobel Population* (Cambridge: Cambridge University Press, 1992). Recent Japanese and Chinese anxiety to win Nobel Science Prizes, moreover, belie the impression of an entirely universalistic world community of science and scientists (see note 13 in chapter 1 above).

29. See Dowling, *Language and Decadence*, 22–31.

30. Strich, *Goethe and World Literature*, 16.

31. Ibid., 149.

32. Jones, "Chinese Literature," 180. Jones's article offers bracingly clear-sighted criticism of Goethe's idea of *Weltliteratur*.

33. Strich, *Goethe and World Literature*, 5.

34. Ibid., 17.

35. Jones, "Chinese Literature," 181.

36. Strich, *Goethe and World Literature*, 58.

37. Ibid., 63.

38. Quoted in Espmark, *The Nobel Prize* (1991), 2.

39. Specter, "The Nobel Syndrome," 55.

40. Rolf Lundén, "Theodore Dreiser and the Nobel Prize," *American Literature* (May 1978): 216–229.

41. Bourdieu, *The Rules of Art*, 61.

42. Feldman, *The Nobel Prize*, 9.

43. Paul Bilic and Robert Winder, "The Prize is Right," *Prospect*, November 1995, 14.

44. Espmark, *The Nobel Prize* (1991), 3.

45. Sture Allén, "Topping Shakespeare? Aspects of the Nobel Prize for Literature." *Artes* (1997): 12.

46. Kjell Espmark, "The Nobel Prize in Literature," December 1999, http://www. Nobel.se.

47. For these, and other Wirsén judgments, see Espmark, *The Nobel Prize* (1991), 9–26.

48. *Academy*, 28 November 1901, 636.

49. Feldman, *The Nobel Prize*, 46.

50. Espmark, *The Nobel Prize* (1991), 30.

51. Ibid., 29.

52. Bunny Suraiya, "A Storm over Poet Tagore's 'Political' Prize Award," *Far Eastern Economic Review*, 1 December 1983, 52.

53. Espmark, *The Nobel Prize* (1991), 62–63.

54. Conversation with Jerry Smith, Professor of Russian at Oxford University, 21 October 2000.

55. Espmark, "The Nobel Prize" (1999), 8.

56. Ibid., 82.

57. Ibid., 80.

58. Ibid., 88.

59. Ibid., 88.

60. Ibid., 91.

61. Ibid., 91.

62. Ibid., 92.

63. Ibid., 92.

64. Ibid., 91.

65. Bourdieu, *The Rules of Art*, 77.

66. Ibid., 79.

67. Espmark, *The Nobel Prize* (1991), 100.

68. Ibid., 101.

69. Ibid., 51.

70. Although they are separated by almost seventy years, there are interesting parallels between the prizes to Bunin and Gao: both were significant as the first award to a writer from their respective nations, both had a politically sensitive background,

and in both cases the Nobel Committee chose writers who were supposedly artistically neutral but who in fact represented political challenges to the Communist regimes ruling their countries at the time.

71. *Ideologicheskie komissii TsK KPSS. 1958–64: dokumenty* (Moscow: ROSSPEN, 1998).

72. Espmark, *The Nobel Prize* (1991), 112.

73. Ibid., 100.

74. Ingmar Björkstén, "Nur sehen, was man sehen will?" *Titel* 4 (1984), quoted in Espmark, *The Nobel Prize* (1991), 101.

75. "Moscow's Pyrrhic Victory," *New York Times*, 30 October 1958, p. 30.

76. Special Correspondent, "Writers' Concern for Fate of Mr Pasternak," (*The London) Times*, 30 October 1958, p. 8.

77. Ronald Torbet, "A Dominican Nobel Prize Winner," *Blackfriars* (January 1959), 30.

78. D. M. Thomas, *Alexander Solzhenitsyn: A Century in His Life* (Little, Brown, 1998), 362.

79. Espmark, "The Nobel Prize" (1999), 5.

80. Lennon, "Why Graham Greene hasn't won," p. 6.

81. Feldman, *The Nobel Prize*, 79.

82. Espmark, *The Nobel Prize* (1991), 108.

83. Ibid., 109.

84. Allén, "Topping Shakespeare," 12.

85. Specter, "The Nobel Syndrome," 48.

86. Espmark, *The Nobel Prize* (1991), 135.

87. Ibid., 135.

88. Ibid., 131.

89. Norman Thomas di Giovanni, "How to win the Nobel Prize for literature," *The Listener*, 11 February 1982, 14.

90. Espmark, *The Nobel Prize* (1991), 132.

91. Ibid., 133.

92. Ibid., 137.

93. Ibid., 141.

94. Lennon, "Why Graham Greene hasn't won," p. 6.

95. di Giovanni, "How to win," 14.

96. Espmark, *The Nobel Prize* (1991), 142; original emphasis.

97. Nobel citations for 1: Sillanpaa, 1939; Mistral, 1945; Seferis, 1963; Asturias, 1967; Kawabata, 1968; Mahfouz, 1988. 2: Kipling, 1907; Gide, 1947; Eliot, 1948; Hemingway, 1954; Camus, 1957; Simon, 1985; Oe, 1994; Gao Xingjian, 2000.

98. Espmark, *The Nobel Prize* (1991), 54.

99. Ibid., 136.

100. di Giovanni, "How to win," 14.

101. Gore Vidal, public lecture at Cambridge Union, 23 October 2000.

102. Specter, "The Nobel Syndrome," 52–53.

103. Conversation with Michel Hockx, Cambridge, 31 October 2000.

104. Specter, "The Nobel Syndrome," 52.

Chapter 3: Ideas of Authorship and the Nobel Prize in China, 1900–1976

1. Taylor, *Sources of the Self,* 4.

2. Fitzgerald, *Awakening China,* 24.

3. Kirk Denton, *The Problematic of Self in Modern Chinese Literature: Hu Feng and Lu Ling* (Stanford: Stanford University Press, 1998), 41.

4. Liu, *Translingual Practice,* 188.

5. See ibid., 195–213.

6. Denton, *The Problematic,* 5.

7. Wang, *Fin-de-Siècle Splendor,* 1–2.

8. Denton, *The Problematic,* 43.

9. Liang Qichao, "Dongji yuedan" (Guidelines to Japanese books) from *Yinbingshi heji-wenji* (Collected writings from the Ice-Drinker's Studio: collected essays) ([Shanghai: China Books, 1936], vol. 4, 91), quoted in Tang, *Global Space,* 32.

10. Leo Ou-fan Lee and Andrew J. Nathan, "The Beginnings of Mass Culture: Journalism and Fiction in the Late Ch'ing and Beyond," in *Popular Culture in Late Imperial China,* ed. David Johnson, Andrew J. Nathan and Evelyn S. Rawski (Berkeley: University of California Press, 1985), 379.

11. Liang Qichao, "Foreword to the Publication of Political Novels in Translation," in Denton, *Modern Chinese Literary Thought,* 73.

12. Liang, "On the Relationship," 75.

13. See Wang, *Fin-de-Siècle Splendor.*

14. Chow Tse-tsung, *The May Fourth Movement: Intellectual Revolution in Modern China* (Cambridge, Mass.: Harvard University Press, 1960), 278–279.

15. Chow, *Woman and Chinese Modernity,* 91.

16. Denton, *The Problematic,* 46.

17. Chow, *Woman and Chinese Modernity,* 92.

18. John Crespi, "A Vocal Minority: New Poetry and Poetry Declamation in China 1915–1975," (Ph.D. diss., University of Chicago, 2001), 52–54.

19. Ibid., 63.

20. Leo Ou-fan Lee, *The Romantic Generation.*

21. Tagore's lectures in southern Chinese cities (Shanghai, Nanjing, Hangzhou) were more enthusiastically received than those in Beijing. See Krishna Dutta and Andrew Robinson, *Rabindranath Tagore: The Myriad-Minded Man* (London: Bloomsbury, 1995), 249–252.

22. Dutta and Robinson, *Rabindranath Tagore,* 251. These comments, originally produced in a leaflet in Chinese, were reprinted in the Calcutta *Bengalee.*

23. *Shanghai Mercury,* 30 May 1924, quoted in Stephen Hay, *Asian Ideas of East and West* (Cambridge, Mass.: Harvard University Press, 1970), 206.

24. Hay, *Asian Ideas,* 129. For Tagore, and the West's views of Asia as a unity, see also Dutta and Robinson, *Rabindranath Tagore,* 247.

25. Mao Zedong, "Talks at the Yan'an Forum on Literature and Art," in Denton, *Modern Chinese Literary Thought,* 483. See Leo Ou-fan Lee, *Voices from the Iron House:*

A *Study of Lu Xun* (Bloomington and Indianapolis: 1987, Indiana University Press) for a thorough analysis of Lu Xun's intellectual biography.

26. Lu Xun, "Zhi Tai Jingnong" (To Tai Jingnong), in *Lu Xun quanji*, vol. 11, 580–581. See also the discussion of Lu Xun's international stature and Nobel candidacy in Paul B. Foster, "The Ironic Inflation of Chinese National Character: Lu Xun's International Reputation, Romain Rolland's Critique of 'The True Story of Ah Q,' and the Nobel Prize," *Modern Chinese Literature and Culture* 13.1 (Spring 2001): 140–168.

27. See Wang Hongzhi, "Nenggou 'rongren duoshao de bushun'—lun Lu Xun de 'yingyi' lilun" (How much awkwardness can be tolerated—on Lu Xun's theory of "hard translation"), in *Ershi shiji Zhongguo fanyi yanjiu* (Hong Kong: Dongfang chuban zhongxin, 1999), 218–239.

28. Chen Chunsheng, "Lu Xun yu Nuobeier wenxuejiang" (Lu Xun and the Nobel Literature Prize), *Lu Xun yanjiu yuekan* no. 8 (2000): 47.

29. Gao Jianping, "Lu Xun: cong wangshang pingxuan shuo kai qu" (Lu Xun: starting from the selection on the Internet), *Shouhuo* no. 1 (2000): 123–124.

30. Denton, *The Problematic*, 61. For more details on the problem of classifying intellectuals in the context of a Chinese Communist revolution, see Yi-tsi Mei Feuerwerker, *Ideology, Power, Text: Self-Representation and the Peasant "Other" in Modern Chinese Literature* (Stanford: Stanford University Press, 1998), 32–35.

31. Denton, *The Problematic*, 65.

32. John Carey, *The Intellectuals and the Masses: Pride and Prejudice among the Literary Intelligentsia, 1880–1939* (London: Faber and Faber, 1992), 16–17.

33. For more detail on the extent and nature of these influences, see, for example, Liu, *Translingual Practice* and Edward Gunn, *Rewriting Chinese: Style and Innovation in Twentieth-Century Chinese Prose* (Stanford: Stanford University Press, 1991).

34. For more details on the tension between elitism and mass politics, see David Holm, *Art and Ideology in Revolutionary China* (Oxford: Clarendon Press, 1991).

35. Leo Oufan Lee, "In Search of Modernity: Some Reflections on a New Mode of Consciousness in Twentieth Century Chinese History and Literature," in *Ideas Across Cultures: Essays on Chinese Thought in Honor of Dr. Benjamin I. Schwartz*, ed. Paul A. Cohen and Merle Goldman (Cambridge, Mass.: Harvard University Press, 1990), 129.

36. *Xiandai zazhi* 1.1 (May 1932): 2, quoted in Lee, *Shanghai Modern*, 135.

37. Liu, *Translingual Practice*, 235.

38. Ibid., 237–238.

39. It would be hard to argue that the timing of Pearl Buck's Nobel—in the midst of the bloody Sino-Japanese War, and one year after the massacre of Nanjing by invading Japanese forces—was coincidental. Awarded in large part for Buck's "rich and truly epic descriptions of peasant life in China," her prize could be seen as a symbol of international recognition and encouragement for the national struggle for survival in which China was at the time engaged. This supposition is further strengthened by the haste with which the Nobel Committee reached its decision to award Buck the prize, indicating that immediate circumstances had an influence on the selection process. For details on the decision, see Espmark, *The Nobel Prize* (1991), 64.

40. He Xianglin, "Xu" (Preface), in *Sai Zhenzhu pinglun ji* (Collected criticism on Pearl Buck), ed. Guo Yingjian (Guangxi: Lijiang chubanshe, 1999), 1. The publication of this critical anthology in 1998 testifies to continuing Chinese interest in Pearl Buck at a mature stage in China's Nobel Complex.

41. Liu Haiping, "Pearl S. Buck's Reception in China Reconsidered," in Elizabeth J. Lipscomb et al., *The Several Worlds of Pearl Buck* (Westport, Conn.: Greenwood Press, 1994), 58.

42. Zou Zhenhuan, "Sai Zhenzhu *Dadi* de fanyi jiqi yinqi de zhengyi" (Debates surrounding the translation of Pearl Buck's *The Good Earth*), in Guo, *Sai Zhenzhu*, 558.

43. Hu Feng, "*Dadi* li de Zhongguo" (The China of *The Good Earth*), in Guo, *Sai Zhenzhu*, 91.

44. Zou, "Sai Zhenzhu *Dadi*," 558.

45. Jonathan Spence, *The Chan's Great Continent: China in Western Minds* (London: Allen Lane, Penguin, 1999).

46. Novels by Westerners include Justin Hill, *The Drink and Dream Teahouse* (London: Weidenfeld and Nicholson, 2001); for details on recent memoirs, see chapter 1, n. 110.

47. Spence, *The Chan's Great Continent*, 95.

48. Pearl Buck, *The Good Earth* (London: Methuen, 1987).

49. Spence, *The Chan's Great Continent*, 182.

50. Florence Ayscough, "The Real China" (*Saturday Review of Literature*, 21 March 1931, 676), quoted in Blake Allmendinger, "Little House on the Rice Paddy," *American Literary History* 10.2 (Summer 1998): 370.

51. Lu Xun, "Zhi Yao Ke" (To Yao Ke), in Guo, *Sai Zhenzhu*, 3.

52. Zhao Jiabi, "Boke furen yu huang long" (Mrs Buck and the yellow dragon), in Guo, *Sai Zhenzhu*, 74.

53. Ibid., 77.

54. Jiang Kanghu, "Yi wei Zhongguo xuezhe dui Buke furen xiaoshuo de guancha" (One Chinese scholar's examination of Mrs Buck's fiction), in Guo, *Sai Zhenzhu*, 14.

55. Yang Changxi, "Bake furen yu Jiang Kanghu lunzhan jiqi dui jidujiao de renshi" (The debate between Mrs Buck and Jiang Kanghu, and the understanding of Christianity), in Guo, *Sai Zhenzhu*, 44.

56. Yi Xian, "Ping *Dadi*" (Considering *The Good Earth*), in Guo, *Sai Zhenzhu*, 29–30.

57. Mao Zedong, "Report on an Investigation of the Peasant Movement in Hunan," quoted in Charles W. Hayford, "*The Good Earth*, Revolution, and the American Raj in China," in Lipscomb et al., *The Several Worlds*, 22.

58. Charles Hayford, "What's So Bad About *The Good Earth*?" *Education about Asia* 3.3 (Winter 1998): 5. Pearl Buck's viewpoint echoed her husband's findings on his agronomist survey of Chinese villages, in which he discovered limited evidence to support apocalyptic Marxist analyses of China's rural malaise, reporting almost no capitalist farming and very few large landlords. The general picture of rural China that emerges, Jack Gray summarizes, "is not one of glaring inequalities. There was no aristocracy with vast estates. . . . There is no evidence of increasing polarization of land ownership or of agricultural incomes." Taxation was getting lighter and Buck's

farmers were almost unanimous in asserting that their standard of living had improved over the last few years. When asked to give their opinions as to the causes of adverse conditions in agriculture, almost one-third of peasants stated that "they were aware of no adverse factors. Almost one-half of the rest named bandits or soldiers as the worst evil. More than a third (thirty-nine percent) named natural disasters. If this survey is valid, then the diagnosis of rural ills produced by the peasants . . . does not, surely, express a revolutionary frame of mind." Jack Gray, *Rebellions and Revolutions: China from the 1800s to the 1980s* (Oxford: Oxford University Press, 1990), 159–160.

59. Pearl Buck, "China the Eternal" (*International Review of Missions*, October 1924, 573–584), quoted in Hayford, "*The Good Earth*," 24.

60. Pearl Buck's sympathetic view of the countryside and rural traditions is to an extent echoed in some of Mao Dun's (1896–1981) historical fiction, in particular the 1932 novel *Chuncan* (Spring silkworms), in which his celebration of the peasants' patient endurance appears to dominate his Marxist belief in the revolutionary motor of history. For a discussion of the contradictions in Mao Dun's historical novels, see "Fictive History: Mao Dun's Historical Fiction," in David Der-wei Wang, *Fictional Realism in Twentieth-Century China: Mao Dun, Lao She, Shen Congwen* (New York: Columbia University Press, 1992), 25–66.

61. Hayford, "What's So Bad?" 6.

62. Hu, "*Dadi* li de Zhongguo," 98–99.

63. Xu Yuxin, "Sai Zhenzhu — Mei diguozhuyi wenhua qinlue de ji xianfeng" (Pearl Buck — the vanguard of American imperialist cultural aggression), in Guo, *Sai Zhenzhu*, 134–143.

64. Zou, "Sai Zhenzhu *Dadi* de fanyi," 560–561.

65. Holm, *Art and Ideology*, 9.

66. Zhou Qiying, "Guanyu wenxue dazhonghua," (*Beidou*, 2.3/4 [July 1932]), quoted in Holm, *Art and Ideology*, 36.

67. Holm, *Art and Ideology*, 57.

68. Ibid., 65.

69. Ding Ling, "Shihe qunzhong yu qumei qunzhong" (Adapting to and fawning on the masses), (*Ding Ling wenji* [Changsha: Hunan renmin chubanshe, 1983–1984], vol. 4, 36), quoted in Denton, *The Problematic*, 66.

70. Zhang Daofan, "Women suo xuyao de wenyi zhengce" (The literary policy we need), in *Xiangtu wenxue taolunji* (Collected discussions of nativist literature), ed. Wei Tiancong (Taipei: Wei Tiancong, 1978), 815–845.

71. Wang Shiwei's protest against party cultural policy turned him into the principal target of the 1942 Rectification Campaign; after several years' imprisonment, he was executed in Yan'an in 1948. For more detail, see Dai Qing, *Wang Shiwei and "Wild Lilies": Rectification and Purges in the Chinese Communist Party 1942–1944* (New York: M. E. Sharpe, 1994).

72. Huang Xiuji, *Zhao Shuli pingzhuan* ([Xuzhou: Jiangsu renmin chubanshe, 1981], 5), quoted in Feuerwerker, 115. See Feuerwerker, *Ideology*, 100–145, for details of Zhao's life and works.

73. Edward Gunn, *Unwelcome Muse: Chinese Literature in Shanghai and Peking 1937–1945* (New York: Columbia University Press, 1980), 263.

74. Qian Zhongshu, *Xie zai rensheng bianshang* (Written on the margin of life) ([Shanghai, 1941], 63–64), quoted in Gunn, *Unwelcome Muse*, 243–244.

75. Qian Zhongshu, "Linggan" (Inspiration) in *Qian Zhongshu zuopinji* vols. 3–4 (one volume) (Taipei: Shulin chuban youxian gongsi, 1989), 128–150. Subsequent numbers in parentheses refer to the pages in this edition.

76. Kraus and Larson, "China's Writers," 148. For more details, see Lothar von Falkenhausen's review of Göran Malmqvist, *Bernard Karlgren: Ett Forskarporträtt*, in *China Review International* 8.1 (Spring 2001): 15–33.

77. Chen Duxiu, *Duxiu wencun* (Duxiu's writings) ([Shanghai: Shanghai yadong tushuguan, 1922], vol. 2, 366), quoted in Marston Anderson, *The Limits of Realism: Chinese Fiction in the Revolutionary Period* (Berkeley: University of California Press, 1989), 27.

78. Chen Duxiu, "Wenxue geming lun" (On literary revolution), (in Zhao Jiabi, *Zhongguo xin wenxue daxi* [Shanghai: Liangyou, 1935–1936], vol. 1, 47), quoted in Liu, *Translingual Practice*, 188.

79. Lu Xun, "Si hou," in *Lu Xun quanji*, vol. 2, 209–213.

80. Wang, *Fictional Realism*, 113.

81. See examples given in Link, *The Uses of Literature*, 114. For a discussion of the competition between trends of professionalism and amateurism in the early years of the PRC, see Lars Ragvald, "Professionalism and Amateur Tendencies in Post-revolutionary Chinese Literature," in Göran Malmqvist ed., *Modern Chinese Literature and its Social Context* (Stockholm: Nobel Foundation, 1975), 152–179.

82. For details on the functioning of the Writers' Association, see Richard Kraus, *The Party and the Arty in China: The New Politics of Culture* (Lanham, Md.: Rowman and Littlefield, 2004) and Link, *The Uses of Literature*, 118–122.

83. Zhou Yang, "Build China's Own Marxist Literary Theory and Criticism" (*Renmin ribao*, 29 August 1958), quoted in Goldman, *Literary Dissent*, 241.

84. Guo Morou, "Hit Back with a Vengeance at the Rightist!" (New China News Agency, 15 July 1957), quoted in Goldman, *Literary Dissent*, 241.

85. For more details on these figures, see Link, *Roses and Thorns*, 7.

86. For contemporary details of the Stalin Prizes won by Ding Ling and other Chinese writers in 1951, see, for example, anon., "Ding Ling, Zhou Libo deng rong huo Sidalin jiang" (Ding Ling, Zhou Libo et al. are awarded the Stalin Prize), *Wenyi bao*, 25 March 1952, p. 15; anon., "Sulian dashiguan daibiao Sidalin jiangjin weiyuanhui shouyu Ding Ling deng Sidalin jiangjin" (the Soviet embassy on behalf of the Stalin Prize committee present Ding Ling et al. with the Stalin Prize), *Wenyi bao*, 25 June 1952, p. 7.

87. See, for example, Michael B. Yahuda, *China's Role in World Affairs* (London: Croom Helm, 1978), 235–268.

88. For more details, see Jonathan D. Pollack, "The Opening to America," in Roderick MacFarquhar and John K. Fairbank eds., *The Cambridge History of China Volume 15: Revolutions within the Chinese Revolution 1966–1982* (Cambridge: Cambridge University Press, 1991), 402–472.

89. Ding Ling, "Kua dao xin de shidai lai" (Striding into the new era) (Peking, 1951, 210), quoted in Goldman, *Literary Dissent*, 102.

90. Feng Xuefeng, *Lunwenji* (Collected essays) (Peking, 1952, vol. 1, 239), quoted in Goldman, *Literary Dissent*, 121.

91. Goldman, *Literary Dissent*, 141–142.

92. Denton, *The Problematic*, 96.

93. Ibid., 99.

Chapter 4: China's Search for a Nobel Prize in Literature, 1979–2000

1. The desire for China to "march towards the world" was both explicitly and implicitly expressed in many intellectual forums of the 1980s, manifesting an intense concern that China assume a place in global modernity. This feeling climaxed with the 1988 television series, *Heshang* (River elegy). See, for example, discussions in Wang, *High Culture Fever*, 37–136 and Zhao, "Chinese Intellectuals' Quest," 727. For the script of the series itself and further critical essays, see Su Xiaokang and Wang Luxiang, *Deathsong of the River: A Reader's Guide to the Chinese TV Series* Heshang, trans. Richard W. Bodman and Pin P. Wan (Ithaca, N.Y.: Cornell University, East Asia Series, 1991).

2. For a discussion of "Misty poetry," see van Crevel, *Language Shattered*, 3–76 and William Tay, "Obscure Poetry: A Controversy in Post-Mao China," in *After Mao: Chinese Literature and Society 1978–1981*, ed. Jeffrey Kinkley (Cambridge, Mass.: Harvard University Press, 1990), 133–157.

3. Zhong, *Masculinity Besieged?*, 169.

4. Li Feng, interview by author, Beijing, 6 April 2000. Li's comments about the gendered nature of the Nobel Complex have held true all the way up to 2000. All of China's front-running, oft-nominated candidates were male: Ai Qing, Ba Jin, Bei Dao, Gao Xingjian, Gu Cheng, Li Rui, Mo Yan, and Shen Congwen.

5. For more details, see Bonnie S. McDougall, "Breaking Through: Literature and the Arts in China 1976–1986," in her *Fictional Authors*, 171–204.

6. See Yang Yu, "Wenxue: Shique hongdong xiaoying yihou" (After literature has lost its sensational effect), *Wenyi bao*, 30 January 1988, p. 2.

7. Chen, *Occidentalism*, 5.

8. Ibid., 8.

9. It would be an exaggeration to claim that China's post-Mao literary community has been uniformly or consistently fascinated by the Nobel Prize and the ramifications of the Nobel Complex. Firstly, as has been pointed out above, modern Chinese cultural nationalism and the Nobel Complex have been predominantly male preoccupations. Secondly, it could be argued that, particularly in the 1980s, many of the forums for discussing the Nobel Complex were literary newspapers and magazines such as *Wenyi bao* (Literary Gazette) and *Renmin ribao* (People's Daily) that do not represent the main core of professional literary production in Mainland China. This would suggest that serious writers and critics have been far more concerned with creative literary issues than with the highs and lows of Nobel angst. However, my interviews with a wide range of writers and critics indicated that the Nobel Complex was in fact an issue that occupied an important position in the post-Mao literary con-

sciousness, even if individuals were themselves unwilling openly to admit to concern with it.

10. See Howard Goldblatt, ed., *Chinese Literature for the 1980s* (New York: M. E. Sharpe, 1982).

11. Xu Chi, "Xishou waiguo wenyi jinghua zonghe: Wei *Waiguo wenxue yanjiu* jikan chuangkan hao er zuo (Absorb the synthetic essence of foreign arts: Written for the inaugural issue of *Foreign Literature Research*), *Waiguo wenxue yanjiu*, no. 1 (1978): 1.

12. See Meng Fanhua, "1978 de pingxuan zhidu" (The awards system of 1978) in *1978: Jiqing suiyue* (1978: A time of excitement) (Shandong: Jiaoyu chubanshe, 1998), 238–249.

13. Huang Qingyun, "Xifang de weixiao he dongfang de hunli" (The Western smile and the Eastern wedding), *Yangcheng wanbao*, 21 November 1981, p. 2.

14. Xin Weiling, "1978 niandu Nuobeier wenxuejiang huodezhe — Xin'ge" (The winner of the 1978 Nobel Literature Prize — Singer), *Guowai shehui kexue cankao ziliao*, no. 2 (1979): 10. Shao Ying, trans., "Yijiuqijiu nian Nuobeier wenxuejiangjin huodezhe jianjie" (A brief introduction to the winner of the 1979 Nobel Literature Prize), *Guowai shehui kexue dongtai*, no. 11 (1979): 27.

15. Yu Hua, interview by author, Beijing, 19 April 2000.

16. Yao Jian, "Cong wenxue jiaodu kan wo guo dui waiwenhua jiaoliu" (Viewing our country's exchange with foreign culture from a literary angle), *Waiguo wenxue yanjiu*, no.3 (1982): 74–75.

17. Mu Jun, "Ershi shiji wenxue jingying — lun Nuobeier wenxuejiang" (The elite of the twentieth century — the Nobel Prize for Literature), *Waiguo wenxue xinshang*, no. 3 (1983): 38.

18. Ba Jin, "Women de wenxue yinggai zhan zai shijie de qianlie — zai Zhongguo zuojia xiehui di si ci huiyuan daibiao dahui shang de kaimuci" (Our literature should stand in the front ranks of the world — inaugural speech at the fourth representatives' meeting of the Writers' Association), *Renmin ribao*, 30 December 1984, p. 3.

19. See Shi Bo, "Zou xiang shijie wentan — ji zhongguo nuzuojia shenghui" (Marching towards the world literary scene — reporting from the meeting of Chinese women writers), *Renmin ribao*, 29 June 1981, p. 8. For more details of the "culture fever," see Wang, *High Culture Fever* and Zhang, *Chinese Modernism*.

20. Kraus and Larson, "China's Writers," 149.

21. For example, Bang Fu trans., "Nuobeier jiang pingxuan weiyuanzhang deng tan Nuobeier jiang de pingxuan" (The Nobel Prize Committee discusses Nobel Prize selection), *Waiguo wenxue dongtai*, no. 5 (1986): 23–25.

22. Espmark (1991), 138.

23. See Ying Hong, "Zhalan men zai Zhongguo tudi shang dakai" (The railings are opened on China's home soil), *Wenyi bao*, 8 November 1986, p. 1; Gao Ning, "Zhongguo wenxue zheng zai zou xiang shijie" (Chinese literature is marching towards the world), *Renmin ribao*, 22 November 1986, p. 6; Ying Hong, "Hanxuejia tan zhongguo zuojia weihe wei huo Nuobeier jiang" (Sinologists discuss why a Chinese writer has never won the Nobel Prize), *Wenyi bao*, 15 November 1986, p. 1; Li Man, "Zhongguo zuojia heshi wending Nuobeier wenxuejiang?" (When will a Chinese writer win the

Nobel Literature Prize?), *Shijie bolan*, no. 1 (1987): 34–36. See also the discussion in Kraus and Larson, "China's Writers," 154–155.

24. Bai Jieming (Geremie Barmé), "Mianxiang shijie de dangdai dalu wenxue" (Contemporary Mainland literature faces the world), *Jiushi niandai*, no. 12 (December 1986): 83.

25. In the Anglophone reading market, this initiative produced *Notes from the City of the Sun*, a volume of translations of Bei Dao by McDougall (Ithaca: Cornell University China-Japan Program, 1983).

26. McDougall, telephone interview by author, 10 July 2002.

27. Zhu Jingdong, "Zou xiang shijie de chenggong changshi" (A successful march towards the world), *Zuojia*, no. 12 (1988): 73.

28. Wang Meng, *Qiuxing qiyu ji* (Strange tales of a football star), *Renmin wenxue*, no. 10 (1988): 4–41.

29. Qiu Huadong, interview by author, Beijing, 28 April 2000.

30. Feng Yidai, "Nuobeier wenxuejiang de wo jian" (My view of the Nobel Prize), *Qunyan*, no. 2 (1987): 32–33.

31. He Feng, "'Nuobeier wenxuejiang' de pianpo yu 'Zhonghua wenxue dajiang' de sheli" (The bias of the Nobel Literature Prize and the establishment of the Chinese Literature Prize), *Bianyi cankao*, no. 2 (1987): 35–37.

32. Wang Ning, "Ruidian huangjia wenxueyuan yuanshi Aisipamake tan Nuobeier wenxuejiang" (Swedish Academician Epsmark discusses the Nobel Literature Prize), *Wenyi bao*, 18 July 1987, p. 6.

33. Deng Youmei, "Zhongguo zuojia, qingjin!" (Chinese writers, please come in!), *Wenyi bao*, 12 December 1987, p. 1.

34. Kraus and Larson, "China's Writers," 160.

35. In-house report, "Yue Gang Ao zuojia juxing di er jie lianyihui" (The second friendship association meeting of Guangdong, Hong Kong, and Macao writers), *Renmin ribao (haiwaiban)*, 22 June 1988, p. 6.

36. Chow, *Writing Diaspora*, 97.

37. Jin Jianfan, "Guoji bihui yu Wei Jingsheng he Bei Dao" (International Pen, Wei Jingsheng and Bei Dao), *Wenyi lilun yu piping*, no. 1 (1990): 75.

38. Yu Bin, "Zou xiang shijie yu 'xiyang qingjie'" (Marching towards the world and the "Western complex"), *Renmin ribao*, 9 January 1990, p. 6.

39. Wen Hui, "Tan wenxue de minzuxing yu shijiexing" (On national and global qualities in literature), *Beijing shehui kexue*, no. 1 (1990): 73.

40. Xu, "From Modernity to Chineseness."

41. Zhao, "Chinese Intellectuals' Quest," 731.

42. Zhang Quan, "Lun Nuobeier wenxuejiang jiqi yu Zhongguo" (On the Nobel Literature Prize and China), *Beijing shehui kexue*, no. 4 (1992): 88.

43. Zi Zhongjun, "Nuobeier wenxuejiang you shijie yiyi ma?" (Does the Nobel Literature Prize have global significance?), *Dushu*, no. 7 (1996): 73.

44. He Song, "*Dajia*: rang Nuobeier wenxuejiang zoukai" (*Dajia*: tell the Nobel Prize to go away), *Dajia*, no. 1 (1998): 205

45. Ling Shuiming, "Buyong wei Li Ao danyou" (No need to worry about Li Ao), *Zhonghua dushu bao*, 10 May 2000, p. 8.

46. Li Yongyin, "Dangdai Zhongguo wenxue de huihuang mengxiang" (The glorious dream of contemporary Chinese literature), *Yunnan shehui kexue*, no. 3 (1996): 85–91.

47. Zhang Yiwu, "Hongyuan yu momeng: Nuobeier wenxuejiang yu Zhongguo" (Great aspirations and secret dreams: China and the Nobel Literature Prize), *Waiguo wenxue*, no. 5 (1997): 10–11.

48. Liu Zaifu, "Bainian Nuobeier wenxuejiang he Zhongguo zuojia de quexi" (One hundred years of the Nobel Prize and the absence of a Chinese writer). *Lianhe wenxue*, no. 1 (1999): 44–77.

49. Han Shaogong, interview by author, Hunan, 3 June 2000; Mo Yan, interview by author, Beijing, 3 April 2000.

50. Xi Chuan, interview by author, Beijing, 19 April 2000.

51. Dai Jinhua, *Yinxing shuxie* (Hidden writing) (Jiangsu: Renmin chubanshe, 1999), 48.

52. Wang, *High Culture Fever*, 116.

53. Gregory Guildin, *Anthropology in China* ([New York: M. E. Sharpe, 1990], 22), quoted in Edward Friedman, "Reconstructing China's National Identity: A Southern Alternative to Mao-Era Anti-Imperialist Nationalism," *Journal of Asian Studies* 53.1 (February 1994): 71.

54. Li Tuo, interview by author, Beijing, 20 April 2000.

55. Feng Jicai, interview by author, Tianjin, 25 May 2000.

56. Chen Liao, "Zou xiang shijie yihou" (After having marched towards the world), *Wenyi pinglun*, no. 4 (1986): 20.

57. Jian Jinsong, "Zhongguo wenxue ruhe zou xiang shijie" (How can Chinese literature march towards the world?), *Renmin ribao (haiwaiban)*, 2 May 1988, p. 7.

58. Dai Jinhua, interview by author, Beijing, 31 May 2000.

59. Dai, *Yinxing shuxie*, 263.

60. Chen, "Zou xiang shijie yihou," 23.

61. Mu, "Ershi shiji wenxue de jingying," 35–37.

62. Li Tuo, interview.

63. McDougall, interview. For more details on her circle of acquaintances, see "Breaking Through: Literature and the Arts in China 1976–1986," in her *Fictional Authors*, 171–204.

64. McDougall, interview.

65. Perry Link, *Evening Chats in Beijing*, for example 10–13, 117, 123, 201–212, 249–255, 292–293.

66. "Yao qiaru qifen de kandai Nuobeier wenxuejiang" (View the Nobel Literature Prize appropriately), in *Xuanchuan dongtai 1986 nian xuanbian* (Trends in propaganda: 1986 anthology) (Beijing: Jingji ribao chubanshe, 1987).

67. For details on links between establishment and intellectuals in the 1980s, see, for example, Merle Goldman, *Sowing the Seeds of Democracy in China: Political Reform in the Deng Xiaoping Era* (Cambridge, Mass.: Harvard University Press, 1994). Most professional writers participated at least to a limited extent in the official literary scene in the 1980s: even Bei Dao joined the Writers' Association, if only to facilitate

getting a passport. Examples of writers who combined high establishment positions with fairly liberal, reformist stances include Wang Meng, Liu Xinwu, and Feng Jicai.

68. References to Goethe and his World Literature were made in the influential 1985 essay "Lun ershi shiji Zhongguo wenxue" (On twentieth-century Chinese literature), *Wenxue pinglun*, no. 5 (1985): 3–13, by Chen Pingyuan et al. Books such as Zeng Xiaoyi's *Zou xiang shijie wenxue* (Marching towards world literature), (Hunan: Hunan renmin chubanshe, 1985) indicated a concern to place modern Chinese literature within a broad "international" (principally Western) channel of influence.

69. Liu Xinwu "Shijie zai nali?" (Where is the world?), *Wenyi bao*, 24 January 1987, p. 4.

70. Chen Xiaoming, interview by author, Beijing, 4 April 2000.

71. Like almost all Nobel Literature laureate announcements in the post-Mao period, Soyinka's prize generated a collection of articles introducing him to Chinese readers; see, for example, Jiang Yuying, "Tiancai zuojia he ziyou zhanshi — 1986 nian Nuobeier wenxue jiang huodezhe Suoyingka" (Genius writer and freedom fighter — Soyinka, the winner of the 1986 Nobel Literature Prize), *Shulin*, no. 6 (1987): 39–40; Gu Yaoming, "Dui Feizhou wenxue de baojiang — fang Niriliya zuojia Woer. Suoyingka" (An award to African literature — an interview with the Nigerian writer Wole Soyinka), *Renmin ribao* 16 December 1986, p. 7. However, his Nobel award did not fuel excitement comparable to the Latin American literary fever of 1980s China.

72. Chen Sihe, interview.

73. Kraus and Larson, "China's Writers," 155.

74. Dai, interview, 2000.

75. Key writers and works associated with the roots-seeking movement include Han Shaogong, *Bababa* (Dadada), *Renmin wenxue, no.* 6 (1985): 83–102; Ah Cheng, *Qiwang*, in *Shanghai wenxue*, no. 7 (1984): 15–35; Jia Pingwa's Shangzhou stories (*Shangzhou xilie*), for example "Shangzhou chulu" (Records of Shangzhou, One), *Zhongshan*, no. 10 (1982).

76. For more details, see discussions in Zhang, *Chinese Modernism* and Wang, *High Culture Fever*.

77. Li Tuo, "1985," trans. Anne Wedell-Wedellsborg, in *Under-sky Underground*, ed. Henry Y. H. Zhao and John Cayley (London: The Wellsweep Press, 1994), 126–127.

78. Yu, interview.

79. Tay, "Obscure Poetry," 146.

80. Liu Xinwu, "Zai 'xin qi guai' mianqian: du *Xiandai xiaoshuo jiqiao chutan*" (Facing "the new, the strange, and the grotesque": On reading Reading *The preliminary enquiry into the techniques of modern fiction*) (from *Xifang xiandai pai wenxue lunzheng ji*, vol. 2, 528), quoted in Wang, *High Culture Fever*, 145–146.

81. Kraus and Larson, "China's Writers," 154.

82. Bonnie S. McDougall and Kam Louie, *The Literature of China in the Twentieth Century* (London: Hurst & Company, 1997), 430.

83. Jing Wang characterizes the late 1980s debates over aesthetic modernity in China as "none other than the desire to look different." See *High Culture Fever*, 137–194.

84. Zhong Chengxiang, "Xun 'gen': yu shijie wenhua de fazhan tongbu" (Searching

out "roots": In step with the development of world culture), *Dangdai wentan*, no. 11 (1985): 42–43.

85. Chen, "Zouxiang shijie yihou," 21–23.

86. Li Yukun, "'Minzu hua' yu 'shijiexing'" ("Nationalization" and "global quality"), *Zhongguo wenhua bao*, 27 May 1987, p. 3.

87. Chen, "Zouxiang shijie yihou," 22.

88. Han Shaogong, "Wenxue de gen" (The roots of literature), *Zuojia*, no. 4 (1985): 2–5.

89. Zheng Yi, "Kuayue wenhua de duanliedai" (Leaping over the cultural rupture zone), *Wenyi bao*, 13 July 1985, p. 3.

90. Catherine V. Yeh, "Root Literature of the 1980s: May Fourth as a Double Burden" (paper presented at International Conference on the Burdens of the May Fourth Cultural Movements, Charles University, Prague, August 1994).

91. Zhong, *Masculinity Besieged?*, 52–170. This interpretation is interesting but not exclusive. Bingzai also carries echoes of Ah Q; his "aesthetic language" consists solely of the phrases "dadada" and "***mama."

92. Ibid., 167.

93. Ibid., 169.

94. Han, interview.

95. Chen Xiaoming, interview; Chen Sihe, interview.

96. Daruvala, *Zhou Zuoren*, 12.

97. Ibid., 252.

98. Li Tuo, "Yixiang de jiliu" (A surging current of imagery: outline), unpublished, photocopy.

99. See Wang, "Imaginary Nostalgia," in his *Fictional Realism*, 247–289. The traceable influence of Shen Congwen's "imaginary nostalgia" for the countryside on roots-seeking is not considered by Xueping Zhong.

100. Dai, interview, 2000.

101. Gao Yingpin, "Zou xiang shijie de xin yidai zuojia — Jiang Zilong jiqi zuopin zai guowai" (A new generation of writers marching towards the world — Jiang Zilong and his works abroad). *Mengya*, no. 11 (1985): 29.

102. Ibid., 31.

103. Dai, interview, 2000.

104. Although she had already been published in China, the Chinese literary world only started to take notice of her and accepted her into the Writers' Association after she had been translated. (Can Xue, interview by author, Hunan, 4 June 2000.)

105. Jianying Zha, *China Pop: How Soap Operas, Tabloids, and Bestsellers Are Transforming a Culture* (New York: The New Press, 1995), 81.

106. Dai, interview, 2000.

107. See, for example, Wei Kefeng, "Zhai jiang: Fang Ruidian xueyuan Ma Yueran yuanshi tan Nuobeier wenxuejiang" (Plucking the prize: An interview with Swedish Academician Göran Malmqvist about the Nobel Prize for Literature), *Lianhe wenxue*, no. 1 (1999): 81–82.

108. Li Dawei, interview by author, Beijing, 21 April 2000.

109. Dai, interview, 2000.

110. Owen, "What is World Poetry?"

111. Ibid., 32.

112. See discussion in Rey Chow, *Primitive Passions: Visuality, Sexuality, Ethnography, and Contemporary Chinese Cinema* (New York: Columbia University Press, 1995), 155–156.

113. Talal Asad, "Introduction," in *Anthropology and the Colonial Encounter*, ed. Asad (London: Ithaca Press, 1973), 16.

114. Chow, *Primitive Passions*, 142–172.

115. For roots-seeking interest in Shen, see Li, "Yixiang de jiliu." For official concern about Shen, see Shao Pu, "Zhongyang lingdao guanxin gaishan lao zuojia Shen Congwen de shenghuo" (The central leadership concerns itself over improving the life of the aged writer Shen Congwen), *Wenyi bao*, 14 June 1986, p. 1. On Goran Malmqvist's interest in Shen as a Nobel candidate and reaction to news of his death, see Liu, "Bainian Nuobeier," especially p. 65.

116. Xu, "From Modernity to Chineseness," 216.

117. Wang Hui, "Contemporary Chinese Thought and the Question of Modernity," trans. Rebecca El Karl, *Social Text* 55 (Summer 1998): 36.

118. See discussion in Barmé, "To Screw Foreigners is Patriotic," in *In the Red*, 255–280.

119. Ibid., 258.

120. Xin Chao, "Nuobeier wenxue de xiandai renlei wenhua yishi" (The modern human cultural consciousness of Nobel literature), *Waiguo wenxue yanjiu*, no. 11 (1991): 84.

121. Zhao Li, "Dongfang wenxue moli yu Nuobeier wenxuejiang" (The magic of Eastern literature and the Nobel Literature Prize), *Dongbei shida xuebao*, no. 6 (1997): 66. See also similar analysis in Wei Shanhao, "Shiji zhi jiao de 'dongfang Nuobeier wenxuejiang qingjie' — Da Jiang Jian San Lang huojiang de qishi" (The East's Nobel Prize complex at the turn of the century — lessons to be learnt from Oe Kenzaburo's prize), *Guowai wenxue*, no. 1 (1998): 42–46

122. Geographical factors and the events of the past one hundred and ten years have rendered exceptionally fraught the national relationship between China and Japan. The proximity of the two countries has fostered a basic tendency towards mutual comparison and competition in both nations' race for global modernity; Japan's victory in the 1894–1895 Sino-Japanese War, and its invasion of China during World War II and subsequent unwillingness to apologize (to Chinese satisfaction) for atrocities committed have intensified Chinese unease into a powerful sense of insecurity and resentment that periodically erupts into open hostility. (For discussion of the Sino-Japanese relationship and modern nationalism, see Gries, *China's New Nationalism*, especially 35–40, 90–98, and 121–125.)

123. Chinese "face" was to a certain extent saved by the fact that both Japanese Nobel literature laureates, and especially Oe, could be identified as opponents of modern Japanese nationalism and aggression towards China. Chinese critics also drew comfort from Oe's frequently expressed admiration for Chinese literature and for the novelist Mo Yan in particular: Oe's comment "If I were to choose a Nobel laureate, it would be Mo Yan," adorns the cover of a recent collection of Mo Yan's short

stories translated into English. Mo Yan, *Shifu, You'll Do Anything for a Laugh*, trans. Howard Goldblatt (London: Methuen, 2002).

124. Li Feng, interview by author, Beijing, 23 March 2001.

125. Cai Yi, "Nuobeier wenxuejiang yu Zhongguo wenxue" (The Nobel Literature Prize and Chinese literature), *Yunnan wenyi pinglun*, no. 1 (1995): 10.

126. Wang Hongtu, "Xifang wenhua de baquan he Dongfang de bianyuanxing" (Western cultural hegemony and Eastern marginality), *Shanghai wenxue*, no. 12 (1992): 75.

127. Ibid., 76.

128. Ibid.

129. Ibid.

130. For discussions of the "Wang Shuo phenomenon," see Barmé, *In the Red* and Wang, *High Culture Fever*.

131. Jia Pingwa, *Feidu* (Beijing: Beijing chubanshe, 1993).

132. Zha, *China Pop*, 137.

133. Dai Jinhua, interview by author, Beijing, 26 March 2001.

134. Dai, interview, 2000.

135. Zhang Rongyi, "Disan shijie wenxue yu 'tazhe bianma'" (Third-world literature and "encoding as the other"), *Wenshi zhi*, no. 3 (1995): 73.

136. Ibid., 74.

137. Ibid., 75.

138. Ibid.

139. Wang Lijiu, "Shilun wenxue de minzuxing yu shijiexing" (An enquiry into the national and global aspects of literature), *Guiyang shizhuan xuebao*, no.3 (1992): 35.

140. Goran Malmqvist, interview by Gregory Lee, Stockholm, 14 May 1990.

141. Ouyang Jianghe, interview by author, Beijing, 27 April 2000.

142. van Crevel, *Language Shattered*, 99–101.

143. Yang Lian, "The Writer and the Party," *Times Literary Supplement*, 6 November 1998, p. 18.

144. Yang Lian, interview by author, London, 7 October 1999.

145. Yang Lian, "The Writer and the Party," p. 18.

146. van Crevel, *Language Shattered*, 98.

147. Yang Lian, "Chi rensheng zhe zhi zhizhu" (This life-eating spider), preface to Chinese edition of Yang Rae, *Spider Eaters*, 10 August 1999, prepublication copy obtained from Yang Lian.

148. For more details of Yang's ideas about poetic language, see for example "Zhili de kongjian" (The intelligent space), "Tongxinyuan" (Concentric circles) in *Yang Lian zuopin 1982–1997, sanwen, wenlun juan: Guihua — zhili de kongjian* (Yang Lian works, 1982–1997, essays: Ghost talk — the intelligent space), (Shanghai: Wenyi chubanshe, 1998).

149. For both collections, see *Yang Lian zuopin 1982–1997: shige juan: Dahai tingzhi zhi chu* (Yang Lian works, 1982–1997, poetry: Where the sea stands still), (Shanghai: Wenyi chubanshe, 1998). *Dahai tingzhi zhi chu* is translated in *Where the Sea Stands Still*, trans. Brian Holton (Newcastle, Eng.: Bloodaxe, 1999).

150. Yang, "Tongxinyuan," in *Yang Lian zuopin 1982–1997: sanwen, wenlun juan,* 166.

151. See Brian Holton's translations and essay on translation, "Translating Yang Lian," in *Where the Sea Stands Still*, 173–189.

152. Ibid., 11 and 71, respectively.

153. Ibid., 150.

154. Ouyang, interview.

155. For instance, Bei Dao's various highly accomplished translators would certainly dispute the "easy translatability" of his poetry.

156. Michelle Yeh, "The 'Cult of Poetry' in Contemporary China," *Journal of Asian Studies* 55.1 (February 1996): 53.

157. Wang Jiaxin, interview by author, Beijing, 1 May 2000.

158. Yeh, "The 'Cult of Poetry,'" 67.

159. Ouyang, interview.

160. Wang Jiaxin, interview.

161. Ouyang, interview.

162. See Maghiel van Crevel, "'Intellectuals' vs. 'The People': A Late 1990s Controversy in Chinese Poetry," conference paper, 2001).

163. Dai, interview, 2001.

164. Claire Huot, "Here, There, Anywhere: Networking by Young Chinese Writers Today," in *The Literary Field of Twentieth-century China*, ed. Michel Hockx (Surrey: Curzon Press, 1999), 200.

165. Zhu Wen comp., "Duanlie: Yi fen wenjuan he wushiliu fen dajuan," (Rupture: One questionnaire and fifty-six responses), *Beijing wenxue*, no. 10 (1998): 19–47. Examples of Zhu Wen's peer group include the novelists Han Dong (1961–), Li Dawei, Li Feng, Dong Xi (1966–).

166. Wang, "Culture as Leisure," 89.

167. Ibid., 98–99.

168. Dai Jinhua, "Behind Global Spectacle and National Image Making," *Positions* 9 (Spring 2001): 173.

169. Xu Xiaobin, interview by author, Beijing, 24 April 2000.

170. Xu Xiaobin, "Cong Nuobeier wenxuejiang tankaiqu" (Starting with the Nobel Literature Prize), *Waiguo wenxue*, no. 5 (1997): 6.

171. Mian Mian, interview by author, Shanghai, 12 April 2000.

172. Li Feng, interview, 2000.

173. Li Tuo, interview.

174. Chen Xiaoming, interview.

175. Jin Jianfan, interview by author, Beijing, 31 March 2000.

176. Mo, interview.

177. Dai, interview, 2000.

178. Li Feng, interview, 2000.

179. Li Tuo, interview.

180. Wang Xiaoming, interview by author, Shanghai, 12 April 2000.

181. Jin, interview.

182. Ibid.

183. Bing Ling, "Wei de shi Zhongguo wenxue zou xiang shijie" (In order for Chinese literature to march towards the world), *Qingnian zuojia*, no. 9 (1998): 58.

184. Dai, interview, 2000.

185. Eric Eckholm, "China Reacts to Nobel Choice with Surprise, Elation and Suspicion," *International Herald Tribune*, 14–15 October 2000, p. 4.

186. Yan Huandong, "Shiji zhi jiaohua 'Nuojiang'" (The Nobel Prize: Topic of the century) *Zhongguo jingji shibao*, 13 October 2000.

187. Jin, interview.

188. See Brownell, *Training the Body*.

189. See ibid. for the dissident and nationalist appropriation of sporting events.

190. See, for example, Zhang Tingquan, "Beijing 2000—Aolinpike xin jieduan—Chen Xitong tan Beijing juban Aoyunhui de shenyuan yiyi" (Beijing 2000—a new phase for the Olympics—Chen Xitong discusses the deep significance of Beijing hosting the Olympic Games), *Renmin ribao*, 22 September 1993, p. 1.

191. Wu Wenbin, Wang Chuanbao, "Zhong-Mei Beijing Aoyunhui shenban cujin hui fabiao shenming: Qianze Mei zhongyuan ganshe Aolinpike shiwu" (Sino-American Committee for the Promotion of Beijing's 2000 Olympic bid condemns interference by the House of Representatives in Olympic matters), *Renmin ribao*, 2 August 1993, p. 6.

192. A professor at Beijing University pointed out to me a spray-painted area of grass in spring 2001; for details of brutality against a handicapped Beijing resident, see Nicholas D. Kristof and Sheryl Wudunn, *China Wakes: The Struggle for the Soul of a Rising Power* (London: Nicholas Brealey, 1995), 94–99.

193. See, for example, Zhang, "Beijing 2000."

194. Brownell, *Training the Body*, 313.

195. Wu Shaozu, "Aolinpike jingshen zhi tedian" (Characteristics of the Olympic spirit), *Renmin ribao*, 9 July 1996, p. 8.

196. For three of the earliest articles, see Xing Runchuan and Liu Jinyi, "Zhongnian kexuejia yu Nuobeier jiangjin huodezhe" (Middle-aged scientists and Nobel laureates), *Guangming ribao*, 10 October 1979; Chen Chao, "Nuobeier jiang shi zenme pingxuan de" (How the Nobel Prize is judged?), *Beijing kejibao*, 14 September 1979; Jiang Liangde, "Kexuejia de zui gao rongyu (Nuobeier jiangjin jianjie)" (The highest honor for scientists [a brief introduction to the Nobel Prize]), *Jiefang ribao*, 26 October 1979.

197. See Sun Haidong, "Bainian Nuobeier" (One hundred years of the Nobel Prize), *Beijing wanbao*, 27 May 2000, p. 17.

198. Xu Jiayue, "Keyan bentuhua: Tongxiang Nuobeier jiang zhi lu (shang)" (The nativization of scientific research: Heading for the Nobel Prize [one]), *Kexue xue yu kexue jishu guanli*, no. 7 (1996): 4.

199. Ge Henglin and Sun Jingshui, "Zhongguo weihe zhijin yu kexue Nuobeier jiang wu yuan" (Why China has never won a Nobel Science Prize), *Zhongguo guoqing guoli*, no. 10 (2001): 40–42; Chen Ying and Mao Xia, "Lun chuangxin jiaoyu: Cong Zhongguo meiyou Nuobeier jiang tan qi" (On creative education: Thoughts on China's failure to win a Nobel Prize), *Jiaoyu tansuo*, no. 4 (2001): 14–16.

200. Fan Yuejin and Yin Yuji, "Zhongguo jingjixue ruhe tiaozhan Nuobeier jiang" (How Chinese economics can contend for the Nobel Prize), *Jingji xuejia*, no. 1 (2001).

201. See, for example, Ge and Sun, "Zhongguo weihe"; Chen and Mao, "Lun chuangxin jiaoyu"; Fan and Yin, "Zhongguo jingjixue"; Liu Haifeng, "Wo guo kexuejia wuyuan Nuobeier jiang de yuanjin ji chongji duice" (The reasons why our scientists have never won a Nobel Prize and strategies for remedying this) *Nanjing shehui kexue*, no. 2 (1999): 45–47. For a general discussion of these issues, see Cong Cao, "Chinese Science and the 'Nobel Prize Complex,'" *Minerva* 42 (2004): 151–172.

202. These attitudes are exemplified in Ge and Sun, "Zhongguo weihe."

203. This is not the place to debate this contentious proposition in detail. Crawford in *Nationalism and Internationalism in Science* conducts an interesting debate on the subject, referring in the process to nationalistic intrusions into nineteenth- and twentieth-century science. John Cornwell, *Hitler's Scientists: Science, War, and the Devil's Pact* (London: Viking, 2003) provides a detailed account of the participation of German scientists in Germany's twentieth-century state-building project. For an account of the political uses to which science was put in Maoist China and Stalinist Russia, see Jasper Becker, *Hungry Ghosts: China's Secret Famine* (London: John Murray, 1996), 58–82.

204. Zhong Weigang and Li Hongyin, "Zou jin Nuobeier" (Drawing close to a Nobel), *Ziran bianzhengfa yanjiu*, no. 5 (1999): 65.

205. Fan and Yin, "Zhongguo jingjixue."

206. The same point cannot be made quite so straightforwardly in the case of post-Mao Chinese economics. Although by the late 1990s, approximate consensus had been reached within the PRC about the general correctness of the market economy as a path of development for China, earlier debates about the economy were far more ideologically contentious. For a general introduction to the issues, see Roderick MacFarquhar, ed., *The Politics of China: The Eras of Mao and Deng* (Cambridge: Cambridge University Press, 1997); Zhang Lun, *La Vie Intellectuelle en Chine depuis la Mort de Mao* (Paris: Fayard, 2003).

207. For more instances of the politicization of modern science, see note 203 above.

208. Felix Belair Jr., "Swedes 'Protect' Two Nobel Winners: Chinese Physicists Arrive from U.S. — Red Embassy Aides Are Fended Off," *New York Times*, 9 December 1957, p. 25.

209. Anon., "Liu wei Huayi Nuobeier jiang huodezhe zhanwang 21 shiji" (Six ethnic Chinese Nobel Prize winners look ahead to the twenty-first century), *Zhongguo minying keji yu jingji*, no. 21 (2000): 6–7.

Chapter 5: The Nobel Prize, 2000

1. On beginning the interviews, I learned that some of my interviewees had been criticized for voicing opinions on Gao's prize. This, in combination with the fact that all Gao's works were banned in China after the announcement of his prize, led me to conclude that omission of all names would be the safest policy.

2. Gao Xingjian, interview by author, London, 9 March 2001.

3. The work of Henry Zhao and Syren Quah on his drama stands out particularly; on his fiction, Mabel Lee has done work in translation and criticism; her translation of *Lingshan* came out in 2000. See Kwok-kan Tam, *Soul of Chaos: Critical Perspectives on Gao Xingjian* (Hong Kong: Chinese University Press, 2001) and *Modern Chinese Literature and Culture* 14 (Fall 2002) for useful collections of critical essays on Gao's work.

4. Gao Xingjian, *Meiyou zhuyi* (No-ism) (Hong Kong: Cosmos Books, 1996), 2.

5. Ibid., 19.

6. Ibid., 4.

7. Ibid., 21.

8. Ibid., 111.

9. Gao Xingjian, "The Case for Literature," Nobel Lecture 2000.

10. Gao Xingjian, *Chezhan* (Bus-stop), *Shiyue* no. 3 (1983), 119–138.

11. Gao Xingjian, *Lingshan* (Soul Mountain) (Taipei: Lianjing, 1990); Gao, "The Case for Literature."

12. Syren Quah, "The Theatre of Gao Xingjian: Experimentation within the Chinese context and towards new modes of representation," Ph.D. diss., University of Cambridge, 1999.

13. For Gao's post-exile work, see *Gao Xingjian xiju liuzhong* (Six plays by Gao Xingjian) (Taipei: Dijiao, 1995); *The Other Shore: Plays by Gao Xingjian*, trans. Gilbert C. F. Fong (Hong Kong: The Chinese University Press, 2000).

14. Henry Zhao, *Towards a Modern Zen Theatre: Gao Xingjian and Chinese Theatre Experimentalism* (London: School of Oriental and African Studies, 2000), 207.

15. Ibid., 207–214.

16. Gao Xingjian, *Soul Mountain*, trans. Mabel Lee (New York: HarperCollins, 2000), 452–453. Numbers in parentheses in this section on *Lingshan* refer to pages in this edition.

17. Quah, "Gao Xingjian," 14.

18. Yang, "The Writer and the Party," *Times Literary Supplement*, 6 November 1998, p. 18.

19. Zhang Xianliang, *Xiguan siwang* (Getting used to dying) (Taipei: Yuansheng, 1989). The similarity between the novels of Gao and Zhang is an insight I owe to Michel Hockx.

20. Xinhua, "Nuobeier wenxuejiang bei yong yu zhengzhi mudi shiqu quanweixing," *Renmin ribao*, 14 October 2000, p. 2.

21. Yang Lian, "Liuwang de shengli" (The victory of exile), *Zhongguo shibao*, 14 October 2000, p. 37.

22. Moli, "Miandui Ruidian wenxueyuan de 'jiezuo'" (Facing the Swedish Academy's "masterwork"), 25 February 2001 (13 March 2001). http://www.whxf .com/wenxue.

23. Chinesenewsnet. 2000. "Liang'an zuojia zonglun Gao Xingjian" (Chinese writers on both sides of the straits discuss Gao Xingjian), 14 October 2000 (15 October 2000). http://www4.Chinesenewsnet.com/Feature/GaoXinJian/.

24. See, for example, critical comments in chapter 4 above.

25. See Yang, "The Writer and the Party," 18.

26. Shu Yi, interview by author, Beijing, 28 March 2001.

27. For details of the story about Lao She and the Nobel Prize, see, for example, Shu Yun, "Lao She weishenme mei ling dao Nuobeier wenxuejiang" (Why Lao She didn't win the Nobel Literature Prize), *Yanhuang chunqiu* no. 9 (1994): 70–71.

28. Writer B avoided referring to another story concerning the relationship between Gao and Malmqvist that circulated in the weeks following the announcement of Gao's prize, namely that a few months before the prize was awarded, Malmqvist persuaded Gao to transfer the publishing rights for his Swedish translations of Gao's works to a company run by a personal friend. In the press, Malmqvist was suspected of improper insider dealing, of disclosing in advance the outcome of that year's Nobel to the profit of his friend. While the timing of the switch was, with hindsight, unfortunate, it seems improbable that someone in Malmqvist's public position would contemplate the kind of underhanded behavior of which he was accused. On 23 November 2000, Malmqivst presented an explanation of his actions on the "Modern Chinese Literature and Culture" Internet discussion list, in which he pointed out that by switching from a large to a small publisher, his own translator's fee was reduced by 50 percent.

29. Eric Eckholm, "Jiang Portrays China's Ties with U.S. as Showing 'Positive' Desire," *International Herald Tribune*, 10 August 2001, p. 1.

30. Li Feng, interview, 2001.

31. Ibid.

Afterword

1. Martin Amis, *Experience* (New York: Vintage, 2000), 46.

GLOSSARY OF CHINESE TERMS

Ah Q zheng zhuan　阿Q正传

Ai Qing　艾青

Ba Jin　巴金

Bei Dao　北岛

Beijing ren zai Niuyue　北京人在纽约

bense　本色

biji　笔记

Bingzai　丙崽

Cai Yuanpei　蔡元培

Chen Duxiu　陈独秀

Chen Kaige　陈凯歌

Chen Shuibian　陈水遍

Chenzhong de chibang　沉重的翅膀

Chezhan　车站

chiru　耻辱

Dadi　大地

Da hai tingzhi zhi chu　大海停止之处

Deng Xiaoping　邓小平

Ding Ling　丁玲

Duihua yu fanjie　对话与反詰

Duo Duo　多多

fengtu　风土

Feng Xuefeng　冯雪峰

fuqiang　富强

gaizao guominxing　改造国民性

geren　个人

Gu Cheng　顾城

Gu Hongming　辜鸿铭

Guo Moruo　郭沫若

Hanlin　翰林

Heshang　河殇

houxue　后学

Hu Shi　胡适

Hu Yaobang　胡耀邦

Jiang Zemin　江泽民

Jinshan　金山

Jintian　今天

Junshi bowuguan　军事博物馆

"Kuangren riji"　狂人日记

Lao She　老舍

leng de wenxue　冷的文学

li　礼

Liang Qichao　梁启超

Lin Yutang　林语堂

Liu Bannong　刘半农

Liu Suola　刘索拉

Liu Xinwu　刘心武

Long Yingtai　龙应台

Lu Ling　路翎

Mao Dun　茅盾

Mao Zedong　毛泽东

menglong shi　朦胧诗

Mingbao yuekan　明报月刊

minjian xiezuo　民间写作

Nuobeier qingjie　诺贝尔情节

*Nuobeier wenxue jiangjin huodezhe
　zuojia zuopin xuan*
　诺贝尔文学奖金获得者作家作品选

pingmin　平民

quwei　趣味

quxiao shijian　取消时间

ren de wenxue　人的文学

Renmin ribao　人民日报

Shangzhou xilie　商州系列

Shen Congwen　沈从文

Sheng si zhi jie　生死之界

shijie wenxue　世界文学

Shi Zhecun　施蛰存

223

"Shuo qun"　说群
Tai Jingnong　台静农
Taowang　逃亡
Tongxinyuan　同心圆
wang qian kan　往前/钱看
Wang Shiwei　王实味
Wang Shuo　王朔
Wang Yichuan　王一川
wei renmin fuwu　为人民服务
wenhua duanlie　文化断裂
wenhua re　文化热
wenhua yishu chubanshe
　文化艺术出版社
wenxue　文学
Wenyi bao　文艺报
wu fu　五府
Xiandai xiaoshuo jiqiao chutan
　现代小说技巧初谈
Xiandai zazhi　现代杂志
Xiaoshuo yuebao　小说月报
xin ganjue pai　新感觉派
xin min　新民
xin shengdai　新生代
xin shiqi　新时期
Xu Zhimo　徐志摩
xugou　虚构
xungen pai　寻根派
Yan Fu　严复
Yang Jiang　杨绛
Yeyou shen　夜游神

youhuan yishi　忧患意识
Yu Dafu　郁达夫
Yu Jian　于坚
yue shi minzu de yue shi shijie de
　越是民族的越是世界的
Zhang Ailing　张爱玲
Zhang Fa　张法
Zhang Yimou　张艺谋
Zhao Shuli　赵树理
Zheng Yi　郑义
zhishi fenzi　知识分子
zhishifenzi xiezuo　知识分子写作
zhong　中
Zhongguo huanxiang　中国幻想
Zhongguo keyi shuo bu　中国可以说不
Zhongguo yu shijie jiegui
　中国与世界接轨
Zhonghua dushu bao　中华读书报
Zhong-Mei Beijing 2000 nian aoyunhui
　shenban cujin hui
　中美北京2000年奥运会申办促进会
Zhongyang dianshitai　中央电视台
Zhou Yang　周扬
Zhou Zuoren　周作人
zijue　自觉
ziyou zuojia　自由作家
zou xiang Nuobeier　走向诺贝尔
zou xiang shijie　走向世界
zuo gei waiguo ren kan　作给外国人看
Zuojia xiehui　作家协会

BIBLIOGRAPHY

Ah Cheng 阿成. *Qiwang* 棋王 (The chess king). *Shanghai wenxue*, no. 7 (1984): 15–35.

Ahmad, Aijaz. "Jameson's Rhetoric of Otherness and the 'National Allegory.'" In idem, *In Theory: Classes, Nations, Literatures*, 92–122. London: Verso, 1992.

Allén, Sture. "Topping Shakespeare? Aspects of the Nobel Prize for Literature." *Artes* (1997): 11–18.

Allmendinger, Blake. "Little House on the Rice Paddy." *American Literary History* 10.2 (Summer 1998): 360–377.

Amis, Martin. *Experience*. New York: Vintage, 2000.

Anderson, Benedict. *Imagined Communities: Reflections on the Origin and Spread of Nationalism*. London: Verso, 1991.

Anderson, Marston. *The Limits of Realism: Chinese Fiction in the Revolutionary Period*. Berkeley: University of California Press, 1989.

Ang, Ien. *On Not Speaking Chinese*. London: Routledge, 2001.

Anon. "Liu wei huayi Nuobeier jiang huodezhe zhanwang 21 shiji" 六位华裔诺贝尔奖获得者展望21世纪 (Six ethnic Chinese Nobel Prize winners look ahead to the twenty-first century). *Zhongguo minying keji yu jingji*, no. 21 (2000): 6–7.

Appadurai, Arjun. "Disjuncture and Difference in the Global Cultural Economy." In *Global Culture*, edited by Mike Featherstone, 295–310. London: Sage Publications, 1990.

Arrighi, Giovanni, Takeshi Hamashita, and Mark Selden, eds. *The Resurgence of East Asia: 500, 150 and 50 year perspectives*. London: Routledge, 2003.

Asad, Talal. "Introduction." In *Anthropology and the Colonial Encounter*, edited by Talal Asad, 9–19. London: Ithaca Press, 1973.

Bai Jieming 白杰明 (Geremie Barmé). "Mianxiang shijie de dangdai dalu wenxue" 面向世界的大陆文学 (Contemporary Mainland Chinese literature faces the world). *Jiushi niandai*, no. 12 (December 1986): 82–85.

Bain, R. Nisbet. *Gustavus III and His Contemporaries, 1746–1792*. Vol. 2. London: K. Paul, Trench, Trubner & Co., 1894.

de Balzac, H. *Traité de la vie élégante*. Paris: Delmas, 1952.

Bang Fu 邦富, trans. "Nuobeier jiang pingxuan weiyuanzhang deng tan Nuobeier jiang de pingxuan" 诺贝尔奖评选委员长等谈诺贝尔奖的评选 (The Nobel Prize Committee members discuss Nobel Prize selection). *Waiguo wenxue dongtai*, no. 5 (1986): 23–25.

Barmé, Geremie. *In the Red: On Contemporary Chinese Culture.* New York: Columbia University Press, 1999.

Barmé, Geremie, and John Minford, eds. *Seeds of Fire: Chinese Voices of Conscience.* Newcastle, Eng.: Bloodaxe, 1989.

Bayly, C. A. *The Birth of the Modern World, 1780–1914: Global Connections and Comparisons.* Oxford: Blackwell, 2004.

Becker, Jasper. *Hungry Ghosts: China's Secret Famine.* London: John Murray, 1996.

Bei Dao. *Notes from the City of the Sun: Poems by Bei Dao.* Translated and edited, with an introduction by Bonnie S. McDougall. Ithaca, N.Y.: Cornell University China-Japan Program, 1983.

Berman, Marshall. *All That Is Solid Melts Into Air: The Experience of Modernity.* London: Verso, 1983.

Bhabha, Homi K. "DissemiNation: time, narrative and the margins of the modern nation." In *Nation and Narration,* edited by Bhabha, 291–320. London: Routledge, 1990.

Bilic, Paul, and Robert Winder. "The Prize is Right." *Prospect* (November 1995): 14–15.

Bing Ling 冰凌. "Wei de shi Zhongguo wenxue zou xiang shijie" 为的是中国文学走向世界 (In order for Chinese literature to march towards the world). *Qingnian zuojia,* no. 9 (1998): 56–58.

Bourdieu, Pierre. *The Field of Cultural Production.* Edited by Randall Johnson. Cambridge: Polity Press, 1993.

———. *The Rules of Art.* Translated by Susan Emanuel. Cambridge: Polity Press, 1996.

Brownell, Susan. *Training the Body for China: Sports in the Moral Order of the People's Republic.* Chicago: University of Chicago Press, 1995.

Buck, Pearl. *The Good Earth.* London: Methuen, 1987.

Buell, Frederick. *National Culture and the New Global System.* Baltimore: Johns Hopkins University Press, 1994.

Burke, Peter, ed. *New Perspectives on Historical Writing.* Cambridge: Polity Press, 2001.

Cai Yi 蔡毅. "Nuobeier wenxuejiang yu Zhongguo wenxue" 诺贝尔文学奖与中国文学 (The Nobel Literature Prize and Chinese literature). *Yunnan wenyi pinglun,* no. 1 (1995): 10–18.

Calinescu, Matei. *Five Faces of Modernity: Modernism, Avant-Garde, Decadence, Kitsch, Postmodernism.* Durham, N.C.: Duke University Press, 1987.

Can Xue 残雪. Interview by author, 4 June 2000, Hunan.

Carey, John. *The Intellectuals and the Masses: Pride and Prejudice among the Literary Intelligentsia, 1880–1939.* London: Faber and Faber, 1992.

Chan, Red. "Politics of Translation: Mainland Chinese Novels in the Anglophone World in the Post-Mao Era." Ph.D. dissertation, Oxford University, 2003.

Chang, Jung. *Wild Swans: Three Daughters of China.* London: HarperCollins, 1991.

Chatterjee, Partha. *Nationalist Thought and the Colonial World: A Derivative Discourse?* London: Zed Books, 1986.

———. *The Nation and Its Fragments: Colonial and Postcolonial Histories.* Princeton: Princeton University Press, 1993.

Chen Chunsheng 陈春生. "Lu Xun yu Nuobeier wenxuejiang" 鲁迅与诺贝尔文学奖. *Lu Xun yanjiu yuekan*, no. 8 (2000): 47–50.

Chen, Da. *Sounds of the River.* London: William Heinemann, 2003.

Chen Liao 陈辽. "Zou xiang shijie yihou" 走向世界以后 (After having marched towards the world). *Wenyi pinglun*, no. 4 (1986): 20–23.

Chen Pingyuan 陈平原, Huang Ziping 黄子平, and Qian Liqun 钱理群. "Lun ershi shiji Zhongguo wenxue" 论二十世纪中国文学 (On twentieth-century Chinese literature). *Wenxue pinglun*, no. 5 (1985): 3–13.

Chen Sihe 陈思和. Interview by author, 8 April 2000, Shanghai.

Chen Xiaomei. *Occidentalism: A Theory of Counter-discourse in Post-Mao China.* Oxford: Oxford University Press, 1995.

Chen Xiaoming 陈晓明. Interview by author, 4 April 2000, Beijing.

Chen Ying 陈英, and Mao Xia 毛霞. "Lun chuangxin jiaoyu: Cong Zhongguo meiyou Nuobeier jiang tanqi" 论创新教育：从中国没有诺贝尔奖谈起 (On creative education: Thoughts on China's failure to win a Nobel Prize). *Jiaoyu tansuo*, no. 4 (2001): 14–16.

Cheng, Nian. *Life and Death in Shanghai.* London: Grafton, 1986.

Chi, Pang-yuan, and David Der-wei Wang, eds. *Chinese Literature in the Second Half of a Modern Century: A Critical Survey.* Bloomington: Indiana University Press, 2000.

Chin, Annping. *Four Sisters of Hofei.* London: Bloomsbury, 2003.

Chinesenewsnet. "Liang'an zuojia zonglun Gao Xingjian" 两岸作家纵论高行健 (Chinese writers on both sides of the straits discuss Gao Xingjian). 14 October 2000. http://www4.Chinesenewsnet.com/Feature/GaoXinJian/ (accessed 15 October 2000).

Chow, Rey. *Woman and Chinese Modernity.* Minneapolis: University of Minnesota Press, 1991.

———. *Writing Diaspora.* Bloomington: Indiana University Press, 1993.

———. *Primitive Passions: Visuality, Sexuality, Ethnography, and Contemporary Chinese Cinema.* New York: Columbia University Press, 1995.

———. *Ethics After Idealism.* Bloomington: Indiana University Press, 1998.

Chow Tse-tsung. *The May Fourth Movement: Intellectual Revolution in Modern China.* Cambridge, Mass.: Harvard University Press, 1960.

Cong Cao. "Chinese Science and the 'Nobel Prize Complex.'" *Minerva* 42 (2004): 151–172.

Cornwell, John. *Hitler's Scientists: Science, War, and the Devil's Pact.* London: Viking, 2003.

Crawford, Elisabeth. *Nationalism and Internationalism in Science, 1880–1939: Four Studies of the Nobel Population.* Cambridge: Cambridge University Press, 1992.

Crespi, John. "A Vocal Minority: New Poetry and Poetry Declamation in China 1915–1975." Ph.D. dissertation, University of Chicago, 2001.

Dai Jinhua 戴锦华. *Yinxing shuxie* 隐形书写 (Hidden writing). Jiangsu: Renmin chubanshe, 1999.

————. Interview by author, 31 May 2000, Beijing.

————. Interview by author, 26 March 2001, Beijing.

————. "Behind Global Spectacle and National Image Making." *Positions* 9, no. 1 (Spring 2001): 161–186.

Dai Qing. *Wang Shiwei and "Wild Lilies": Rectification and Purges in the Chinese Communist Party, 1942–1944.* New York: M. E. Sharpe, 1994.

Daruvala, Susan. *Zhou Zuoren and an Alternative Chinese Response to Modernity.* Cambridge, Mass.: Harvard University Press, 2000.

Denton, Kirk. *The Problematic of Self in Modern Chinese Literature: Hu Feng and Lu Ling.* Stanford: Stanford University Press, 1998.

————, ed. *Modern Chinese Literary Thought: Writings on Literature, 1893–1945.* Stanford: Stanford University Press, 1996.

di Giovanni, Norman Thomas. "How to win the Nobel Prize for Literature." *The Listener*, 11 February 1982, 12–14.

Dirlik, Arif. *The Postcolonial Aura: Third World Criticism in the Age of Global Capitalism.* Boulder, Co.: Westview Press, 1997.

Dirlik, Arif, and Xudong Zhang. "Introduction: Postmodernism and China." *boundary 2* 24.3 (1997): 1–18.

Dowling, Linda. *Language and Decadence in the Victorian Fin de Siècle.* Princeton: Princeton University Press, 1986.

Duara, Prasenjit. *Rescuing History from the Nation.* Chicago: University of Chicago Press, 1995.

Duke, Michael S. "The Problematic Nature of Modern and Contemporary Chinese Fiction in English Translation," in Goldblatt, *Worlds Apart*, 198–227.

Dutta, Krishna, and Andrew Robinson. *Rabindranath Tagore: The Myriad-Minded Man.* London: Bloomsbury, 1995.

Espmark, Kjell. *The Nobel Prize in Literature: A Study of the Criteria Behind the Choices.* Boston: G. K. Hall, 1991.

————. 1999. "The Nobel Prize in Literature." December 1999. http://www.Nobel. se (accessed 20 January 2000).

Fairbank, John K., ed. *The Chinese World Order.* Cambridge, Mass: Harvard University Press, 1968.

Fairbank, John K., and S. Y. Teng. "On the Ch'ing Tributary System." *Harvard Journal of Asiatic Studies* 6.2 (1942): 135–246.

von Falkenhausen, Lothar. Review of Göran Malmqvist, *Bernard Karlgren: Ett Forskarporträtt*, in *China Review International* 8.1 (Spring 2001): 15–33.

Fan Yuejin 范跃进, and Yin Yuji 尹玉吉. "Zhongguo jingjixue ruhe tiaozhan Nuobeier jiang" 中国经济学如何挑战诺贝尔奖 (How can Chinese economics contend for the Nobel Prize). *Jingji xuejia*, no. 1 (2001).

Feldman, Burton. *The Nobel Prize: A History of Genius, Controversy, and Prestige.* New York: Arcade, 2000.

Feng Jicai 冯骥才. Interview by author, 25 May 2000, Tianjin.

Feng Yidai 冯亦代. "Nuobeier wenxuejiang de wo jian" 诺贝尔文学奖的我见 (My view of the Nobel Prize). *Qunyan*, no. 2 (1987): 32–33.

Feuerwerker, Yi-tsi Mei. *Ideology, Power, Text: Self-Representation and the Peasant "Other" in Modern Chinese Literature*. Stanford: Stanford University Press, 1998.

Fitzgerald, John. *Awakening China: Politics, Culture, and Class in the Nationalist Revolution*. Stanford: Stanford University Press, 1996.

Foster, Paul B. "The Ironic Inflation of Chinese National Character: Lu Xun's International Reputation, Romain Rolland's Critique of 'The True Story of Ah Q,' and the Nobel Prize." *Modern Chinese Literature and Culture* 13.1 (Spring 2001): 140–168.

Friedman, Edward. "Reconstructing China's National Identity: A Southern Alternative to Mao-Era Anti-Imperialist Nationalism." *Journal of Asian Studies* 53.1 (February 1994): 67–91.

Gandhi, Leela. *Postcolonial Theory: A Critical Introduction*. Edinburgh: Edinburgh University Press, 1998.

Gao Anhua. *To the Edge of the Sky*. London: Viking, 2000.

Gao Jianping 高建平. "Lu Xun: Cong wangshang pingxuan shuo kai qu" 鲁迅：从网上评选说开去 (Lu Xun: Starting from the selection on the Internet). *Shouhuo*, no. 1 (2000): 120–124.

Gao Xingjian 高行健. *Chezhan* (Bus stop). *Shiyue*, no. 3 (1983): 119–138.

———. *Lingshan* 灵山 (Soul Mountain). Taipei: Lianjing, 1990.

———. *Gao Xingjian xiju liu zhong* 高行健戏剧六种 (Six Plays by Gao Xingjian). Taipei: Dijiao, 1995.

———. *Meiyou zhuyi* 没有主义 (No-ism). Hong Kong: Cosmos Books, 1996.

———. *Yige ren de shengjing* 一个人的圣经 (One man's bible). Taipei: Lianjing, 1999.

———. *Soul Mountain*. Translated by Mabel Lee. New York: HarperCollins, 2000.

———. *The Other Shore: Plays by Gao Xingjian*. Translated by Gilbert C. F. Fong. Hong Kong: The Chinese University Press, 2000.

———. "The Case for Literature." Nobel Lecture, 2000.

———. Interview by author, 9 March 2001, London.

Gao Yingpin 高应品. "Zou xiang shijie de xin yidai zuojia—Jiang Zilong jiqi zuopin zai guowai" 走向世界的新一代作家—蒋子龙及其作品在国外 (A new generation of writers marching towards the world—Jiang Zilong and his works abroad). *Mengya*, no. 11 (1985): 29–31.

Ge Henglin 葛恒林, and Sun Jingshui 孙敬水. "Zhongguo weihe zhijin yu kexue Nuobeier jiang wuyuan" 中国为何至今与科学诺贝尔奖无缘 (Why China has never won a Nobel Science Prize). *Zhongguo guoqing guoli*, no. 10 (2001): 40–42.

Gellner, Ernest. *Nations and Nationalism*. Oxford: Blackwell, 1983.

Goldblatt, Howard, ed. *Chinese Literature for the 1980s*. New York: M. E. Sharpe, 1982.

———. *Worlds Apart: Recent Chinese Writing and Its Audiences*. New York: M. E. Sharpe, 1990.

———. *Chairman Mao Would Not Be Amused: Fiction from Today's China*. New York: Grove Press, 1995.

Goldman, Merle. *Literary Dissent in Communist China.* Cambridge, Mass.: Harvard University Press, 1967.

———. *Sowing the Seeds of Democracy in China: Political Reform in the Deng Xiaoping Era.* Cambridge, Mass.: Harvard University Press, 1994.

Gray, Jack. *Rebellions and Revolutions: China from the 1800s to the 1980s.* Oxford: Oxford University Press, 1990.

Greenfeld, Liah. *Nationalism: Five Roads to Modernity.* Cambridge, Mass.: Harvard University Press, 1992.

Gries, Peter Hays. *China's New Nationalism: Pride, Politics, and Diplomacy* (Berkeley: University of California Press, 2004).

Gunn, Edward. *Unwelcome Muse: Chinese Literature in Shanghai and Peking, 1937–1945.* New York: Columbia University Press, 1980.

———. *Rewriting Chinese: Style and Innovation in Twentieth-Century Chinese Prose.* Stanford: Stanford University Press, 1991.

Guo Yingjian 郭英剑, ed. *Sai Zhenzhu pinglun ji* 赛珍珠评论集 (Collected criticism on Pearl Buck). Guangxi: Lijiang chubanshe, 1999.

Ha Jin. *Waiting.* New York: Random House, 1999.

Hamashita, Takeshi. "Tribute and Treaties: Maritime Asia and Treaty Port Networks in the Era of Negotiation, 1800–1900." In Arrighi et al., *The Resurgence of East Asia,* 17–50.

Han Shaogong 韩少功. "Wenxue de gen" 文学的根 (The roots of literature). *Zuojia,* no. 4 (1985): 2–5.

———. *Bababa* 爸爸爸 (Dadada). *Renmin wenxue,* no. 6 (1985): 83–102.

———. Interview by author, 3 June 2000, Hunan.

———. *A Dictionary of Maqiao.* Translated by Julia Lovell. New York: Columbia University Press, 2003.

Hay, Stephen. *Asian Ideas of East and West.* Cambridge, Mass.: Harvard University Press, 1970.

Hayford, Charles. "*The Good Earth,* Revolution, and the American Raj in China." In Lipscomb et al., *The Several Worlds,* 19–27.

———. "What's So Bad About *The Good Earth?*" *Education About Asia* 3.3 (Winter 1998): 4–7.

He Feng 贺风. "'Nuobeier wenxuejiang' de pianpo yu 'Zhonghua wenxue dajiang' de sheli" 诺贝尔文学奖的偏颇于中华文学大奖的设立 (The bias of the Nobel Literature Prize and the establishment of the Chinese Literature Prize). *Bianyi cankao,* no. 2 (1987): 35–37.

He Song 何松. "*Dajia*: Rang Nuobeier wenxuejiang zoukai" 大家：让诺贝尔文学奖走开 (*Dajia*: Tell the Nobel Prize to go away). *Dajia,* no. 1 (1998): 205–207.

He Xianglin 贺祥麟. "Xu" 序 (Foreword). In Guo, *Sai Zhenzhu,* 1–4.

Held, David, and Anthony McGrew. "The Great Globalization Debate: An Introduction." In *The Global Transformations Reader: An Introduction to the Globalization Debate,* edited by Held and McGrew, 1–45. Cambridge: Polity Press, 2000.

Held, David, Anthony McGrew, David Goldblatt, and Jonathan Perraton. *Global Transformations: Politics, Economics and Culture.* Cambridge: Polity Press, 1999.

Hill, Justin. *The Drink and Dream Teahouse*. London: Weidenfeld and Nicholson, 2001.

Hitchens, Christopher. *Unacknowledged Legislation*. London: Verso, 2001.

Holm, David. *Art and Ideology in Revolutionary China*. Oxford: Clarendon Press, 1991.

Hong Ying. *Daughter of the River*. Translated by Howard Goldblatt. London: Bloomsbury, 1998.

Hsia, C. T. "Appendix 1: Obsession with China: The Moral Burden of Modern Chinese Literature." In idem, *A History of Modern Chinese Fiction*, 2d ed., 533–554. New Haven: Yale University Press, 1971.

Hu Feng 胡风. "*Dadi* li de Zhongguo" 大地里的中国 (The China of *The Good Earth*). In Guo, *Sai Zhenzhu*, 91–100.

Huang, Philip C. C. "Liang Ch'i-ch'ao: The Idea of the New Citizen and the Influence of Meiji Japan." In *Transition and Permanence: Chinese History and Culture. A Festschrift in Honour of Dr. Hsia Kung-ch'uan*, edited by David C. Buxbaum and Frederick T. Mote, 71–102. Hong Kong, privately printed, 1972.

Huot, Claire. "Here, There, Anywhere: Networking by Young Chinese Writers Today." In *The Literary Field of Twentieth-Century China*, edited by Michel Hockx, 198–215. Surrey: Curzon Press, 1999.

Hutcheon, Linda. *A Poetics of Postmodernism: History, Theory, Fiction*. New York: Routledge, 1988.

———. *The Politics of Postmodernism*. London: Routledge, 1989.

Ideologicheskie komissii TsK KPSS. 1958–64: dokumenty. Moscow: ROSSPEN, 1998.

Ignatieff, Michael. *Empire Lite: Nation-Building in Bosnia, Kosovo, Afghanistan*. London: Vintage, 2003.

Jacques, Martin. "The Interregnum." *London Review of Books*, 5 February 2004.

Jameson, Fredric. "Third-World Literature in the Era of Multinational Capitalism." *Social Text* 15 (Fall 1986): 65–88.

———. "A Brief Response." *Social Text* 17 (Fall 1987): 26–27.

———. *Postmodernism, or the Cultural Logic of Late Capitalism*. Durham, N.C.: Duke University Press, 1991.

———. "Preface." In Jameson and Miyoshi, *The Cultures of Globalization*, xi–xvii.

Jameson, Fredric, and Masao Miyoshi, eds. *The Cultures of Globalization*. Durham, N.C.: Duke University Press, 1998.

Jenner, W. J. F. "Insuperable Barriers? Some Thoughts on the Reception of Chinese Writing in English Translation." In Goldblatt, *Worlds Apart*, 177–197.

Jia Pingwa 贾平凹. "Shangzhou chulu" 商州初录 (Records of Shangzhou, one). *Zhongshan* 10 (1982).

———. *Feidu* 废都 (The ruined capital). Beijing: Beijing chubanshe, 1993.

Jiang Kanghu 江亢虎. "Yi wei Zhongguo xuezhe dui Buke furen xiaoshuo de guancha" 一位中国学者对布克夫人小说的观察 (One Chinese scholar's examination of Mrs Buck's fiction). In Guo, *Sai Zhenzhu*, 12–15.

Jiang Yuying. "Tiancai zuojia he ziyou zhanshi—1986 nian Nuobeier wenxuejiang huodezhe Suoyingka" 天才作家和自由战士—1986年诺贝尔文学奖获得者索应

卡 (Genius writer and freedom fighter—Soyinka, the winner of the 1986 Nobel Literature Prize), *Shulin*, no. 6 (1987): 39–40.

Jin Jianfan 金坚范. "Guoji bihui yu Wei Jingsheng he Bei Dao" 国际笔会与魏京生和北岛 (International Pen, Wei Jingsheng, and Bei Dao). *Wenyi lilun yu piping*, no. 1 (1990): 73–75.

——. Interview by author, Beijing, 31 March 2000.

Jones, Andrew. "Chinese Literature in the 'World' Literary Economy." *Modern Chinese Literature* 8.1–2 (Spring/Fall 1994): 171–190.

Jusdanis, Gregory. *Belated Modernity and Aesthetic Culture: Inventing National Literature*. Minneapolis: University of Minnesota Press, 1991.

Kaldor, Mary. *Global Civil Society: An Answer to War*. London: Polity, 2003.

Kinkley, Jeffrey. "A Bibliographic Survey of Publications on Chinese Literature in Translation from 1949 to 1999." In *Chinese Literature in the Second Half of a Modern Century: A Critical Survey*, edited by Pang-yuan Chi and David Der-wei Wang, 239–286. Bloomington: Indiana University Press, 2000.

Kinzer, Stephen. "America Yawns at Foreign Fiction." *New York Times*, 26 July 2003. http://www.nytimes.com/2003/07/26/books/26BOOK.html (accessed 2 October 2003).

Kraus, Richard. *The Party and the Arty in China: The New Politics of Culture*. Lanham, Md.: Rowman and Littlefield, 2004.

Kraus, Richard, and Wendy Larson. "China's Writers, the Nobel Prize, and the International Politics of Literature." *The Australian Journal of Chinese Affairs* 21 (January 1989): 143–160.

Kristof, Nicholas D., and Sheryl Wudunn. *China Wakes: The Struggle for the Soul of a Rising Power*. London: Nicholas Brealey, 1995.

Lardy, Nicholas R. *Integrating China into the Global Economy*. Washington, D.C.: The Brookings Institution, 2002.

Lee, Gregory. *Troubadours, Trumpeters, Troubled Makers*. London: Hurst and Company, 1996.

Lee, Leo Ou-fan. *The Romantic Generation of Modern Chinese Writers*. Cambridge, Mass.: Harvard University Press, 1973.

——. *Voices from the Iron House: A Study of Lu Xun*. Bloomington: Indiana University Press, 1987.

——. "In Search of Modernity: Some Reflections on a New Mode of Consciousness in Twentieth-Century Chinese History and Literature." In *Ideas Across Cultures: Essays on Chinese Thought in Honor of Dr. Benjamin I. Schwartz*, edited by Paul A. Cohen and Merle Goldman, 109–135. Cambridge, Mass.: Harvard University Press, 1990.

——. *Shanghai Modern: The Flowering of a New Urban Culture in China 1930–1945*. Cambridge, Mass.: Harvard University Press, 1999.

Lee, Leo Ou-fan, and Andrew J. Nathan. "The Beginnings of Mass Culture: Journalism and Fiction in the Late Ch'ing and Beyond." In *Popular Culture in Late Imperial China*, edited by David Johnson, Andrew J. Nathan, and Evelyn S. Rawski, 378–395. Berkeley: University of California Press, 1985.

Bibliography

Lennon, Peter. "Why Graham Greene hasn't won a Nobel Prize and Solzhenitsyn has." *Washington Post* (Book World), 28 December 1980.

Levenson, Joseph R. "The Genesis of *Confucian China and Its Modern Fate*." In *The Historian's Workshop: Original Essays by Sixteen Historians*, edited by L. P. Curtis, Jr., 277–291. New York: Knopf, 1970.

Lewis, Pericles. *Modernism, Nationalism, and the Novel*. Cambridge: Cambridge University Press, 2000.

Li Dawei 李大卫. Interview by author, 21 April 2000, Beijing.

Li, Dian. "Ideology and Conflicts in Bei Dao's Poetry." *Modern Chinese Literature* 9.2 (Fall 1996): 369–384.

Li Feng 李冯. Interview by author, 6 April 2000, Beijing.

———. Interview by author, 23 April 2001, Beijing.

Li Hui. *Going Through Together: Yang Xianyi and Gladys Yang*. Hong Kong: The Chinese University Press, 2001.

Li Man 李曼. "Zhongguo zuojia heshi wending Nuobeier wenxuejiang?" 中国作家何时问鼎诺贝尔文学奖 (When will a Chinese writer win the Nobel Literature Prize?). *Shijie bolan*, no. 1 (1987): 34–36.

Li Rui. *Silver City*. Translated by Howard Goldblatt. New York: Holt, 1997.

Li Tuo 李陀. "1985." Translated by Anne Wedell-Wedellsborg. In *Under-sky Underground*, edited by Henry Y. H. Zhao and John Cayley, 115–130. London: The Wellsweep Press, 1994.

———. "Yixiang de jiliu" (A surging current of imagery: outline). Obtained in Prof. Leo Ou-fan Lee's "Seminar in Modern Chinese Literature." Winter 1989, University of Chicago. Photocopy, no publisher available.

———. Interview by author, 20 April 2000, Beijing.

Li Yongyin 李咏吟. "Dangdai Zhongguo wenxue de huihuang mengxiang" 当代中国文学的辉煌梦想 (The glorious dream of contemporary Chinese literature). *Yunnan shehui kexue*, no. 3 (1996): 85–91.

Liang Qichao 梁启超. "Dongji yuedan" (Guidelines to Japanese books). In idem, *Yinbingshi heji-wenji* (Collected writings from the Ice-Drinker's Studio: collected essays), vol. 4. Shanghai: China Books, 1936.

———. "Foreword to the Publication of Political Novels in Translation." Translated by Gek Nai Cheng. In Denton, *Modern Chinese Literary Thought*, 71–73.

———. "On the Relationship Between Fiction and the Government of the People." Translated by Gek Nai Cheng. In Denton, *Modern Chinese Literary Thought*, 74–81.

Link, Perry. *Evening Chats in Beijing*. New York: Norton, 1992.

———. *The Uses of Literature: Life in the Socialist Literary System*. Princeton: Princeton University Press, 2000.

———, ed. *Roses and Thorns: The Second Blooming of the Hundred Flowers in Chinese Fiction, 1979–1980*. Berkeley: University of California Press, 1984.

Lipscomb, Elizabeth J., Frances E. Webb, and Peter Conn, eds. *The Several Worlds of Pearl Buck*. Westport, Conn.: Greenwood Press, 1994.

Liu Haifeng 刘海峰. "Wo guo kexuejia wuyuan Nuobeier jiang de yuanyin ji chongji duice" 我国科学家无缘诺贝尔奖的原因及冲击对策 (The reasons why our scientists have never won a Nobel Prize and strategies for remedying this). *Nanjing shehui kexue*, no. 2 (1999): 45–47.

Liu Haiping. "Pearl S. Buck's Reception in China Reconsidered." In Lipscomb et al., *The Several Worlds*, 55–67.

Liu Kang. "Is There an Alternative to (Capitalist) Globalization? The Debate about Modernity in China." In Jameson and Miyoshi, *The Cultures of Globalization*, 164–188.

Liu, Lydia H. *Translingual Practice: Literature, National Culture, and Translated Modernity; China, 1900–1937*. Stanford: Stanford University Press, 1995.

Liu Zaifu 刘再复. "Bainian Nuobeier wenxuejiang he Zhongguo zuojia de quexi" 百年诺贝尔文学奖和中国作家的缺席 (One hundred years of the Nobel Prize and the absence of a Chinese writer). *Lianhe wenxue*, no. 1 (1999): 44–77.

Lodén, Torbjörn. "Why Pure Literature? Random Thoughts on Aestheticism in Contemporary Chinese Literature." In *Inside Out: Modernism and Postmodernism in Chinese Literary Culture*, edited by Wendy Larson and Anne Wedell-Wedellsborg, 156–160. Aarhus, Denmark: Aarhus University Press, 1993.

Lu Xun 鲁迅. *Lu Xun quanji* 鲁迅全集 (Complete works of Lu Xun). 16 vols. Beijing: Renmin wenxue chubanshe, 1982.

———. "Zhi Yao Ke" 致姚克 (To Yao Ke). In Guo, *Sai Zhenzhu*, 3.

Lundén, Rolf. "Theodore Dreiser and the Nobel Prize." *American Literature* (May 1978): 216–229.

Lyotard, Jean-Francois. *The Postmodern Condition: A Report on Knowledge*. Manchester: Manchester University Press, 1984.

MacFarquhar, Roderick, ed. *The Politics of China: The Eras of Mao and Deng*. Cambridge: Cambridge University Press, 1997.

MacFarquhar, Roderick, and John K. Fairbank, eds. *The Cambridge History of China. Volume 15: Revolutions Within the Chinese Revolution 1966–1982*. Cambridge: Cambridge University Press, 1991.

McDougall, Bonnie S. *The Introduction of Western Literary Theories into Modern China, 1919–25*. Tokyo: Centre for East Asian Cultural Studies, 1971.

———. Telephone interview by author, 10 July 2002, Cambridge-Edinburgh.

———. *Fictional Authors, Imaginary Audiences: Modern Chinese Literature in the Twentieth Century*. Hong Kong: The Chinese University Press, 2003.

McDougall, Bonnie S., and Louie Kam. *The Literature of China in the Twentieth Century*. London: Hurst & Company, 1997.

Malmqvist, Göran. Unpublished interview by Gregory Lee, 14 May 1990, Stockholm. Transcript obtained from Gregory Lee.

———, ed. *Modern Chinese Literature and Its Social Context*. Stockholm: Nobel Foundation, 1975.

Marx, Karl. *The Communist Manifesto*. London: Harmondsworth, 1967.

Meng Fanhua 孟繁华. *1978: Jiqing suiyue* 1978: 激情岁月 (1978: A time of excitement). Shandong: Jiaoyu chubanshe, 1998.

Mian Mian 棉棉. Interview by author, 12 April 2000, Shanghai.

Min, Anchee. *Red Azalea: Life and Love in China*. London: Victor Gollancz, 1993.

Mo Yan 莫言. *Red Sorghum: A Novel of China*. Translated by Howard Goldblatt. New York: Viking, 1993.

———. Interview, 3 April 2000, Beijing.

———. *Shifu, You'll Do Anything for a Laugh*. Translated by Howard Goldblatt. London: Methuen, 2002.

Moffett, Sebastian. *Japanese Rules*. London: Yellow Jersey Press, 2002.

Moli 茉莉. "Miandui Ruidian Wenxueyuan de 'jiezuo'" 面对瑞典文学院的杰作 (Facing the Swedish Academy's "masterwork"). 25 February 2001. http://www.wxhf.com/wenxue (accessed 13 March 2001).

Mu, Aiping. *The Vermilion Gate*. London: Little, Brown, 2000.

Mu Jun 穆俊. "Ershi shiji wenxue jingying—lun Nuobeier wenxuejiang" 二十世纪文学精英—论诺贝尔文学奖 (The elite of the twentieth century—the Nobel Prize for Literature). *Waiguo wenxue xinshang*, no. 3 (1983): 34–39.

Ng, Mau-sang. *The Russian Hero in Modern Chinese Fiction*. Hong Kong: The Chinese University Press, 1988.

Nolan, Peter. *China and the Global Economy: National Champions, Industrial Policy and the Big Business Revolution*. New York: Palgrave Macmillan, 2001.

Odelberg, W., ed. *Nobel the Man and His Prizes*. New York: American Elsevier Press, 1972.

Österling, Anders. "The Literary Prize." In Odelberg, *Nobel the Man*, 73–137.

Ouyang Jianghe 欧阳江河. Interview by author, 27 April 2000, Beijing.

Owen, Stephen. "What is World Poetry? The Anxiety of Global Influence." *The New Republic*, 19 November 1990, 28–32.

Pauli, Herta. *Alfred Nobel*. London: Nicholson & Watson, 1947.

Pollack, Jonathan. "The Opening to America." In MacFarquhar and Fairbank, *The Cambridge History*, 402–472.

Polman, Linda. *We Did Nothing: Why the Truth Doesn't Always Come Out when the UN Goes In*. Translated by Rob Bland. London: Penguin, 2003.

Pomeranz, Kenneth. *The Great Divergence: China, Europe, and the Making of the Modern World Economy*. Princeton: Princeton University Press, 2000.

Prakash, Gyan. "Writing Post-Orientalist Histories of the Third World: Perspectives from Indian Historiography." *Comparative Studies in Society and History* 32.2 (April 1990): 383–408.

Qian Zhongshu 钱钟书. "Linggan" 灵感 (Inspiration). In *Qian Zhongshu zuopinji*, vols. 3–4 (one volume), 128–150. Taipei: Shulin chuban youxian gongsi, 1989.

Qiu Huadong 邱华栋. Interview by author, 28 April 2000, Beijing.

Quah, Syren. "The Theatre of Gao Xingjian: Experimentation within the Chinese context and towards new modes of representation." Ph.D. dissertation, Cambridge University, 1999.

Ragvald, Lars. "Professionalism and Amateur Tendencies in Post-Revolutionary Chinese Literature." In Malmqvist, *Modern Chinese Literature and Its Social Context*, 152–179.

Said, Edward. *Orientalism*. New York: Random House, 1978.

Sardar, Ziauddin. *Postmodernism and the Other*. London: Pluto Press, 1998.

Schwarcz, Vera. *The Chinese Enlightenment: Intellectuals and the Legacy of the May Fourth Movement of 1919.* Berkeley: University of California Press, 1986.

Shao Ying 少英, trans. "Yijiuqijiu nian Nuobeier wenxue jiangjin huodezhe jianjie" 一九七九年诺贝尔文学奖金获得者简介 (A brief introduction to the winner of the 1979 Nobel Literature Prize). *Guowai shehui kexue dongtai*, no. 11 (1979): 27.

Shu Yi 舒乙. Interview by author, 28 March 2001, Beijing.

Shu Yun 舒云. "Lao She weishenme mei ling dao Nuobeier wenxuejiang" 老舍为什么没领到诺贝尔文学奖 (Why Lao She didn't win the Nobel Literature Prize). *Yanhuang chunqiu*, no. 9 (1994): 70–71.

Siu, Helen, and Zelda Stern, eds. *Mao's Harvest: Voices from China's New Generation.* New York and Oxford: Oxford University Press, 1983.

Skagegård, Lars-Åke. *The Remarkable Story of Alfred Nobel and the Nobel Prize.* Uppsala, Sweden: Konsultförlaged AB, 1994.

Specter, Michael. "The Nobel Syndrome." *The New Yorker*, 5 October 1998, 46–55.

Spence, Jonathan. *The Chan's Great Continent: China in Western Minds.* London: Allen Lane, Penguin, 1999.

Statutes of the Nobel Foundation. Stockholm: The Nobel Foundation, 1994.

Stokes, Gale. "The Fates of Human Societies." *American Historical Review*, 102.2 (April 2001): 508–525.

Strich, Fritz. *Goethe and World Literature.* Translated by C. A. M. Sym. New York: Kennikat Press, 1972.

Studwell, Joe. *The China Dream: The Elusive Quest for the Greatest Untapped Market on Earth.* London: Profile, 2002.

Su Xiaokang, and Wang Luxiang. *Deathsong of the River: A Reader's Guide to the Chinese TV Series.* Translated by Richard W. Bodman and Pin P. Wan. Ithaca, N.Y.: Cornell University, East Asia Series, 1991.

Sun Wanning. *Leaving China: Media, Migration, and Transnational Imagination.* Lanham, Md.: Rowman and Littlefield, 2002.

Suraiya, Bunny. "A Storm over Poet Tagore's 'Political' Prize Award." *The Far Eastern Economic Review*, 1 December 1983.

Swedish Academy. http://www.nobel.se/literature/laureates/2000/index.html.

———. "Press Release: The Nobel Prize for Literature," 12 October 2000. http://www.nobel.se/literature/laureates/2000/press.html.

———. http://www.nobel.se/literature/laureates/2000/presentation-speech.html.

Tam, Kwok-kan. *Soul of Chaos: Critical Perspectives on Gao Xingjian.* Hong Kong: The Chinese University Press, 2001.

Tang, Xiaobing. *Global Space and the Nationalist Discourse of Modernity: The Historical Thinking of Liang Qichao.* Stanford: Stanford University Press, 1996.

Tay, William. "Obscure Poetry: A Controversy in Post-Mao China." In *After Mao: Chinese Literature and Society 1978–1981*, edited by Jeffrey Kinkley, 133–157. Cambridge, Mass.: Harvard University Press, 1990.

Taylor, Charles. *Sources of the Self.* Cambridge, Mass.: Harvard University Press, 1989.

Thomas, D. M. *Alexander Solzhenitsyn: A Century in His Life.* Little, Brown, 1998.

Torbet, Ronald. "A Dominican Nobel Prize Winner." *Blackfriars*, January 1959, 30–32.

Twitchett, Dennis, and Michael Loewe, eds. *The Cambridge History of China. Volume 1: The Ch'in and Han Empires, 221 B.C.–A.D. 220.* Cambridge: Cambridge University Press, 1986.

van Crevel, Maghiel. *Language Shattered: Contemporary Chinese Poetry and Duoduo.* Leiden: Research School CNWS, 1996.

———. "'Intellectuals' vs. 'The People': A Late 1990s Controversy in Chinese Poetry." Conference paper, privately obtained from author, 2001.

Wang, David Der-wei. *Fictional Realism in Twentieth-Century China: Mao Dun, Lao She, Shen Congwen.* New York: Columbia University Press, 1992.

———. *Fin-de-Siècle Splendor: Repressed Modernities in Late Qing Fiction.* Stanford: Stanford University Press, 1997.

Wang, David Der-wei, and Jeanne Tai, eds. *Running Wild: New Chinese Writers.* New York: Columbia University Press, 1994.

Wang Hongtu 王宏图. "Xifang wenhua de baquan he dongfang de bianyuanxing" 西方文化的霸权和东方的边缘性 (Western cultural hegemony and Eastern marginality). *Shanghai wenxue*, no. 12 (1992): 73–77.

Wang Hongzhi 王宏志. "Nenggou 'rongren duoshao de bushun'—lun Lu Xun de 'yingyi' lilun" 能够容忍多少的不顺—论鲁迅的硬译理论 (How much awkwardness can be tolerated—on Lu Xun's theory of 'hard translation'). In *Ershi shiji Zhongguo fanyi yanjiu*, 218–239. Hong Kong: Dongfang chuban zhongxin, 1999.

Wang Hui. "Contemporary Chinese Thought and the Question of Modernity." Translated by Rebecca E. Karl. *Social Text* 55 (Summer 1998): 9–44.

Wang Jiaxin 王家新. Interview by author, 1 May 2000, Beijing.

Wang, Jing. *High Culture Fever: Politics, Aesthetics, and Ideology in Deng's China.* Berkeley: University of California Press, 1996.

———. "Culture as Leisure and Culture as Capital," *Positions* 9, no. 1 (Spring 2001): 69–104.

———, ed. *China's Avant-garde Fiction: An Anthology.* Durham, N.C.: Duke University Press, 1998.

Wang Lijiu 王力久. "Shilun wenxue de minzuxing yu shijiexing" 试论文学的民族性与世界性 (An enquiry into the national and global aspects of literature). *Guiyang shizhuan xuebao*, no. 3 (1992): 30–36.

Wang Meng 王蒙. *Qiuxing qiyu ji* 球星奇遇记 (Strange encounters of a football star). *Renmin wenxue*, no. 10 (1988): 4–41.

Wang Shuo. *Playing for Thrills: A Mystery.* Translated by Howard Goldblatt. London: No Exit Press, 1997.

———. *Please Don't Call Me Human.* Translated by Howard Goldblatt. London: No Exit Press, 2000.

Wang Xiaoming 王晓明. Interview by author, 12 April 2000, Shanghai.

Wei Hui. *Shanghai Baby.* Translated by Bruce Humes. London: Robinson, 2001.

Wei Kefeng 魏可风. "Zhai jiang: Fang Ruidian xueyuan Ma Yueran yuanshi tan Nuobeier wenxuejiang" 摘奖访瑞典学院马悦然院士谈诺贝尔文学奖 (Plucking the prize: An interview with Swedish Academician Göran Malmqvist about the Nobel Prize for Literature). *Lianhe wenxue*, no. 1 (1999): 78–84.

Wei Shanhao 魏善浩. "Shiji zhi jiao de 'dongfang Nuobeier wenxuejiang qingjie'—Da Jiang Jian San Lang huojiang de qishi" 世纪之交的 '东方诺贝尔文学奖情结'—大江健三郎获奖的启示 (The East's Nobel Prize complex at the turn of the century—lessons to be learnt from Oe Kenzaburo's prize), *Guowai wenxue*, no. 1 (1998): 42–46.

Wei Tiancong 尉天聰, ed. *Xiangtu wenxue taolunji* 乡土文学讨论集 (Collected discussions on nativist literature). Taipei: Wei Tiancong, 1978.

Wen Hui 闻慧. "Tan wenxue de minzuxing yu shijiexing" 谈民族的文学性与世界性 (On national and global qualities in literature). *Beijing shehui kexue*, no. 1 (1990): 68–73.

Wesseling, Henk. "Overseas History," in Burke, *New Perspectives*, 71–96.

Wong, R. Bin. *China Transformed: Historical Change and the Limits of European Experience* (Ithaca, N.Y.: Cornell University Press, 1997).

Wood, Ellen Meiksins. *Empire of Capital*. London: Verso, 2003.

Xi Chuan 西川. Interview by author, 19 April 2000, Beijing.

Xin Chao 辛潮. "Nuobeier wenxue de xiandai renlei wenhua yishi" 诺贝尔文学的现代人类文化意识 (The modern human cultural consciousness of Nobel literature). *Waiguo wenxue yanjiu*, no. 11 (1991): 84–91.

Xin Weiling 辛未岭. "1978 niandu Nuobeier wenxuejiang huodezhe—Xingge" 1978年诺贝尔文学奖获得者—辛格 (The winner of the Nobel Literature Prize 1978—Singer). *Guowai shehui kexue cankao ziliao*, no. 2 (1978): 10.

Xu Ben. "From Modernity to Chineseness": The Rise of Nativist Cultural Theory in Post-1989 China." *Positions* 6, no. 1 (1998): 203–237.

Xu Chi 徐迟. "Xishou waiguo wenyi jinghua zonghe: wei *Waiguo wenxue yanjiu* jikan chuangkan hao er zuo" 吸收外国文艺精华综合：为外国文学研究季刊创刊号作 (Absorb the synthetic essence of foreign arts: Written for the inaugural issue of *Foreign Literature Research*). *Waiguo wenxue yanjiu*, no. 1 (1978): 1–2.

Xu Jiayue 徐家跃. "Keyan bentuhua: tongxiang Nuobeier jiang zhi lu (shang) 科研本土化：通向诺贝尔奖之路 (上) (The nativization of scientific research: Heading for the Nobel Prize [one]). *Kexue xue yu kexue jishu guanli*, no. 7 (1996): 4–6.

Xu Xiaobin 徐小斌. "Cong Nuobeier wenxuejiang tankaiqu" 从诺贝尔文学奖谈开去 (Starting with the Nobel Literature Prize). *Waiguo wenxue*, no. 5 (1997): 3–6.

———. Interview by author, 24 April 2000, Beijing.

Xu Yuxin 徐育新. "Sai Zhenzhu—Mei diguozhuyi wenhua qinlue de ji xianfeng" 赛真珠—美帝国主义文化侵略的急先锋 (Pearl Buck—the vanguard of United States imperialist cultural aggression). In Guo, *Sai Zhenzhu*, 134–143.

Xuanchuan dongtai 1986 nian xuanbian 宣传动态1986年选编 (Trends in propaganda: 1986 anthology). Beijing: Jingji ribao chubanshe, 1987.

Yahuda, Michael B. *China's Role in World Affairs*. London: Croom Helm, 1978.

Yang Changxi 杨昌溪. "Bake furen yu Jiang Kanghu lunzhan jiqi dui Jidujiao de renshi" 巴克夫人与江亢虎论战及其对监督教之认识 (The debate between Mrs

Buck and Jiang Kanghu, and the understanding of Christianity). In Guo, *Sai Zhenzhu*, 43–45.

Yang Lian 杨炼. *Yang Lian zuopin 1982–1997* 杨炼作品1982–1997 (Yang Lian works, 1982–1997). 2 vols. (poetry and prose). Shanghai: Wenyi chubanshe, 1998.

———. *Where the Sea Stands Still*. Translated by Brian Holton. Newcastle, Eng.: Bloodaxe, 1999.

———. "Chi rensheng zhe zhi zhizhu" 吃人生这只蜘蛛 (This life-eating spider). Preface to Chinese edition of Yang Rae, *Spider Eaters*, 10 August 1999. Prepublication copy obtained from Yang Lian.

———. Interview by author, 7 October 1999, London.

Yao Jian 姚见. "Cong wenxue jiaodu kan wo guo dui waiwenhua jiaoliu" 从文学角度看我国对外文化交流 (Viewing our country's exchange with foreign culture from a literary angle). *Waiguo wenxue yanjiu*, no. 3 (1982): 70–75.

Ye Zhaoyan. *Nanjing 1937: A Love Story*. Translated by Michael Berry. London: Faber and Faber, 2003.

Yeh, Catherine V. "Root Literature of the 1980s: May Fourth as a Double Burden." Paper presented at International Conference on the Burdens of the May Fourth Cultural Movements, Charles University, Prague, August 1994.

Yeh, Michelle. "The 'Cult of Poetry' in Contemporary China." *Journal of Asian Studies* 55.1 (February 1996): 51–80.

———. "International Theory and the Transnational Critic: China in the Age of Multiculturalism." *boundary 2* 25.3 (1998): 193–222.

Yi Xian 宜闲. "Ping *Dadi*" 评大地 (Considering *The Good Earth*). In Guo, *Sai Zhenzhu*, 29–30.

Yu Hua 余华. Interview by author, Beijing, 19 April 2000.

Yu Ying-Shih. "Han Foreign Relations." In Twitchett and Loewe, *The Cambridge History*, 377–462.

Zeng Xiaoyi 曾小逸. *Zou xiang shijie wenxue* 走向世界文学 (Marching towards world literature). Hunan: Hunan renmin chubanshe, 1985.

Zha, Jianying. *China Pop: How Soap Operas, Tabloids, and Bestsellers Are Transforming a Culture*. New York: The New Press, 1995.

Zhang Daofan 张道藩. "Women suo xuyao de wenyi zhengce" 我们所需要的文艺政策 (The literary policy we need). In Wei, *Xiangtu wenxue taolunji*, 815–845.

Zhang Lun. *La Vie Intellectuelle en Chine depuis la Mort de Mao*. Paris: Fayard, 2003.

Zhang Quan 张泉. "Lun Nuobeier wenxuejiang jiqi yu Zhongguo" 论诺贝尔文学奖及其与中国 (On the Nobel Prize and China). *Beijing shehui kexue*, no. 4 (1992): 84–92.

Zhang Rongyi 张容翼. "Disan shijie wenxue yu 'tazhe bianma'" 第三世界文学与他者编码 (Third-world literature and 'encoding as the other'). *Wenshi zhi*, no. 3 (1995): 73–79.

Zhang Xianliang 张贤亮. *Xiguan siwang* 习惯死亡 (Getting used to dying). Taipei: Yuansheng, 1989.

Zhang, Xudong. *Chinese Modernism in the Era of Reforms: Cultural Fever, Avant-garde Fiction and the New Chinese Cinema*. Durham, N.C.: Duke University Press, 1997.

Zhang Yiwu 张颐武. "Hongyuan yu momeng: Nuobeier wenxuejiang yu Zhongguo" 宏愿与默梦：诺贝尔文学奖与中国 (Great aspirations and secret dreams: China and the Nobel Literature Prize). *Waiguo wenxue*, no. 5 (1997): 10–11.

Zhao, Bin. "Consumerism, Confucianism, Communism: Making Sense of China Today." *New Left Review* 222 (1997): 43–59.

Zhao, Henry Y. H. (Zhao Yiheng). *The Lost Boat: Avant-garde Fiction from China.* London: The Wellsweep Press, 1993.

———. *Towards a Modern Zen Theatre: Gao Xingjian and Chinese Theatre Experimentalism.* London: School of Oriental and African Studies, 2000.

Zhao Jiabi 赵家璧. "Boke furen yu huang long" 勃克夫人与黄龙 (Mrs Buck and the yellow dragon). In Guo, *Sai Zhenzhu*, 73–81.

Zhao Li 赵立. "Dongfang wenxue moli yu Nuobeier wenxuejiang" 东方文学魔力与诺贝尔文学奖 (The magic of Eastern literature and the Nobel Literature Prize). *Dongbei shida xuebao*, no. 6 (1997): 65–68.

Zhao, Suisheng. "Chinese Intellectuals' Quest for National Greatness and Nationalistic Writing in the 1990s." *China Quarterly* 152 (December 1997): 725–745.

Zhao Yiheng 赵毅衡. "'Houxue' yu Zhongguo xin baoshou zhuyi" 后学与中国新保守主义 ("Post-isms" and China's new conservatism). *Ershiyi shiji* 27 (February 1995): 4–15.

Zhao Zhizhong 赵志忠. "Shen Congwen yu Nuobeier wenxuejiang" 沈从文与诺贝尔文学奖 (Shen Congwen and the Nobel Literature Prize). *Waiguo wenxue*, no. 4 (2000): 87–90.

Zhong Chengxiang 仲呈祥. "Xun 'gen': yu shijie wenhua de fazhan tongbu" 寻根：与世界文化的发展同步 (Searching out "roots": In step with the development of world culture). *Dangdai wentan*, no. 11 (1985): 42–43.

Zhong Weigang 仲伟纲, and Li Hongyin 李宏印. "Zou jin Nuobeier" 走近诺贝尔 (Drawing close to a Nobel). *Ziran bianzhengfa*, no. 5 (1999): 65–69.

Zhong, Xueping. *Masculinity Besieged? Issues of Modernity and Male Subjectivity in Chinese Literature of the Late Twentieth Century.* Durham, N.C.: Duke University Press, 2000.

Zhou Changcai 周长才. "Ba Jin he Nuobeier wenxuejiang" 巴金和诺贝尔文学奖 (Ba Jin and the Nobel Literature Prize). *Waiguo wenxue*, no. 5 (2000): 43–51.

Zhu Jingdong 朱景冬. "Zou xiang shijie de chenggong changshi" 走向世界的成功尝试 (A successful march towards the world). *Zuojia*, no. 12 (1988): 73–79.

Zhu Wen 朱文, comp. "Duanlie: Yi fen wenjuan he wushiliu fen dajuan" 断裂：一份文卷和五十六份答卷 (Rupture: One questionnaire and fifty-six responses). *Beijing wenxue*, no. 10 (1998): 19–47.

Zi Zhongjun 资中筠. "Nuobeier wenxuejiang you shijie yiyi ma?" 诺贝尔文学奖有世界意义吗? (Does the Nobel Literature Prize have global significance?). *Dushu*, no. 7 (1996): 71–73.

Zou Zhenhuan 邹振环. "Sai Zhenzhu *Dadi* de fanyi jiqi yinqi de zhengyi" 赛真珠大地的翻译及其引起的争议 (Debates surrounding the translation of Pearl Buck's *The Good Earth*). In Guo, *Sai Zhenzhu*, 558–561.

INDEX

Gong Li, 142
Gordimer, Nadine, 64, 116
Gorky, Maxim, 58, 61
Grass, Gunther, 45
Great Leap Forward, 80, 102
Greenfeld, Liah, 10, 15
Gu Cheng, 114, 121
Gu Hongming, 81–82
Guomindang (GMD), 14, 84, 88, 96, 97
Guo Moruo, 102
Gyllensten, Lars, 59, 62

Ha Jin, 34, 135
Han Chinese, 119, 129
Han dynasty, 11
Han Shaogong, 117; *Bababa* (Dadada),
    129; and roots-seeking literature, 127,
    130
Hayford, Charles, 93
He Song, 117
Heaney, Seamus, 150
Hedin, Sven, 83, 85
Hegel, G. W. F., 10–11, 190n.23
Held, David, 19
Herder, Johann Gottfried von, 21, 49,
    190n.23, 193n.48
Hesse, Herman, 59
Hill, Justin, 34
Hsia, C. T., 5–6, 32. *See also* "obsession
    with China"
Hu Feng, 76, 89, 94, 97, 104–106
Hu Shi, 80, 101
Hu Yaobang, 137
Huang Qingyun, 112

Ibsen, Henrik, 56
imperialism, 12, 14–16, 74
India, 81, 123
individualism, 11, 13, 74; and Lu Xun, 83;
    in modern Chinese literature, 74–78,
    79–80, 97, 104, 105; and nationalism,
    18, 158; and post-Mao Chinese intel-
    lectuals, 111, 121–122, 125–126, 132;
    and revolution, 86–87, 96, 102
intellectuals, modern Chinese: am-

bivalence towards the West, 7, 17–18,
26–27, 81–82, 107–108, 156; attitudes
towards modernity, 4–10; comparison
with Western counterparts, 86–87;
definitions of, 5–6; dominant anxieties of, 4; identity, 8; literary, 5, 75, 105,
110; male, 6, 76, 109; marginality in
the 1990s, 137; "marginality complex,"
17–18, 109, 122–123, 129, 142, 143–144,
150–152, 168, 175, 181; and Marxism,
86, 96; overlapping with Communist state ideology, 118, 153, 181; and
"post-isms," 25–27; return to public
life post-Mao, 107, 118; "worrying
consciousness," 121–122, 182. *See also*
globalization; literature, modern
Chinese; nationalism
intellectuals, premodern Chinese: assumptions, 13; traditional views of
China's place in the world order,
11–12, 73

Jacques, Martin, 19
James, Henry, 56
Jameson, Fredric, 21, 24, 25, 37–38
Jenner, W. J. F., 33, 36
Jia Pingwa, 131, 141–142
Jian Jinsong, 119
Jiang Kanghu, 92
Jiang Zemin, 162, 181
Jiang Zilong, 132–133
Jin Jianfan, 115, 154, 155, 157
Jinshan Conference, 113, 114, 120, 134
Jintian (Today), 144–145
Joyce, James, 37, 58, 73, 175
Jusdanis, Gregory, 16

Kafka, Franz, 23
Kawabata, Yasanuri, 28, 65, 68, 112, 139,
    180
Kinkley, Jeffrey, 33
Kipling, Rudyard, 23, 72

Lao She, 3, 102, 180
Lawrence, D. H., 86

May Fourth, 5, 12, 13, 35; anti-tradition-
alism of, 87, 96; elitism in, 87, 96;
ideas about literature, 75, 79–81, 86,
101, 124, 130, 177; writers and communism, 95, 103–106
McDougall, Bonnie, 30, 113, 121, 188n.9
McGrew, Anthony, 19
Mian Mian, 154
Mingbao yuekan, 117
Mistral, Gabriela, 65
Misty poetry (*Menglong shi*), 108, 113,
125, 126, 132, 134, 144, 151, 162, 189n.12
Mo Yan, 116, 117, 154–155, 162, 183,
215n.123
modernism, Chinese, 124–125, 127, 130,
131; ambivalence about Westernization of, 126; and Gao Xingjian, 168,
171
modernism, Western, 35
modernity, 8–11, 124, 192nn.39, 42; Chinese, 4–5, 12–13, 93, 118–119, 123, 185;
literary, 87, 124; and modernization,
15, 137–138, 153
Morrison, Toni, 70
Mu Jun, 112, 120

Nabokov, Vladimir, 65
nationalism, 10–17, 190n.20
nationalism (Chinese): cultural, 5, 7,
26, 100, 108; and economics, 6–7, 138,
157; 159–161; incorporation of diverse
cultural forms, 13; links with globalization, 10–11, 14, 18; modern intellectual, 4–10, 12, 14, 25–27, 75, 107–108,
129–130, 154, 164, 175–180, 181, 185–186,
188n.12; post-Mao formulations of,
119, 188n.10; resurgence in China
post-1989, 115, 116, 138, 140, 153–154,
195n.83; schizophrenia towards West,
4, 7, 17–18, 154; and science, 157, 159–
162; and sport, 157–159
Nationalist Party, 14. *See also*
Guomindang
nation-building, 8, 12–15, 74, 131
Neoperceptionist writers, 86

Neruda, Pablo, 45, 62, 64, 67
New Era (*Xin shiqi*), 116, 119, 140
New Generation (*Xin Shengdai*) writers, 152
New World Press, 33
Nixon, Richard, 103
Nobel, Alfred, 27, 41, 45–46, 53
Nobel Complex, Chinese, 3, 4–6, 26,
76, 84–85, 107–162 passim; and Africa, 123; ambivalence towards West,
107–110, 114–115, 122–124, 134, 138; as
bulwark against Maoism and Communist Party-state, 109–110, 113–114,
120–122, 124, 132; criticisms of, 140–
141; critics debate, 139–141; and debate
about Chinese literary modernity,
125–126; historical overview of, 111–
118; insecurity within, 120; and Japan,
139–140; motivation behind, 121; and
the Nobel Prize 2000, 163, 164; official
attitudes towards, 112, 114, 115, 121,
138, 156; skepticism about, 117; state
at end of twentieth century, 154–155;
and translation, 134–135; waning of,
182–183
Nobel Complex, Dutch, 4, 70
Nobel Complex, English, 71
Nobel Complex, Japanese, 189n.13,
201n.28
Nobel Economics Prize, 50; in China,
107, 157, 159–161
Nobel Literature Prize, 17, 18, 28–29, 30,
38–39, 41–72 passim, 73, 75, 98–99;
adjudication and nomination procedure, 43–45; and China, 73, 75, 80–85,
90, 98–100, 107–162 passim; and Cold
War, 61–65; and communist writers,
58, 61, 63–64; contradictory philosophy behind, 45–54, 71–72; criticisms
of, 55; Eurocentrism of, 52–53, 65–70,
123–124, 139, 151, 178; and experimental writers, 58–59; history of, 56–60;
and "idealism," 3, 41, 55–56, 64–65;
and non-Western authors, 28–29, 60,
65–70, 166–167; prestige of, 43–44;

102; and Bei Dao, 212n.67; and Nobel Complex, 107, 108, 113, 115, 118, 121, 152, 153, 154, 155; and Nobel Literature Prize 2000, 172

Xi Chuan, 118
Xia dynasty, 11
Xiao Hong, 76
Xu, Ben, 26
Xu Chi, 111
Xu Zhimo, 81

Yan Fu, 13
Yan'an, 95–97
Yang Changxi, 92
Yang, Chen Ning, 161–162
Yang Jiang, 97
Yang Lian, 113, 144–152, 169–171, 172
Yao Jian, 112
Yeats, W. B., 82
Yeh, Catherine, 128
Yeh, Michelle, 150
Yi Xian, 93
Yu Dafu, 88
Yu Hua, 112, 125, 143, 183
Yu Jian, 152

Zhang Ailing, 97
Zhang Daofan, 96
Zhang Fa, 25

Zhang Jie, 174, 197n.99
Zhang Quan, 116
Zhang Rongyi, 143–144
Zhang Xianliang, 141, 170
Zhang, Xudong, 25–26
Zhang Yimou, 117, 133–134, 136, 142–144, 175, 181
Zhang Yiwu, 25, 116, 117, 137
Zhao, Bin, 14–15
Zhao, Henry, 26, 166
Zhao Jiabi, 88, 92
Zhao Li, 139
Zhao Shuli, 97
Zhao, Suisheng, 116
Zheng Yi, 128
Zhong, Xueping, 17, 109, 122, 129–130, 168, 170, 188n.9. *See also* intellectuals, modern Chinese
Zhongguo keyi shuo bu (China can say no), 154
Zhonghua dushu bao (China Reading Times), 117
Zhou Yang, 95, 102
Zhou Zuoren, 84, 88, 101, 130–131
Zhu Jingdong, 114
Zhu Wen, 153
Zi Zhongjun, 117
Zola, Émile, 47, 56, 59, 101
Zou Zhenhuan, 89